Comprehension Process Instruction

Solving Problems in the Teaching of Literacy

Cathy Collins Block, *Series Editor*

Comprehension Process Instruction

Creating Reading Success in Grades K–3

Cathy Collins Block

Lori L. Rodgers

Rebecca B. Johnson

The Guilford Press

New York   London

We gratefully acknowledge Modern Signs Press, Inc., for permission to use their
signs, which are the basis for our Comprehension Process Motions. The art for
each of the motions is from *Signing Exact English* by Gerilee Gustason and
Esther Zawolkow, illustrated by Lilian Lopez. Copyright 1993 by Modern Signs
Press, Inc. Reprinted by permission of the publisher.

Library of Congress Cataloging-in-Publication Data

Block, Cathy Collins.
    Comprehension process instruction: creating reading success in grades K–3 /
Cathy Collins Block, Lori L. Rodgers, Rebecca B. Johnson.
        p.   cm. — (Solving problems in the teaching of literacy)
    Includes bibliographical references and index.
    ISBN 1-59385-023-9 (pbk.) — ISBN 1-59385-024-7 (hard)
    1. Reading comprehension—Study and teaching (Primary)   2. Reading
(Primary)—Curricula.   I. Rodgers, Lori L.   II. Johnson, Rebecca B.   III.
Title.   IV. Series.
    LB1525.7.B58 2004

                                                    2003027735

*This book is dedicated
to all young readers
and their teachers,
who make a difference!*

About the Authors

Cathy Collins Block, PhD, is a Professor of Education at Texas Christian University and a member of the board of directors of the International Reading Association. She has also served on the board of directors for the National Reading Conference, IBM's Educational Division, Nobel Learning Communities, India's International Learning Society, and the National Center for Learning Disabilities, as well as on the editorial boards for *Reading Research Quarterly*, *Reading Teacher*, the *Journal of Educational Psychology*, and the *Phi Delta Kappan*. Dr. Block is listed in *Who's Who in the World*, in *Who's Who among American Teachers*, and as one of the 2,000 most outstanding scholars for the 21st century in *Who's Who in America*, and has received numerous teaching and writing awards. She also received the Paul A. Witty Outstanding Service Award from the International Reading Association, Outstanding Teaching Award from Texas Christian University, Outstanding Research and Creative Activity Award from Texas Christian University, and Outstanding Teaching Award from the University of Notre Dame. Dr. Block has directed eight nationally funded research projects related to comprehension instruction, teaching comprehension, teacher education, and professional development. She has conducted more than 300 professional development sessions for school districts, taught all grade levels from preschool to high school, and published 29 books and 90 research articles.

Lori L. Rodgers, MS, has taught kindergarten for 9 years. Her master's degree in education and curriculum is from Texas Christian University. She has presented at numerous national association conferences. Ms. Rodgers is an active member of the Texas State Reading Association, the International Reading Association, and the National Association for the Education of Young Children, and has served on several of their committees. She has conducted a national study to validate the effectiveness of the materials contained in this book, and is the director of a national network of educators working to advance the comprehension instruction of young children.

Rebecca B. Johnson, MS, completed her master's degree at Texas Christian University. She has taught primary-age children for several years and has worked in managerial positions for early childhood daycare and healthcare facilities. Ms. Johnson was involved in the creation of the comprehension process approach and participated in the research under which the lessons in this book were created. She presently teaches in Southlake Carroll Independent School District, Southlake Carroll, Texas, and is an active member in several professional associations. Her latest publication was the chapter "The Thinking Approach to Teaching Comprehension" in *Comprehension Instruction* (Jossey-Bass, 2003).

Preface

Teachers of kindergarten- and primary-age students recognize the gifts that young children possess and the heights to which they can succeed. In our efforts to prepare students for future educational challenges, our quest for effective instructional materials is often limited to (1) integrated studies on a variety of topics, (2) phonics lessons, (3) phonemic awareness exercises, and (4) thematic arts and crafts activities. Materials that build young children's higher-order thinking skills and reading comprehension are rare. Curricula and professional development books that do exist on this topic are generally not age appropriate.

This book is designed to fill this void. It is intended as a college textbook for graduate and undergraduate reading methodology courses, and as a professional development text for inservice teachers and administrators. The Comprehension Process Instruction (CPI) model, introduced in Chapter 1, comprises three comprehension lesson "strands." These strands enable young learners to develop their comprehension abilities, no matter what their current reading level is. Strand 1 lessons are teacher directed and provide rich, engaging demonstrations of comprehension processes in action. These lessons are taught before students need to apply these processes in their reading experiences. Strand 2 lessons' purposes differ markedly. They provide opportunities for students to receive personalized, direct instruction through mini-interventions as they read. Such one-on-one instruction occurs in shared readings, paired literacy activities, independent silent reading periods, guided practice sessions, and in small-group settings. The goal of Strand 2 lessons is to afford more time for students to practice reading texts silently in monitored conditions at school. Through them, individualized instruction can be given when comprehension challenges emerge for particular students. Such lessons do not occur regularly in most of today's primary classrooms.

A new direction in reading comprehension instruction is addressed in Strand 3 lessons: Students choose which comprehension process to study. The lessons in this strand are based on the premise that readers usually (1) recognize when comprehension breaks down in their reading and (2) experience an increased value for learning new comprehension processes *after* these points of need have been experienced. Strand 3 lessons occur on a weekly basis so all young readers can *select* which comprehension processes they need or want to learn to increase their understanding and enjoyment while reading.

Of particular interest to teachers are the Comprehension Process Motions (CPMs): tools that complement the three strands of instruction. These motions were created to represent each comprehension process employed by expert readers while reading. They also engage young readers in visual stimuli, kinesthetic movement, and metacognitive reporting. Research has demonstrated that the comprehension process abilities of young children increased significantly compared to students not receiving the benefits of the visual, kinesthetic, and metacognitive dimensions of CPI motions. Integrating CPMs into CPI lessons also provides comprehension instruction that meets readers' developmental and intellectual needs.

CPMs are currently being used in numerous classrooms in Colorado, Illinois, Indiana, Nebraska, and Texas. After attending conferences where one of us (Cathy Collins Block) introduced the research effectiveness data, 31 educators (including literacy coordinators, a curriculum specialist, a reading specialist, and classroom teachers working in grades 1–4) requested information on the motions. Several of these educators have already implemented this research in their classrooms and district inservices. We welcome the opportunity to publicly thank each of these educators for their dedication in helping young readers. We particularly extend our deep gratitude to Kathryn Aschliman, Mary Lynne Bailey, Stephen J. Donndelinger, Carole Johnson, Cathy Koeplin, Aimee Mullis, Cindy Schwaninger, John Stoffel, and Diane Vyhnalek.

This research could not have been conducted without the support of Marsha Sonnenberg and Clairita Porter of the Reading Department of the Fort Worth (Texas) Independent School District. We would like to thank Principal Mary Jane Marshall and the teachers and staff of Waverly Park Elementary in Fort Worth for eagerly accepting the challenge of instituting new reading comprehension research in their classrooms. Christine Marshall and Heidi Bruns provided additional information from their students to assist us in meeting the needs of all children.

A special thank you to Shelley Chester for her willingness to share her daily successes and modifications in the kindergarten lessons she teaches, and to Jennifer Brown for her assistance in creating motions that avoided confusion in the conceptual understandings of hearing-impaired students.

Contents

Comprehension Process Instruction

CHAPTER 1

Daily Comprehension Instruction in a New Era for Our Changing Students

Ms. Hisel, a second-grade teacher dedicated to helping students increase their comprehension, is using the research-based practices presented in this book. Ms. Hisel understands her responsibilities to help the new generation of students. Katherine and Kyleigh are members of her class. Katherine had this to say about Ms. Hisel: "She doesn't just give us instructions or tell us what to do, she truly teaches!"

Kyleigh told Ms. Hisel that she is *such a good* teacher! Kyleigh explained: "I feel as if I can see inside her brain. I work really hard every day so my brain will work just like Ms. Hisel's."

Chapter Overview

In the past, many comprehension programs were comprised of questions that followed the reading of a fiction or nonfiction text. Today, comprehension instruction encompasses the ability to construct meaning as the text is read (Snow, 2002). This book describes literal, inferential, and metacognitive comprehension instruction, as taught by the Comprehension Process Instruction (CPI) model.

CPI is based on the proposition that the comprehension abilities of students in grades K–3 depend greatly on the instruction they receive, the quality of their past and present literary experiences, and the degree to which they understand and elicit comprehension processes. CPI contains three distinct categories or "strands" of lessons—referred to as Strands 1, 2, and 3—that provide innovative, targeted, daily instruction addressing the most salient comprehension needs of our youngest generation of readers. These needs, coupled with the data from research about how students in grades K–3 best learn to understand fiction and nonfiction, formed the foundation of the CPI model (Block & Rodgers, in press; Block & Johnson, 2002; Block, Oaker, & Hurt, 2002).

In teaching CPI lessons, goals include:

1. Presenting vivid demonstrations of how the mind contemplates text (Strand 1 lessons).
2. Building a learning environment that elicits students' natural energy and inclination to explore new ideas in texts (Strand 2).
3. Scheduling time for, and providing experiences that allow students to describe how they comprehend and to choose what they want to learn next (Strand 3).

Rather than teaching a series of isolated strategies as the goal of comprehension instruction, CPI identifies its goal as the development of students' ability to initiate their own cognitive processes (Block, 1999).

Comprehension Process Instruction incorporates three conceptual changes. The first change concerns our past sole focus on creating an end product—for example, by instructing children to underline the main idea in a paragraph. In CPI, alternatively, teachers instruct children in grades K–3 about the process the author went through in constructing a main idea. In the course of learning, the underlying thought process can be visually depicted by using the Comprehension Process Motion charts shown in Appendix B, which can be posted in your classroom. These charts enable each reader to follow the author's train of thought and identify the main ideas more automatically and independently as he or she reads. CPI focuses on teaching *how* authors and their readers get to the main idea and to other end products of comprehension, such as drawing conclusions, understanding causes and effects, and so forth. Children understand what the main point is *as well as* the mental steps they took to get to that end product. This focus on process is a significant change from past instructional procedures.

The second conceptual change involves teaching young students to comprehend by *not* insisting that all students follow the same mental processes to gain meaning. The thoughts chosen by any two people who read the same book, or the thoughts employed by authors who write two books on the same topic, will differ considerably. Therefore, CPI describes, demonstrates, and models several mental processes that can be followed to obtain meaning. For example, CPI teaches young readers that the mind does not process text in a linear fashion. While a student is working to understand text, his or her mental energy naturally ebbs and flows. It begins to flow with less concentration when this child enters a section of text that does not demand as many decoding and comprehension processing tools (i.e., the child will not have to use as many cognitive or metacognitive processes to obtain meaning). At these points, young readers can experience the relatively effortless joy of becoming engrossed in reading and entering a state of "eustress" (defined as being in such a focused state that time seems to be standing still).

CPI lessons reflect the belief that every child can be taught to recognize these times in which less versus more effort needs to be exerted to glean rich understandings. The lessons also recognize that no two children will enter and depart from these deeply pleasurable reading states at the same time, even though all children are reading from the same book for the same amount of time.

Equally important, CPI enables teachers to aid a significantly greater number of students at the exact moment that comprehension challenges emerge. For example, when a child misunderstands or becomes confused by a section of text, he or she then must select multiple metacognitive processes to overcome that particular barrier. When children know that a wide variety of processes could be utilized at various points in a text, they are more likely to exert effort to find the exact one they need at a precise spot. They are willing to think hard and apply more cognitive processes because they know that in a few moments (after they or their teacher's mini-intervention [Strand 2 lessons] has eliminated the confusion), the amount of effort necessary to comprehend will decrease and reading will become more pleasurable. This is the natural ebb and flow of mental energy that occurs for all readers. CPI makes this rhythm tangible for children.

The third conceptual change is that CPI enables children to internalize comprehension processes, *not* through repetition, drill, or memory, but by developing an understanding of the processes that they themselves can initiate to obtain meaning. In CPI lessons, students no longer merely tell teachers the answers that they think their teachers want to hear. Instead, students are taught to tailor their comprehension processes to meet their own needs and address their challenges within each novel text that they select, or that their teacher asks them to read.

Three types of comprehension processes are taught: literal, inferential, and metacognitive. *Literal* comprehension is defined as extracting the details of the text and recognizing the author's purpose. Students must have a clear understanding of the material, as presented by the author. In addition, they must be able to recognize the way in which the author orders information throughout the text. Mastery of the literal comprehension process is usually a prerequisite for inferential comprehension.

Inferential comprehension requires students to create meaning from the text and move beyond the author's purpose by combining the textual information with their own thoughts. This form of comprehension is not a one-step process. It entails the creation of a complete mental picture that enables students to think intently about a text, relate it to their personal experiences, and connect it to other information (Baker, 2002; Kintsch, 1999; Omanson, Warren, & Trabasso, 1978).

A step beyond inferential comprehension is *metacognition*. In general, metacognition involves thinking about one's own thinking or controlling one's learning. Metacognitive processes help students (1) remove road blocks that interrupt comprehension (Block, 2000c; Block & Johnson, 2002; Block & Pressley, 2002; Keene & Zimmerman, 1997) and (2) reflect on what they have learned and what they want to learn next. Students must receive explicit instruction on metacognition or they will not engage in these processes (Baker, 2002; Block, 1998; Paris, Wasik, & Turner, 1991).

This new approach is timely and important. The National Reading Panel (2000) reviewed the data-driven studies concerning comprehension instruction for grades K–3 and found the following:

- Reading comprehension is an active process, directed by intentional thinking that allows young readers to make connections between their thinking processes, the textual content, and their own knowledge, expectations, and purposes for reading.
- Meaning resides in the "intentional, problem-solving, thinking processes of the reader as that reader participates in an interchange with a text. This meaning making process is influenced by the text, and by the reader's prior knowledge that is brought to bear

on it by the reader" (National Reading Panel, 2000, pp. 34–39). The teacher's direction as well as each lesson's instructional goal contribute further influence.

• The goal of comprehension instruction in grades K–3 is to build readers' thinking processes so that they can read a text with understanding, construct memory and metacognitive representations of what they understand, and put their new understandings to use when communicating with others.

During the past 20 years, the explicit instruction of reading comprehension has focused on teaching individual cognitive strategies to students (National Reading Panel, 2000). Many programs and recent teacher reference books (Owocki, 2003) have described multiple strategies for teaching comprehension. Researchers have begun to explore the ways in which professional development can help teachers learn how to teach comprehension in the ways that teachers were taught themselves as students. This book addresses this contemporary need. Furthermore, the research underlying CPI instruction demonstrated that comprehension strategy instruction alone is inadequate to develop automaticity in young readers (Block & Rodgers, in press).

Many students have weak literacy abilities and cannot develop comprehension processes unaided (Chall, 1998; Durkin, 1978). Moreover, "it is clear that children who can not comprehend tend to fall further behind their peers [in their comprehension abilities] by third grade, regardless of their decoding skill level" (Chall, 1998, p. 98). Studies have demonstrated that students who received the comprehension instruction presented in this book significantly outperformed schoolmates on measures of comprehension, vocabulary, decoding, problem solving, cooperative group skills, and self-esteem, as determined by the Iowa Test of Basic Skills, the Harter Test of Self-Concept, informal reading inventories, and standardized reasoning tests (Block & Rodgers, in press; Block, 1999; Collins, 1991. This newly evolved CPI model offers print-rich, developmentally appropriate lessons that actively engage students so that they initiate their own thinking processes to untangle the confusions and complexities in printed ideas.

To summarize, CPI lessons enable teachers to aptly explain how comprehension develops—how students and authors work together to build understanding (Block, 1999; Leslie & Allen, 1999; Lipson & Wixson, 1997). The process-based lessons are based on the assumption that during each meaning-making endeavor, a reader's purpose, state of mind, knowledge of English, and background experiences are as important to comprehension as are the printed words and the social, historical, and political contexts in which that text is read (Bakhtin, 1993; Bloome, 1986; Rosenblatt, 1978).

CPI lessons provide a balanced focus on facilitating (1) individual interpretation and literal comprehension, (2) avid reading of fiction and nonfiction, (3) student self-selected reading and direct instruction, and (4) *efferent* (i.e., appreciating new knowledge) and *aesthetic* (i.e., appreciating the emotions that a book elicits) responses to reading. These lessons also demonstrate how young children can develop meaning by moving along a continuum of thoughts, marked on one end by an author's intended message and on the other by an application of specific insights the text generated for a particular reader. The three strands of instruction—(1) teaching students how to combine multiple thinking processes, (2) encouraging students to enjoy reading, and (3) increasing students' abilities to recognize their own comprehension weaknesses—require that teachers go beyond merely "telling" students what to do: Teachers do not simply instruct, they demonstrate by thinking aloud about how they select and initiate successful comprehension processes, thereby modeling their thinking strategies. According to Laura Parks, reading specialist in Keller, Texas, "Everybody has a desire to have their needs met immediately. It is our job to meet students' needs *and* to ensure that they know that these needs are important to us. I have assumed the five responsibilities [discussed in the following section] and as a result, for the first time, I am able to meet my students' needs the moment they are expressed" (Parks, personal communication, May 5, 2001).

After reading this chapter, you will be able to assume important new responsibilities that can bring comprehension alive for your students. You will also learn what Comprehension Process Instruction (CPI) is and how to teach highly effective comprehension process lessons for beginning readers. Specifically, you will be able to answer the following questions:

1. With whom, in what situations, and in what ways can you teach comprehension processes both explicitly and implicitly?
2. How can you go beyond think-alouds to assign the control for making meaning to students?
3. How can you encourage students to initiate their own comprehension processes?
4. What actions do you and your students perform as you proceed through the three strands of CPI lessons?

New Responsibilities for Teachers

CPI involves teaching students (1) how to identify the thinking processes and meaning-making tools needed to understand a text, and (2) how to initiate several thinking processes at points in a text when understanding is interrupted. CPI lessons establish goals for teachers, curriculum, and pupils that are based on the following research.

Prior to 1990, many teachers taught comprehension by (1) merely giving directions, (2) telling students to "read carefully," (3) assigning workbook pages, or (4) orally asking literal questions after a text was read. By 1991, Pearson and Fielding (1991) argued for a movement away from these time-honored traditions. At that time, some teachers were teaching comprehension as a set of strategies, and only a few educators were highly skilled in demonstrating and explaining comprehension thought processes (what Paris, 1986, labeled "making thinking public," p. 173). CPI was developed after conducting research to analyze the actions of these highly effective teachers of comprehension (Block & Johnson, 2002; Block & Mangieri, 2003).

Canadian researchers Scott, Jamieson, and Asselin (1999) reported that the average amount of time teachers of K–3 grades spent on teaching comprehension was 25.2% of the total time relegated to reading instruction. Their instruction occurred predominantly utilizing small-group skill developmental lessons, think-alouds, read-alouds, guided reading, modeling, guided practice, brainstorming, and metacognitive explanations. Their instruction was significantly better than that of teachers observed by Durkin (1978) two decades earlier, when less than 3% of classroom instructional time was spent in teaching comprehension. Although it is encouraging that today's teachers devote more time to comprehension instruction, much work remains before every child in grades K–3 is enabled to comprehend independently. CPI has proven helpful to many teachers striving to accomplish this goal.

Moreover, although it has been proven that strategy instruction is more effective than isolated drill and practice on separate skills (Guthrie et al., 2000), data suggest that it is not explicit instruction, per se, but teachers' abilities to communicate the thinking processes that significantly increase pupils' comprehension (Block, 2001c; Block, Gambrell, & Pressley, 2002; Block & Pressley, 2002). When educators teach thinking processes, they increase students' involvement in and control over the meaning-making endeavor through the rich demonstrations and conversations that such lessons entail (Applebee & Langer, 1983; Palincsar, 1986; Wood, Bruner, & Ross, 1976).

The type of cognitive demand, interventions, and questions teachers use is also important. Several researchers have examined the most common type of question-and-answer sessions in comprehension lessons. Usually the teacher asks a question, one or more students answer that question, and the teacher evaluates the response(s). No significant differences were found between students' recall and literal interpretation of texts when their reading experiences were followed by this traditional questioning sequence than when no discussion occurred (see, e.g., Cazden, 1991; O'Flahavan, 1989). However, several significant differences were found in other aspects of students' comprehension when teachers' instructional discussions contained the qualities described in this chapter. Then these question-and-answer sessions led to increased attention to text, comprehension process knowledge, control over their own meaning making, and positive self-perceptions of their important role in discussions of text (Block, Schaller, Joy, & Gaines, 2002).

According to Brown and Campione (1998), students must be taught that complex mental thinking evolves gradually during the process of reading authentic texts, not by teachers' delivery of procedural instructions prior to reading. Thus, in CPI Strand 1 lessons, the making of meaning is taught as a process in which complex thoughts and comprehension tools are engaged when a text requires them.

Zecker, Pappas, and Cohen (1998) reported that unguided peer instruction often resembled a barter system, in which students relied on peers who were equally weak. To preclude this problem, CPI Strand 2 lessons assist teachers in (1) providing direct instruction at the exact point in a text that a child needs scaffolding, and (2) developing student independence. In summary, providing too much explicit instruction hinders young students' development of comprehension because they become overreliant on teacher assistance. Alternatively, an inadequate amount of instruction reduces students' ability to transfer comprehension processes to new books. With these problems in mind, the three strands of CPI were developed.

The Three Differentiated Strands of CPI

The three strands of CPI lessons teach students to (1) use two or more comprehension processes to overcome problems before they experience a need for them; (2) ask teachers for mini-interventions when they are reading silently and come to a point in a text when they are confused and cannot independently perform the processes to overcome this challenge; and

(3) choose what they want to learn after they experience a point of need in a specific text. Each of these lessons serves a different purpose in the total CPI program. Together they build a three-pronged power base from which students develop their abilities to make meaning.

Strand 1 Lessons: Teaching before the Point of Need
(Comprehension Process Motions, Thinking Guides, Models, Think-Alouds, and Power of Three)

Strand 1 lessons involved teacher-directed instruction of comprehension processes *before students read*. The goal of this strand is to preteach how to make meaning. Teachers tell stories about how they, and other expert readers, process text. They also explain how to use the "teachers within" (i.e., metacognitive thinking, prior experiences, and personal goals) and the "teachers without" (i.e., teachers, peers, textual clues, as well as printed, visual, and oral media context/format clues) to overcome comprehension difficulties (Cain-Thoreson, Lippman, & McClendon-Magnuson, 1997; Pressley & Afflerbach, 1995). Teachers demonstrate seven key areas of reading comprehension:

1. Using knowledge gained in prior sentences to comprehend upcoming statements.
2. Thinking on literal, inferential, and applied levels interactively.
3. Adding depth and breadth to their knowledge base.
4. Linking efferent and affective thinking processes.
5. Making connections between words, concepts, and inferences.
6. Filling the gaps in an author's writing.
7. "Tilling a text" (described in Chapter 6).

Strand 1 lessons teach students how to use the following comprehension processes interactively:

1. Savoring special sections of a story or text (i.e., feeling, making connections, rereading, and cause-and-effect processes).
2. Making predictions and inferences about what will happen (i.e., utilizing prediction and inference processes).
3. Understanding points of view and creating mental images (i.e., engaging perspective and visualizing processes).
4. Gleaning revelations from printed text (i.e., drawing conclusions and utilizing processes that produce reasons and evidence).
5. Using rhymes, alliterations, figures of speech, and interpretations of word choices to gain meaning (i.e., engaging interpretive and contextual processes).
6. Overcoming confusion and employing metacognition (i.e., engaging clarification processes by asking questions).
7. Developing text sensitivities, such as recognizing inconsistencies, ascertaining an author's goal, determining theme, "tilling the text" (described Chapter 6), and following author's train of thought (i.e., engaging summary and main idea processes).

In Strand 1, thinking/reading processes are taught immediately before students read so that instruction is not detached from content. This contiguity helps students learn to self-initiate these thinking patterns during reading more quickly (Beck & Dole, 1992; J. Mangieri, personal communication, August 31, 1991). Strand 1 lessons enable more students to reach higher levels of understanding than would be possible without this instruction because they learn why such processes are important at specific points in a text. In this way, more students learn how to initiate the processes unprompted, and can explain why they used a particular set of processes as they read a particular text.

Table 1.1 lists the specific lessons in this book that are CPI Strand 1 lessons. Figure 1.1 summarizes the differentiated goals of CPI strand lessons. Each is presented in Chapter 2, but the integration–comprehension process is outlined briefly here as an example. The integration–comprehension process lesson is designed to introduce a new process to students or to demonstrate how two or more previously taught processes can be integrated to build comprehension as students read. Teaching students to (1) think about two comprehension processes as they read, and (2) place adhesive notes at key points in a text as reminders that using that specific comprehension process at that point in the text could enrich their understanding.

Strand 1 lessons begin after you have identified the literary processes that students need to use to comprehend a particular text. Prepare a brief description of these two thinking processes and select a Comprehension Process Motion (CPM), thinking guide (i.e., visual depictions of thinking steps in a comprehension process), or Post-it Note that can graphically depict them. When introducing each process, present at least three examples, or think-alouds, to teach students how to use the process. Next, teach students to think about how these new strategies can be integrated to overcome comprehension problems. Thinking guides or CPMs can be taught at this point to assist students in independently integrating both the processes as they read (Block & Mangieri, 1996a–c; Schraw, 1998).

After the introduction and discussion of the processes, read orally or have the students read silently from a text for 10–20 minutes, depending on grade level. After reading, do not ask literal, interpretive, or application questions. Rather ask questions such as following:

- How did these two processes help you as you read?
- How did they help you think ahead, clarify, remember?
- How did they help you stay involved in the story?
- How did they help you overcome distractions in the room?
- How did they help you overcome confusion in the text?

These questions have one characteristic in common. They cannot be answered unless students comprehend the text. Questions such as "What did you like about this book?" can be answered whether or not the student understood the text. Such questions do not improve students' ability to use two comprehension processes to make meaning.

Conclude the lesson by saying, "Whenever you come to points in a text like this in the future, remember to think in both these ways, and think about what your mind is doing to help you develop the deepest, fullest meaning."

TABLE 1.1. Listing of CPI Lessons by Strands

Lesson	Location
Strand 1: Teaching Students to Use Two or More Comprehension Processes *before the Point of Need*	
Scaffolding	Chap. 2
Comprehension Process Motions	Chaps. 2, 4–8
Comprehension Process Thinking Guides	Chaps. 2, 4–8
Comprehension Process Think-Alouds	Chap. 2
Comprehension Process Bookmarks	Chap. 2
Respondent-Centered Questions	Chap. 2
Responding to Incorrect Answers	Chap. 2
Power of Three	Chap. 2
Integrating Two or More Comprehension Processes	Chaps. 2–8
Clarifying	Chap. 5
Building Background Knowledge	Chap. 5
Establishing a Purpose	Chap. 5
Structured Turn Taking	Chap. 2
Reading Two Books Together—Strands 1 and 2	Chap. 6
Tilling the Text and Using Signal Words	Chap. 6
Attending to Author's Writing Style	Chap. 6
Predicting the Functions of Paragraphs	Chap. 6
Writing Hypotheses and Prediction—Strands 1 and 2	Chap. 7
Diagramming the Inference Process and Inference Motion	Chap. 6
Identifying Gaps in Knowledge—Strands 1 and 3	Chap. 7
Look Up and Away to Image—Strands 1 and 2	Chap. 8
Create Mental Stories Before Students Scribe Them	Chap. 8
Paint Mental Pictures to Visualize	Chap. 8
Teaching Semantic and Syntactic Processes	Chap. 9
Teaching Students to Be Sensitive to Authorial Writing Styles	Chap. 9
Teaching Students to Note the Direction of a Character's Thoughts	Chap. 9
Teaching Students to Compare What Is Read to Similar Events in Their Lives	Chap. 9
Multisensory Additions for Reteaching	Chap. 9
Pulling It Together Metacognitively—Strands 1, 2, and 3	Chap. 9
How You Can Help Students Learn How to Solve Problems While Reading—Strands 1 and 2	Chap. 9
How You Can Help Students Explain How a Story Made Them Feel—Strands 1 and 3	Chap. 9
How You Can Help Students Elaborate on a Story	Chap. 9
Strand 2: Creating Time for Students to "Live within Books" and Delivering Mini-Interventions *at the Point of Need*	
PAR	Chap. 3
Student-Share Lessons	Chaps. 1 and 3
Stop-and-Ask Lessons	Chaps. 1 and 3
Think-Aloud Bookmarks Practice	Chap. 3
Think-Aloud Practice Games	Chap. 2
Adhesive Notes Practice	Chap. 3
Teacher and Students Sharing and Storytelling at the End of Silent Reading	Chap. 3

(cont.)

9

TABLE 1.1 (*cont.*)

Lesson	Location
Buddy Reading Assessments and Game-Like Practice	Chap. 3
Pivotal Point Scaffolding	Chap. 3
Asking Questions	Chap. 5
Making Connections	Chap. 5
Story Frames	Chap. 6
Main Idea Practice Sheet	Chap. 6
Summary Practice Sheet	Chap. 6
Continuous Checks	Chap. 7
Using Photographs and Cartoons to Practice Inferencing	Chap. 7
First-Person Narratives—Strands 2 and 3	Chap. 7
Theatre Storytelling	Chap. 7
Two-Column Notes	Chap. 7
"Ask My Teacher When I'm Confused"	Chap. 9
"Mark Where I'm Confused"	Chap. 9
"Asking Myself Questions as I Read"	Chap. 9
"Writing Similes"	Chap. 8
Translate Audiotapes into Print Practice Sessions and Experience Empathy—Strands 2 and 3 Lesson	Chap. 8
Write Poems with Vivid Words and Phrases Practice	Chap. 8
Create Shadow Boxes and Format Poems and Stories	Chap. 8

Strand 3: Students Choose What They Want to Learn
after They *Experience a Point of Need* in a Strand 2 Lesson

Discovery Discussions	Chap. 4
Teacher–Reader Groups	Chap. 4
Two-Process Motions Lessons	Chap. 4
Buddy Reading Assessments	Chap. 4
Reader of the Day	Chap. 2
Structured Turn Taking	Chap. 2
Midterm Surveys	Chap. 4
Saying How They Used Comprehension Strategies	Chap. 7
Explaining the Reasons Behind Inferences	Chap. 7
Paraphrasing	Chap. 7
Round-Table Technique	Chap. 7
"Roving" Teacher–Reader Groups	Chap. 7
"Telling Which Comprehension Processes I'm Using" Test	Chap. 10

Strand 2 Lessons: Creating Time for Students to "Live within Books" and Delivering Mini-Interventions at Points of Need

The goal of Strand 2 lessons is to provide more time for students to (1) practice engaging the comprehension processes learned in Strand 1 when they need them while they read independently; (b) ask for one-on-one mini-interventions from their teachers when they cannot initiate these processes independently; and (3) enjoy reading more books at school. These lessons come in many forms (described in Chapter 3). Before students begin to read, they are

FIGURE 1.1. **Research-based principles in comprehension process instruction (CPI).**

> **Strand 1: Teaching Students to Use Two or More Comprehension Processes <u>before the Point of Need</u>**

1. CPI makes the **process visible** that students take to reach the end-product of making meaning.

2. CPI teaches students how they can initiate the process that leads to the product.

3. CPI demonstrates to students the ebb and flow of mental energy that occurs while reading.

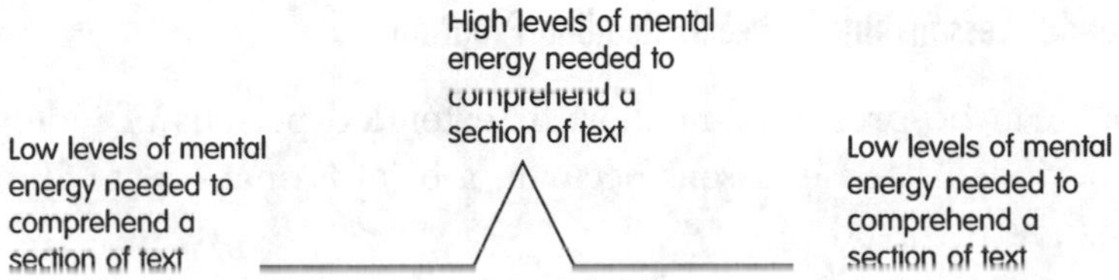

4. CPI enables students to use multiple processes simultaneously.

> **Strand 2: Creating Time for Students to "Live within Books" and Delivering Mini-interventions <u>at Points of Need</u>**

1. CPI enables students to establish their own purposes for every text.

2. CPI eliminates word-calling and teaches students to stop and ask for help when confusion arises.

3. CPI is individualized intervention.

4. CPI increases student metacognition, making students aware of what they need.

> **Strand 3: Students Choose What They Want to Learn after They <u>Experience a Point of Need in a Strand 2 Lesson</u>**

1. CPI includes choice and challenge so that students develop automaticity of each comprehension process.

2. CPI promotes an internalization of processes without drill or memorization.

3. CPI provides individualized instruction and teaches students to tailor their own comprehension processes to every text.

4. CPI does not allow students to merely tell the teacher the answer they think the teacher wants.

reminded to establish their own purpose for reading (described in Chapter 5) and to recall the processes previously taught in prior strand lessons and to initiate these comprehension processes learned in the present Strand 1 lessons. Strand 2 lessons teach them to stop and ask for help when confusion arises. These lessons differ from traditional silent reading periods because students are told to raise their hands when they come to a point in a text when they are confused. Conduct a mini-intervention with each such student to teach him or her how you knew which process to call upon to unlock an unknown meaning. The comprehension process that you used to overcome that confusion is thereby retaught in about 30 seconds.

Using Strand 2 lessons enables students to move to higher levels of understanding more frequently, because their teachers (and peer leaders) become personal coaches, at their sides when they experience confusion.

Incorporating Strand 2 Lessons into a Weekly Reading Program

Strand 2 lessons can be presented in short or extended periods of independent or paired silent reading periods. If these lessons occur in a brief format—5- to 20-minute periods of time—two steps are involved.

> *Step 1*. Have students self-select a book and read silently.
> *Step 2*. Assist students who encounter confusion by providing a brief response. You can use one sentence to provide the meaning needed and a second sentence to reveal the comprehension processes used to gain that meaning. Through these 10-second mini-scaffolds, students' silent reading periods are disturbed only momentarily. As a result, they can enter into a more enjoyable flow of living inside an author's message, and experience the pleasure of loving to read.

If Strand 2 lessons are scheduled for a longer period, they follow one of these two formats (others are listed in Table 1.1 and described in Chapter 3): "student-share lessons" or "stop-and-ask lessons." Student-share lessons are defined as whole-class shared reading experiences. Oral readings are occasionally stopped so that students can share their responses to the ideas being read. These lessons are distinct from traditional shared reading experiences in that teachers pause in their oral reading only if children (1) want to report how they made the author's story their own, or (2) answer other students' questions about how to make meaning. Teachers do not stop for students to talk about the content in the books. Students only describe what they are using to comprehend the material or what they do not understand.

Another difference in a student-share lesson is that teachers do not have the first word after reading—students do. As soon as a story or nonfiction text ends, you close the book and wait for students to tell you what they did to comprehend the material. It is necessary to remain silent when a book ends because whoever leads the dialogue and does most of the talking during these student-share lessons controls the comprehension that occurs. Ideally, students begin and sustain the conversation by discussing (1) a surprise that reverses the book's plot, (2) how they comprehended the sequence in an action-filled segment, (3) how they used tilling the text and story grammar to comprehend a character who repeated an attempt to resolve a problem, or (4) how they used cause-and-effect thinking coupled with inference to understand an event that triggered change in the usual order of things.

Steps in a Student-Share Lesson

Step 1. Read a book, selected by the students, aloud to the whole class.

Step 2. Pause to allow students to make comments about what they are comprehending or to ask questions, as they arise, about what they do not understand or use a recorder to list the questions for later discussion.

Step 3. Have a student lead a discussion about the book.

Step 4. Ask students to select which strategy they want to better learn to hone their comprehension skills.

In the second type of Strand 2 lessons, stop-and-ask lessons, students read silently and ask questions only if they do not understand something. The disruption is so brief that students can be quickly transported back into the action of the story and the pleasure of being engrossed in a book. Teachers can record the questions that students ask during this time to indicate the thinking processes that need to be taught in future Strand 1 lessons or Strand 1 guided reading groups composed of only those students who need to learn more about that specific process.

Steps in a Stop-and-Ask Lesson

Step 1. Have students select a book and read silently and independently.

Step 2. Provide a two-sentence response, when possible, to any question posed by a student.

Step 3. Then the student returns to independent, silent reading.

A completed lesson plan that can be used when teaching Strand 2 lessons is provided at the end of this chapter.

Because Strand 2 lessons are prefaced by instruction in how to set goals, students learn how to establish their own purposes for reading and to turn to books to learn more about topics that they value. Because their teachers answer their comprehension questions right at the time in the text when students are reading, the lessons increase the number of opportunities that students have to "fall in love with" reading. To reiterate: *Comprehension processes are taught at the exact point of need.* Students ask specific questions about the reading process they are engaged in performing, which instantly expands their comprehension abilities. Students who have completed Strand 2 lessons scored higher on standardized comprehension tests than students who simply discussed the content of the texts after they had read (Block, 2003; Block, 1992, 1997a; Graham & Block, 1994; King, 1994).

Strand 3 Lessons: Students Choose What They Want to Learn after They Experience a Point of Need in a Strand 2 Lesson (Discovery Discussions, Teacher–Reader Groups, Buddy Reading Assessments, etc.)

The goal of Strand 3 lessons is to teach students how to identify their own comprehension strengths and weaknesses. The students themselves are the most aware of the level of effort and drive they are willing to expend to become better readers; the outcome of Strand 3 lessons is to increase that level of effort and drive. Strand 3 lessons elicit and foster (1) students' intentional and deliberate thoughts about their level of comprehension, (2) a flexible and adaptable understanding, (3) their ability to select and combine appropriate comprehension processes when new needs arise in texts, and (4) their *metacognitive* reflections.

Recent studies have demonstrated that although good and poor comprehenders use similar comprehension processes, good comprehenders are willing to persist in using and adapting these processes until they ascertain the meaning (Afflerbach, 2002). Without Strand 3 lessons, poorer readers tend to reuse a very few processes; they attempt to comprehend every text using the same limited set of comprehension processes, and reading soon becomes a frustrating task to avoid (Block & Pressley, 2002). Their abilities to discover and savor subtle meanings remain untapped, which in turn limits their capacity to kindle the emotions, drive, and desire that emerge from experiencing meaning.

Students need opportunities to discuss new methods of making meaning, and to identify what they want to learn next to comprehend better. In these lessons, students tell their teachers which skills and strategies they use to read text, as well as what kind of help they need to comprehend material more completely and efficiently. The Strand 3 lessons presented in this book (listed in Table 1.1) enable students to ask more questions of themselves, such as:

- "What processes do I rely upon to comprehend fiction?"
- "What am I learning to do to comprehend better?"
- "What is bothering me about my reading abilities?"
- "What thinking processes do I elicit at a particular point in a text to create a more complete understanding, and how do they help me?"

If Strand 3 lessons are not included in a comprehension program, students' ideas about how they could become better readers may be neglected or overlooked. In contrast, when students express their metacognitive self-perceptions, they make new discoveries about themselves as readers, and their desire to improve their own comprehension abilities expands. They seek to read more difficult text and overcome larger comprehension challenges (Block & Rodgers, in press; Block, 2003). Some types of Strand 3 lessons allow students to choose what they want to learn *about the reading process*, not simply about a particular topic. These types of CPI lessons extend the benefits of book clubs, literature circles, and reading response groups, as is described in Chapter 4.

Incorporating Strand 3 Lessons into a Weekly Reading Program

Use a small-group format to provide instruction after a point of need was experienced in a Strand 2 lesson:

Step 1. Divide students into small groups based on their needs and interests.

Step 2. Work with each small group. Allow each student to describe his or her individual skills and weaknesses relative to a particular comprehension process in which everyone in the group is interested (i.e., learning to draw valid conclusions). Students and teacher suggest methods that other group members could try as a means of improving their abilities relative to that process.

Step 3. Students then report to the class what they learned in their group.

Strand 3 lessons improve readers' abilities to diagnose and overcome their individual comprehension weaknesses (Block & Johnson, 2002) (e.g., students and teachers offer suggestions for overcoming specific reading problems).

Strands 1, 2, and 3 lessons occur in a cycle. In the Strand 1 lessons that begin this cycle, you teach one or more comprehension processes for as many days as needed. You will know it is time to move on to a Strand 2 lesson when students are ready to practice eliciting the process(es) independently. As shown in Figure 1.2, students then engage in several different experiences and lessons, until they can determine which parts of the comprehension process they do well, which parts could be improved with more Strand 1 lessons, and what types of

FIGURE 1.2. Cycle of the three strands of Comprehension Process Instruction.

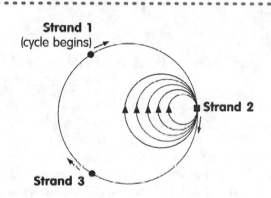

Strand 1: Teaching students to use two or more comprehension processes **before the points of need**
—Introduction of new process(es)

Strand 2: Creating time for students to "live within books" and delivering mini-interventions **at the points of need**
—**Kindergarten**
Teacher-directed daily practice
—**First grade**
½ teacher-directed daily practice + ½ student-selected practice
—**Second grade**
Limited teacher direction; majority is student-selected practice
—**Third Grade**
Almost all student-selected practice with individualized teacher monitoring

Strand 3: Students choose what they want to learn **after they experience a point of need** in a Strand 2 lesson

texts makes it easy or difficult for them to independently elicit that process while making meaning. At this point students are ready to move on to a Strand 3 lesson. In these lessons, students complete self-assessment activities that show you their specific comprehension needs. These needs become the basis for planning the next Strand 1 lesson. Then the cycle begins again.

Summary

Chapter 1 described the research base and components of the CPI model. It also delineates the steps in Strands 1, 2, and 3 of CPI, which are also summarized in Table 1.2. The reasons why students need different types of comprehension instruction were also discussed. When these strands of support are provided through CPI lessons, the synergy they produce fosters a depth and breadth in the meaning-making abilities of young readers that cannot occur when any of these components is missing (Block & Rodgers, in press; Block, 2002a). When you assume the teaching roles described in this chapter, you can (1) maximize students' comprehension competencies and (2) assist them in their attempts to employ numerous comprehension processes independently. In the next chapter, nine forms of Strand 1 lessons are described and illustrated.

Reflecting on What You Have Learned

1. **Interpreting (Summarizing) the Main Points.** List three important comprehension process actions that you have learned from reading this chapter. Rank your present level of ability in each of these actions. A ranking of *1* means that the information was completely new to you; a ranking of *2* means that you have tried the action at times but do not use it as regularly as you could; and a *3* means that you use the action daily. Develop an action plan to increase your abilities in performing the action you ranked lowest.

2. **Making Professional Decisions.** Suppose that you are preparing to teach this chapter to your colleagues. Would you teach it as a Strand 1, 2, or 3 lesson? Defend your answer.

3. **Making Field Applications and Observations.** Try using one of the teaching actions described in this chapter with one or more elementary students. Reflect on your performance, comparing it to the information in this chapter and discussing it with a colleague. Explain why you were successful or less successful in the goal you attempted.

4. **Keeping a Professional Journal.** Many types of journal activities are offered in this section at the end of each chapter. These can be modified and used with students. This one increases the summarization comprehension process: Describe new roles teachers must perform to ensure that all students develop the ability to comprehend. After you and another colleague have made this journal entry, share it with each other and discuss points that you have in common as well as any conflicting values.

TABLE 1.2. Summary of Basic Steps in CPI Strands 1, 2, and 3 Lessons

Steps in Strand 1 Lesson:
Integrating Comprehension Process Lessons before Point of Need:
Thinking Guides, Models, Examples, and Think-Alouds

Step 1. Identify two comprehension processes that students need.

Step 2. Explain and model each process three times in action (e.g., use thinking guides, examples, models, and think-alouds as you read a book orally).

Step 3. Read aloud and ask several students to perform a think-aloud to demonstrate each comprehension process.

Step 4. Ask students to read silently for 10–20 minutes. As they use a comprehension process, they should mark the location in the text. As they read, move from desk to desk and ask each student to tell you where in the book that he or she used one or both comprehension processes and what he or she was thinking as the student used these processes to make meaning.

Step 5. Ask how the processes helped the students to comprehend better. Inquire into the following areas:

- How did these two processes help you as you read?
- How did they help you think ahead, clarify, remember?
- How did they help you stay involved in the story?
- How did they help you overcome distractions in the room?
- How did they help you overcome confusion in the text?

Step 6. With the students, develop a plan for using these processes together as they read in the future.

Steps in Strand 2 Lessons: Time to "Live within Books"
(Instruction at the Point of Need: Student-Share and Stop-and-Ask Lessons)

Strand 2 lessons can occur as short silent reading periods that contain two steps.

Step 1. Have students select a book and read silently.

Step 2. Assist students when they encounter a confusing passage by providing a mini-intervention (i.e., a brief response).

Strand 2 lessons can also be conducted in a longer format; several formats are described in Chapter 3.

Steps in Strand 3 Lessons: Students Choose What They Want to Learn
(Instruction after Point of Need: Teacher–Reader Groups)

Step 1. Divide students into small groups based on their needs and interests.

Step 2. Work with a small group. Allow each student to use his or her individual skills as assets to the entire group.

Step 3. Report back to the class what the group learned.

5. **Making Multicultural Applications.** Identify the benefits of CPI for students who come from diverse cultures and language backgrounds.

6. **Meeting Students' Special Needs.** How can you modify CPI lessons to help students with special needs improve their comprehension?

7. **Checking Key Terms.** Following is a list of the new concepts introduced in this chapter. Place a check of those that you learned by the end of your first reading of this chapter. For those that you do not know you can refer to their definitions on the pages indicated. Of you learned seven of these terms on your first reading, congratulations. These constructed meanings add to your professional knowledge base.

_____Comprehension Process Instruction (CPI) (p. 1)

_____Literal comprehension (p. 3)

_____Inferential comprehension (p. 3)

_____Metacognitive comprehension (p. 3)

_____Efferent responses (p. 4)

_____Afferent responses (p. 4)

_____Strand 1 lessons (p. 7)

_____Strand 2 lessons (p. 10)

_____Strand 3 lessons (p. 13)

_____Cycle of CPI lessons (p. 15)

CHAPTER 2

Strand 1 of CPI in Grades K–3

Instruction *before* the Point of Student Need

Ms. Washington affirmed: "The use of the comprehension process motions definitely has focused the students' energy! Michael and Alyssa, having demonstrated behaviors that interfered with their learning as well as the learning of their classmates, sit in the row nearest me for whole-group reading instruction. But that changed the day I implemented a new approach that associates student-initiated visual and kinesthetic motions with comprehension process skills. Now these students join their classmates in active classroom discussions of the story. All my students make predictions with accountability, ask for clarification of vocabulary and story events, link story references to personal experiences and knowledge, and discuss personal feelings as well as the feelings of the story's characters. Also, this approach has revealed incredible insights into all my students' higher thinking abilities. And it all happened in our kindergarten classroom."

Chapter Overview

When comprehension instruction is not differentiated, struggling readers flounder as they strive to read texts above their reading levels. After repeated failures, many of them retreat to "good enough reading" (Block, 2001b; Mackey, 1997). *Good enough reading* is defined as pronouncing word after word haltingly and making so many compromises in relation to understanding the text that only a general comprehension is managed. Usually these students harbor a hope that complete clarity will somehow, suddenly, magically occur. Other less able readers, of necessity, implement ineffective reading processes. They make inaccurate predictions, generate inappropriate questions, or produce a one-sentence summary just to "be done with it," regardless of their confusion or incomprehension. Alternatively, when the CPI Strand 1 lessons described in this chapter are taught, students became significantly better comprehenders, engaged significantly more thinking processes while reading, and were attentive during reading (Block & Rodgers, in press). Less able students also realized that "good enough reading" was no longer good enough for them.

By the end of this chapter, you will be able to answer the following questions:

1. Why do we need differentiated comprehension instruction?
2. How many types of Strand 1 lessons are there?
3. How do Strand 1 lessons provide students with more time to internalize comprehension processes?
4. How can you teach students to initiate several comprehension processes while reading?
5. How can you diagnose individuals' comprehension weaknesses?

Why Strands 1, 2, and 3 of Differentiated Comprehension Instruction Are Needed

Increasing students' reading comprehension is a priority at the elementary school level, particularly in grades K–3. This is not an easy task. Primary teachers must create a multitude of highly effective lessons that serve multiple intelligence levels, varied personalities, and vast literacy needs in a class full of eager, energetic students every day. CPI lessons were designed to alleviate these burdens.

Strand 1 of this instructional approach is based on the tenet that comprehension occurs on several levels concurrently. Past methods of instruction have not taught how to make meaning at all levels simultaneously. Just as students use a variety of strategies to decode new words, young readers also must be taught how to use numerous comprehension processes interactively. Similarly, when comprehension is taught as a continuous thought process that ebbs and flows according to the changing demands in a text, the making of meaning can come more directly under students' control (Beck & Dole, 1992; Block & Johnson, 2002). CPI lessons provide opportunities for student-initiated thinking, and discussion at the point of confusion or personal interest. During the past year, we have field tested and conducted research concerning numerous process-based comprehension lessons. Each one was designed to encourage students to think strategically as they read. We discovered that when students applied comprehension as a process, in itself, and described parts of the process that they used, their comprehension abilities increased significantly (as measured by standardized and criterion-reference tests, Block, 2000a).

CPI Thinking Guides

CPI thinking guides are graphics that depict the steps in comprehension processes. Many teachers use published versions (e.g., Block & Mangieri, 1996a–c) or make their own to display on overheads, photocopy for students to write on when they read silently in Strands 1 and 2, and mount on poster boards for bulletin boards so that students can reference them continuously, as shown in the accompanying photo.

Many examples of thinking guides are provided in Chapters 5–10. Methods of using each thinking guide as a teaching aid during Strands 1 and 2 are also given. When the teachers

Ms. Parks (and other teachers who conducted CPI research) displayed the thinking guides for comprehension processes so that students could review and reference them easily.

involved in the research that supports the CPI model realized the benefits of the thinking guides described in this book, they made others in response to student needs. Each thinking guide lists and portrays the individual steps that are used to think through comprehension obstacles; it also provides space for students to write descriptions of individual incidents when they employed the steps in that comprehension process.

CPI Comprehension Process Motions (CPMs)

CPMs are diagrams of motions that students perform to portray the mental processes they are using to make meaning. They are compatible with, and use aspects of, American Sign Language (ASL). When singular signs in ASL did not exist, new motions were created to establish a visual and kinesthetic connection to students' internal processes (care was taken *not* to conflict with actual ASL signs).

As a result, primary-age readers experience the sensations of "moving the mind" as they form each motion in their comprehension process. Because these motions reflect the processing in the brain, active participation is stimulated during reading. The motions also enhance students' desire to share or seek information.

We created many types of CPMs and directed studies to determine their effectiveness. Those that demonstrated a significant contribution to students' comprehension achievement appear as full-page reproducible pages in Appendix B of this book. In Chapters 5–10, each is displayed in reproduced form and described in relation to the specific aspects of the basic Strand 1 lesson that can be adapted to build students' abilities in that particular comprehension process.

Teachers who were engaged in the research studies to determine the success of each CPM reported enjoying (1) making copies for students to place on their desks as they read, (2) creating wall-mounted charts for continuous reference, and (3) transforming CPMs into overhead transparencies for use in Strand 1 lessons. The charts that depict each CPM are modeled three times, explained, demonstrated, used in guided practice, and assessed during Strand 1 lessons. The exact means by which this activity occurs is presented throughout sections of Chapters 5–10. Once students learn them, they can use them daily to show that they know *when* they are comprehending and *which* processes they are using to do so, as shown in the accompanying photograph.

Direct Instruction with Think-Alouds

A *think-aloud* is another type of CPI lesson. Think-alouds occur when the teacher verbalizes the comprehension processes used to understand a section of text while reading that selection. In short, the teacher models the silent, mental process of comprehension. Think-alouds differ from prompting, or giving directions. They demonstrate how to select an appropriate comprehension process at a specific point in a particular text. They explain how expert readers elicit comprehension processes separately and collectively. They also describe why a specific thought process would be effective in overcoming a particular confusion or reading difficulty.

In a recent study, 139 second and third graders were asked what their teachers might do to help them comprehend better (Block & Mangieri, 2003). The answer that was given significantly more frequently than any other was a request for their teachers to explain reading processes better. They wanted their teachers to (1) describe what they did to understand the "things that occurred in books," (2) show how they knew which meanings went with which words, and (3) explain "just about everything that they did in their minds to comprehend" (Block & Mangieri, 2003, p. 193).

Another study documented that these needs were greater for English-language learners and struggling readers (Garcia, 2002). These students wanted their teachers to deliver very

Multiple CPI motions occur in single lessons. Brooke and Marcus (the back row of Ms. Parks's classroom) are demonstrating the CPI motion for "feelings," indicating that they have deep feelings that they want to share about the story being read. Roberto, seated ahead of them, has just made a prediction (shown in his CPI motion) that he wants to describe to the class.

specific think-alouds about how to (1) think while they read to confirm or disconfirm what they understand, (2) decode, (3) make inferences, (4) use prior knowledge, (5) notice novelty, (6) paraphrase, (7) predict, (8) question, (9) read ahead, (10) reread, (11) restate, (12) summarize, (13) understand the structure of a text, (14) use context clues, (15) make visual images, and (16) learn new vocabulary words.

Effective teacher think-alouds explain what expert readers do before, during, and after they have read a large section of text. Twelve think-alouds have proven to increase students' comprehension (Block & Israel, 2004). Five demonstrate what expert readers think as they begin to read, four demonstrate the types of thoughts that good comprehenders have during the first few pages of reading, and three portray processes that begin after a large section of text has been completed. The following material describes each of these types that can be included in Strand 1 lessons. All twelve are portrayed in Figure 2.1, as well as in Appendix A.

Looking for Important Information Think-Aloud

Expert readers know how to allocate greater attention to important sentences and how to not be distracted from their reading goals by seductive minor details (Block & Israel, 2004; Pressley & Afflerbach, 1995). To perform this type of think-aloud, hold up a book (preferably a content-area textbook) and turn to a chapter that students have not yet read. You might say:

> "In the beginning of a chapter or book, the author gives clues to help readers find the most important information. The author repeats certain words and makes some statements more frequently than others that are less important. The most important idea may be followed by a sentence containing the words 'for example . . . ,' 'to illustrate . . . ,' or 'let me describe this to you.' " Look for these words for clues to the main idea. Also, when you identify where an author places the main ideas in paragraphs, you can more quickly connect this point to the next most important point. For instance, in this book the author's most important ideas appear at this place in her paragraph [point to a sentence containing a key idea and describe how you knew it was important]."

Then ask students to follow along as you read the next paragraph. Have them identify the clues that indicate the most important sentence in that paragraph. Continue to ask students to perform this think-aloud until most class members can do so independently. Finally, move into a Strand 2 lesson (described in Chapter 3) and monitor students individually as they read silently for the rest of the class period. Ask them to perform this think-aloud for you in one-on-one interactions.

Connecting to an Author's Big Idea Think-Aloud

Expert readers connect ideas in a chapter or section of a book to a central theme. To perform this think-aloud, tell children how you link sentence ideas to the big idea that an author is talking about, and to an idea that is important to you. You might say:

FIGURE 2.1. Flashcards used to enhance students' use of think-aloud strategies during independent reading.

How to select and begin to think about a book

Looking for important information

Connect to author's big ideas

Activate relevant knowledge

Put yourself in the book

Revise prior knowledge and predict

Infer author's intention and depth of writing style

Determine word meanings: Decode, use context, and learn new vocabulary

Think strategically: Question, confirm, and disconfirm

Notice novelties in the structure of the text and converse with author

Summarize, evaluate, reflect, and paraphrase

Use knowledge in the future

Note. 1 = Think-alouds that begin before and as one reads the first few pages; 2 = think-alouds that occur after one has read the first few pages; 3 = think-alouds that occur after a large amount of text has been read.

"When I have read two pages of a book, I pause to ask myself: 'Where do I think the author is going?' By answering this question, I begin to feel that I am on the same train-of-thought as the author. Then I turn to the next page and see if I was correct in identifying what was important to this author. I continue reading. I relate the things I read to my own life, and to the big idea, moral, or theme that the author is conveying. Usually, after I have read three or four pages, I can figure out why the author wrote this particular book. The way I figure out the author's purpose is by seeing how all the important main ideas in each paragraph connect together. For example, the main ideas may be connected in a sequence. In this case, the author thinks it is important to point out that many steps occur to complete something. When I make these connections, I know that the author's purpose is to give the procedure for how to do something. If I'm reading nonfiction, another way I connect to an author's big idea is to keep the title of the book in mind as I read. The title usually names the author's big idea."

For example, Ms. Washington gave this particular think-aloud after reading the first few paragraphs of a second-grade nonfiction text, *Gandhi* (Demi, 2001 p. 4). After rereading the last sentence of those paragraphs—"[Gandhi's] father was a prime minister in the prince's court. His mother was a devout woman who taught her children about their religion, Jainism."—she paused to perform a connection to an author's big idea think-aloud: "Gandhi's father is a prime minister in the prince's court, so that means he's probably pretty important. This helps me understand why Gandhi became influential. Gandhi was taught how to help people, and his parents taught him how to be involved in accomplishing big objectives. This is the author's big idea in this paragraph" (Block & Israel, 2004).

Recognizing Author's Speed and Depth of Writing Style Think-Aloud

Expert readers analyze the depth and speed at which authors introduce ideas. Once students know how to make general predictions, the next goal is to help them infer the topic that is likely to occur in an upcoming sentence or paragraph. An example of this type of think-aloud follows:

"OK, we know something about several of these terms and sentences, but let's see if we can use all the terms together to predict what the next paragraph will be about. Look at the depth and number of new ideas introduced in this paragraph. Use how often this author has changed topics from one paragraph to the next in this chapter as a clue to the speed with which he or she is likely to change from one topic to the next. Do you think the next paragraph will begin a new topic about this subject or continue to talk about the same topic? Give me the reasons for your answer."

Once students have mastered these thought processes, perform another type of recognizing the author's speed and depth of writing style think-aloud. Describe how you used the number of words and the quantity, breadth, and depth of ideas presented in single paragraph to *predict how rapidly new topics will be introduced by a particular author*. This think-aloud can increase students' abilities to make accurate inferences about what the subject of an upcoming sentence is likely to be.

Noticing Novelty in a Text Think-Aloud

Expert readers reflect on an author's ideas and how those ideas are expressed by his or her choice of words. This think-aloud demonstrates how readers can use the novelties in an individual writer's style and a genre's format to flavor a printed message. To teach students to notice novelty, read excerpts from two different genres about the same subject. For example, read a segment from a recipe book and compare it to a poem about strawberry pies. In this think-aloud, describe how you . . .

- Noticed the differences between the genres' formats.
- Identified the subtitles in word choices.
- Used the structure of the first genre (i.e., the recipe book's format) to improve your comprehension (i.e., by noticing details in the photographs of completed recipes and following the sequence of numbered steps).
- Used the format of the poem, "Strawberry Pie in the Making," (i.e., the rhyme and rhythm of the language) to understand its novel meanings.
- Would like to ask the author something about his or her writing style.
- Went back to reread and why.

Strand 1 Lessons That Teach Students to Integrate Two or More Comprehension Processes

Strand 1 lessons are also designed to address the need to develop more self-regulated readers (Pressley, 1999) and to include more research-based lessons in elementary school classrooms (Block, 1999). Strand 1 lessons do so in a different manner from Strands 2 and 3 lessons. The difference between Strands 1 and 2 is that the latter builds students' appreciation of reading by increasing their self-initiated meaning-making processes through teacher mini-interventions in one-on-one settings, whereas Strand 1 teaches them new comprehension processes, that, following repeated practice, they can self-initiate without teacher prompting. The difference between Strands 1 and 3 is that the latter employs many methods by which students diagnose their own comprehension weaknesses, whereas Strand 1 lessons are planned through a teacher's diagnosis of students' needs. Teachers reported being able to answer more students' questions, at the exact point in a text when confusion arose, in Strand 2 lessons because they had previously taught Strand 1 lessons effectively (Block & Rodgers, in press). An example of this type of lesson appears on the facing page.

Integration–comprehension processes and the CPMs are the two most powerful lessons in Strand 1. Their purpose is to introduce new processes and demonstrate how these can be integrated with one or more previously learned processes. Students are taught to think about two comprehension processes as they read by placing adhesive notes at key points in a text to remind them that using a specific comprehension process at that point in the text could enrich their understanding.

After you have identified two literary processes needed to comprehend a particular text, prepare a brief description of them. During each introduction, you can present at least three highly distinctive graphics (e.g., *thinking guides*, *motion charts*), models, examples, or think-

....

Ms. Rodgers is conducting a Strand I lesson with kindergarten students, as Dr. Block collects research data. Students are listening intently to the predictions that fellow classmates are making. Notice that Sean is sharing and that Jason, the fourth child in the back row, has just had a new prediction that he is signaling to share.

alouds to show students how to use each process. Teach students to think about how these new strategies can be integrated with those taught previously (Block & Mangieri, 1996 a–c; Schraw, 1998). The accompanying photo illustrates how intently students concentrate during this segment of Strand 1 lessons.

Incorporating Strand 1 Lessons into a Weekly Program

There are six steps in a Strand 1 lesson of integrating comprehension process lessons (instruction before point of need), as laid out in Table 1.2 earlier.

Step 1

Identify two comprehension processes that students need: for this lesson, prediction and inference are those processes.

Objective: The student can define and successfully apply the prediction and inference comprehension processes.

Step 2

Explain and model each process three times in action: The explanation and modeling should be completed in about 30 seconds each. Students of the 21st century can attend to a 30-second description well, but when longer periods are required they become distracted. By prioritizing the points you want to make, the instruction can fit inside this time limit. The methods of modeling each process include the use of thinking guides, examples, models, and think-alouds (as you read a book orally). You might explain:

"The comprehension process of prediction helps you, the reader, connect story events to your personal knowledge and experiences. This connection provides a thorough understanding of the author's train of thought and helps you forecast future events. Your prediction is based on actual story knowledge supplied by the author and story inferences you draw from prior information. Inferences connect literal concepts to your personal knowledge. The reader must derive meaning by accumulating author clues and adding them to what he or she already has learned from life and prior reading on the topic to be logical or likely to occur next."

Thinking Guides

Display the CPM chart on prediction (see Figure 7.1, p. 116, or Appendix B). Write *Prediction* on chart paper and record "Which picture helped me predict?" and "What did I already know that helped me predict?" Highlight in yellow the words "*picture*," and *I already know*. (Highlighting in yellow has been shown to increase retention [Block, 2002b]). Be sure to display the motion charts and highlighted comprehension process chart for the students to use in future lessons.

Display the comprehension process motion chart for inference (see Figure 7.4, p. 123, or Appendix B). Write *inference* on a chart and record "What I read + What I know = inference." Explain: "Inferences are my understanding of what the author wants me to know without a directly stated description." (Displaying the chart and thinking guide in the classroom for future lessons.)

Model

Demonstrate the prediction motion and then have the students practice it with you as you model the motion three additional times. Explain: "When I predict, I utilize known information that I 'see' in the text [fingertips to eyes] to envision what will happen in the future [turn fingertips forward, as if to look and move through time]."

Now demonstrate the inference motion and have the students practice it with you as you model the motion three additional times. Explain: "Inferences begin with the author's train of thought and move to the unstated. As the reader, I incorporate what the author said [hand held stationary to left of body] and what I know [move hand in an arching motion to the right of body] to infer the meaning."

Think-Alouds

Use the think-aloud to establish the purpose for reading. Using *Alexander and the Terrible, Horrible, No Good, Very Bad Day*, by Judith Viorst (1998) read the first two pages of text and then stop to let students set the purpose for themselves. After reading the first five pages, turn the page and discuss the illustration. State, while demonstrating the prediction motion, "I predict that the teacher will like the friend's picture better than

Anthony's picture because Anthony didn't draw a picture." Read the next five pages and state, while demonstrating the prediction motion, "I predict that Anthony's mother forgot to put dessert in his lunch because things keep happening that make Anthony sad."

On page 13, after Anthony says that next week he's going to Australia, state, while demonstrating the inference motion, "I infer that Anthony wants to go to Australia because he thinks sad things would stop happening if he were in a different place far, far away."

Step 3

Read Aloud and ask several students to perform a think-aloud to demonstrate how they inferred and predicted at a specific point in the book. On page 19, read the paragraph up to "but then the shoe man said . . ." and ask the students to predict what the shoe man said. Remind the students to make the prediction process motion while they answer, "I predict _____ because _____." As you continue reading the story, tell the students to signal when they have a prediction by motioning the prediction process. On page 20, ask the students to infer why Dad said, "Please don't pick him up anymore." Remind the students to motion the inference process as they state, "I infer _____ because _____." Encourage the students to motion the prediction and inference processes to signal their desire to contribute to the story discussion.

Step 4

Ask students to read silently for 10–20 minutes, as described in Table 2.1, and mark the location in the text where they predicted or inferred. As the students read, move from desk to desk and ask each student to tell you where in the book they predicted or inferred and what they were thinking as they used these processes to make meaning.

Kindergarten students can reread orally the book you just read aloud, either with you or a partner.

Step 5

Ask how predicting and inferencing helped the students to comprehend better.

Leading a Student to Initiate the Comprehension Process

At times when you change the role that you assume during CPI lessons, you enable students to become the initiator of improving their own comprehension. For example, you can act as a contributor to, rather than the initiator of, a lesson's goal by preparing surprises or congratulatory instructive statements the day after students demonstrate a comprehension process

TABLE 2.1. Four Categories of Respondent-Centered Questions

Category of question	Best grade level
Elaboration	
Does this selection make you think of anything else you have read?	3
Would you like to be one of the people in this selection? Who? Why?	2
Did you like this selection more or less than the last thing you read? Why?	K
What parts of this selection did you especially like or dislike?	1
What did you mean by _____? Can you give me an example?	K, 1, 2, 3
If _____ happened, what else could happen?	K, 1, 2, 3
Does this story remind you of any other one? Why? What specific characteristics do they have in common?	K
Did the author make you feel any specific emotion?	1, 2
Can you describe the _____?	K, 1, 2, 3
If you had a chance to talk to this author, about what would you speak to him or her?	3
Why do you suppose the author used this title? Can you think of another appropriate title?	2
Why is this an important story to share?	1
Metacognition (thinking about thinking)	
How would you feel if _____ happened?	K
Why did you choose this selection to read?	1, 2, 3
Do you think this story could really happen? Explain.	K
After reading this story, has your perception or view of _____ changed? Explain.	K
What do you know that you did not know before this reading?	1
Did your thoughts and feelings change as you were reading? How and why?	2
Did you have to remember what you already knew? How did you?	3
Problem solving	
What do you need to do next?	K
Can you think of another way we could do this?	2
How would you solve this problem? Why	3
What did you do when you came to difficult words?	K, 1, 2, 3
What do you do when you get stuck?	1
What do you do when you do not understand the content or context?	2, 3
How could you determine whether _____ is true?	3
Supporting answers	
Why is this one better than another?	K, 1, 2, 3
Yes, that's right—but how did you know?	K, 1, 2, 3
What are your reasons for saying that?	K, 1, 2, 3
What do you (or the author) mean by _____?	K, 1, 2, 3
Why does this go here instead of there?	K, 1, 2, 3
Does the author have good evidence for saying that?	K, 1, 2, 3
How did you know that?	1, 2, 3

without your prompting. These surprises become visible displays of how much you value pupils' self-initiated comprehension. Surprising students also develops students' initiative to increase their own comprehension and volition (Block & Beardon, 1997; Block & Mangieri, 2003). On the day after students have initiated a comprehension process without your prompting, add something to the ideas that the students expressed the previous day, or surprise them with a concrete object that highlights the comment that was made. Such surprise actions, teaching tools, and congratulatory statements communicate to the students that they will be acknowledged and supported when they attempt to comprehend a text alone.

For example, Brooke asked Ms. Washington if the class could demonstrate how much they had learned from their nonfiction readings by staging a television news broadcast. She agreed. The next morning Ms. Washington surprised them by displaying a banner with a printed television logo that she had made for them and giving each student an individual name tag of the TV figure that pupil was to become on the broadcast. Because Ms. Washington had visibly shared in their initiative, the enthusiasm for the project mounted and the students read books on the topics of their individual broadcasts, by their own suggestion, to ensure that their speeches were accurate and interesting.

Another way to help K–3 students develop initiative during CPI lessons involves asking them to use their special talents. Brooke wanted to be the news anchor for the broadcast. Ms. Washington not only allowed Brooke to be the news anchor but also helped her write a letter to the local newscaster to learn more about news broadcasting.

Individual comprehension lessons also become more creative when students are encouraged to set their own goals for each lesson (Block & Beardon, 1997). In so doing, students also communicate their preferred learning methods. For instance, to prepare for the broadcast, Kendall asked to watch a TV newscast program and make a list of all the words spoken that he could use in writing the script he would speak. He also wanted to teach the class the newscasting terminology. Brooke made a list of key points about which she would speak, and turned it in as her demonstration of her comprehension of the trade books that she had read. Kristen asked to complete a report that contained more than twice the teacher's minimum requirements. Sean asked if he could write one page of his interpretations instead of using half a page to summarize information in the book and half a page to write his own interpretations.

Scaffolding

Scaffolding occurs when a teacher demonstrates a comprehension process that is beyond a student's understanding (Means & Knapp, 1991). For example, Courtney was unable to read the directions for making an origami crane, but she could comprehend enough of *Creative Origami* to select the animal she wanted to create. To increase Courtney's ability to comprehend printed directions, Ms. Washington used scaffolding by asking Courtney to read aloud only one small part (i.e., one phrase at a time) of each instructional statement. Her teacher read and defined each unknown word and demonstrated how to fold each paper described in each phrase so that Courtney could actually "see" the meaning that was carried in each phrase. Ms. Washington gradually reduced her scaffolding as she passed more of the responsibility for making meaning from each phrase to Courtney.

In scaffolding, you gradually reduce your support from the beginning to the end of Strand 1 lessons, as students become more competent. This technique is aptly named. The temporary scaffolding used in building skyscrapers provides a vivid and concrete image of the support and direction you give students until they can mimic your thinking processes as they create their own meaning from texts.

Recently, researchers have developed new types of scaffolds. These scaffolds are particularly useful during Strands 1 and 2 lessons to help students connect authors' intentions to their life experiences (Langer, 1991; Prawatt, 2001). The following types of scaffolds also enable you to eliminate the dejection that can accompany "failure" and address your students' comprehension difficulties more effectively.

Four Types of Comprehension Scaffolds

The four types of comprehension scaffolds include: (1) demonstrating a complete comprehension process before students begin to read; (2) inviting students to co-create a comprehension process with you by telling each other what you are thinking as you read; (3) beginning a comprehension process first and inviting students to join in when they understand how to think in that way (e.g., teacher begins to summarize a story and describes how she is making the summary until students can tell the teacher how they are making their own summaries); and (4) prompting with the name of a comprehension process to help students identify the process that would be helpful at a specific point in a text (e.g., teacher says, "I had to make a lot of *inferences* as I read this first page because _____. I am thinking that I will probably have to use my inference thinking processes a lot as I read the rest of the pages in this author's book because _____.")

You might say:

> "Try using the 'pausing at the entrance to a playground and taking in all you know so far' image [a comprehension process] after you read the first two pages of a book to think about what the theme of each new book might be, like this [perform a think-aloud after you read the first two pages (a type 3 scaffold, described above)]."

Or you might say:

> "At this point in the text I am beginning to feel as if the author is trying to provide me with information by giving me a fact to convince me of Hosea's valor. I must think about reading to determine the author's perspective. I recommend that you use detective thinking processes as you read this text, and with future texts, when you believe an author is using persuasive writing (a type 4 scaffold, described above)."

Giving Students Choices during Scaffolding

A second way you can avoid the rejection reaction is by offering students choices while you are providing the scaffolding. Offer two or three methods of engaging a specific comprehension process and ask students to select the one they prefer (Block, 2001b; Block & Mangieri,

1996a–c; Read & Roller, 1987). For example, Marcus asked Ms. Washington, "Would you help me? I can't think of how to put my main idea into a title for my story." Ms. Washington added choice to her scaffold by asking a question and then offering options to Marcus, as described below.

> Ms. Washington: What have you tried?
>
> Marcus: I want a short title, but I don't want it to begin with the word *my*, like all of my other titles do.

Marcus's answer told Ms. Washington that he could use summarizing comprehension processes well; this was not the reason for his difficulty in generating a title. What he needed was a thinking tool that he could use in the future to increase his creative thinking. Ms. Washington provided scaffolding by saying:

> "When you want to stop and think about a main idea, or a title, you could do two things. You could change some words to their synonyms, or you could choose words that refer to larger groups of thoughts or objects. For instance, if you don't want your title to be 'My Trip,' you could change the word *My* by substituting a synonym, such as *Marcus's, our, mine,* or *the*. A second strategy you could use is to choose to put the one trip inside a larger group or theme, and write that larger idea first. For example, instead of making your title, 'My Trip,' you could compare the trip to all others you've taken. 'This Trip Was the Best,' 'The Trip That Most Took Marcus by Surprise,' or 'The Most Important Trip.' "

Once this scaffold was complete, Ms. Washington asked Marcus which thinking process he wanted to use to create his title: (1) selecting a synonym or (2) creating a larger theme. Because she had demonstrated both to Marcus, he could select the one he wanted to attempt on his first independent application of creative thinking.

In summary, you can differentiate the types of scaffolds as you deliver them and provide choices so that students can select the particular thinking process they want to use to remediate a comprehension difficulty. When scaffolding is required, your responsibilities include diagnosing the depth of comprehension processing that the student is currently engaging and analyzing which part of a text's content or format became an obstacle for that student.

Increasing Students' Understanding through Respondent-Centered Questions, the Power of Three, and Effective Responses during Discussion

> When children give a wrong answer it is not so often that they are wrong as they are answering another question, and our job is to find out what question they are in fact answering. (Bruner, 1985, p. 34)

Respondent-centered questions, the "power of three" technique, and handling inaccurate answers to questions effectively significantly increase students' depth of comprehension

(Block, Schaller, et al., 2002). *Respondent-centered questions* are those that have more than one correct answer and that require students to answer with precision and elaboration . Respondent-centered questions enable students to (1) explain details, sequence, main ideas, and themes; (2) generate problem–solution sequences, (3) assimilate dissimilar events into their own lives; (4) express affective responses and insights; and (5) justify and defend their positions. (A list of respondent-centered questions is provided in Table 2.1. Teachers have found it helpful to select one question from each category to practice for one month's time. At the end of that month, you could select another question to practice, and continue in this way throughout the school year.)

Pearson and Johnson (1978) were among the first to demonstrate that students understand and remember ideas better when they transform those ideas from one category of thought to another. Asking respondent-centered questions is an effective way of engaging such transformation processes. These types of questions actively engage students in a comprehension endeavor as they create a mental image, elaborate on a point, or justify a position to answer a particular question (Allington, 2001; Au, 1993). Moreover, students tend to mimic your use of respondent-centered questions and ask these questions of themselves, silently, while they read (Block, 2001c). Respondent-centered questions "up the ante" on thinking by asking students to identify the thinking that lies behind their personal comprehension.

Another step toward increasing students' comprehension involves responding effectively to their incorrect answers. Seven helpful responses to students' incorrect answers appear in Table 2.2. Students answer incorrectly for a wide variety of reasons, so a variety of responses is necessary. Once you diagnose the reason why a student responded as he or she did, then you can select the appropriate response. For example, if a student understood the concept but either misheard the question or misread a detail, you could use the sixth strategy in Table 2.2, "That would have been correct if . . ." This response allows the student to regain dignity before his or her peers. For instance, if the question you asked was, "What is the capital of the United States?" and a student answers "Sacramento," you could respond, "Sacramento would be correct if I had asked for the capital of California, but I am asking for the capital city of the entire 50 states." By supplying the question that the student was answering, a student who knows the answer can quickly provide it and regain a strong self-concept, and if the student does not know the answer, the class can quickly understand how an error could have occurred, enabling the student to retain dignity.

Power of three is a teaching technique in which three distinct examples of a comprehension process are given through modeling, demonstrations, and think-alouds. These three examples can be concrete, pictorial, or symbolic; they can include three different pictures of a concept being taught, or model one method of thinking through a comprehension process, then a second way, and finally a third distinctive method. When you use three highly engaging but different examples of comprehension processes in action, you increase students' likelihood of understanding that process before they must do so in the course of reading. After repeated use of this strategy, students develop the ability to explain why they engaged a particular set of comprehension processes and their interrelationships.

At first, some students may not be successful even after four prompts of different examples. In time, however, when contrasting examples are given, many students become enthusiastic about the new realizations that these examples stimulate. As demonstrated in a recent study of 647 exemplary elementary teachers from eight English-speaking countries, the responses these teachers gave to students during discussions increased student comprehension significantly (Block & Mangieri, 2003; Block, Oaker, et al., 2002). These responses (listed in Figure 2.2) demonstrate how they (1) asked students to explain their answers, (2) gave choices to contribute or not, (3) kept single students from dominating or withdrawing from comprehension discussions, and (4) assisted students to lead discussions.

TABLE 2.2. **Responses to Students' Incorrect Answers**

1. *"Think again."* When students have sufficient background knowledge to answer a question, respond to their first "less than correct" attempts by asking them to "think again." This response reassures students that they can produce an effective response, if only allowed a little more time and thought. Use this strategy to respond to a student's insufficient answer when you are 99% certain that the student can respond more effectively with a second try.

2. *Give a relevant prompt.* If students give a partial answer, provide a relevant fact about the topic and then re-ask the question. For example: "Why do you think Cinderella didn't run away from her wicked stepmother and stepsisters?" Students do not answer. You prompt by saying, "Placing yourself in Cinderella's shoes will help you understand what she might have thought."

3. *Reword the question.* When you ask a question, and a student's answer suggests that your wording was vague, acknowledge this student's attempt and say, "Good try. Let me clarify my question. I think it confused you."

4. *"Could you expand your answer for us? Why do you think so?"* When students' answers appear to be off the point, ask them to explain their thinking. In many incidents the answer is relevant when the thoughts that support it are explicated.

5. *"Remember that. I'm going to return and ask for this information again."* When the several answers students give demonstrate that they misunderstand major concepts in a discussion, provide more information. Once you provide this added material, tell students to remember it because you will call on them to state thoughts about it before the class is over. Then as the class ends, you ask their thoughts about that information and the original concepts again.

6. *"That would have been correct if . . ."* If you recognize the reasoning behind a student's answers, follow the insufficient answer with, "That would have been correct if I had asked . . . but I am asking . . . " (restating your original question). For example, if you ask, "What do you do to organize paragraphs when you write?" and a student answers, "Combine sentences to make them less redundant," you respond by saying, "That is an effective sentence-revising strategy, but what I was asking for was a strategy you use at the paragraph level."

7. *Give examples and nonexamples of possible solutions.* This discussion strategy can be used to close a lesson or as a review of previous information. It is based on a multiple-choice testing format in that you supply several answers to a question and students select one of the choices or generate a better solution. To illustrate: You are reviewing a student's language arts portfolio at the end of a grading period. You suggest three future goals, and ask the student to decide which he or she most values.

    Nonexamples are used to stimulate students' thinking by stating what a discussion is not designed to cover. For example, you begin a class dialogue by stating, "Yesterday we covered some of the ways you can decode words. Today we want to extend our discussion. I do not want you to tell me the names of the decoding strategies on your thinking guide. Instead, I want you to tell me a specific word for which you used one of the strategies to decode."

FIGURE 2.2. **Checklist to assess if teachers are assisting students to apply comprehension and decoding strategies independently.**

☐ **The teacher asked students to explain how they successfully comprehended and decoded** (e.g., after a student read a word correctly, the teacher said: "You just read school correctly. How did you know that word?").

☐ **The teacher allowed up to (but usually not more than) six students to express their answers to questions** (e.g., "Why do you think this author picked this title?"), then asked a student to summarize the group's thinking.

☐ **The teacher often gave students a choice to contribute or not to contribute during discussions** (e.g., "Do you want to pass, think about it for a minute, or 'call a friend' for a clue?"). When the teacher judged that a student knew an answer but needed a few moments to recall it, a statement similar to the following was made: "Let's give Brian a moment to write, and when he is finished, we will move on (**silence**)." As soon as Brian finished writing a note on his paper, Brian said, "OK," and this was the signal that the discussion was ready to move on. Brian knew that the time to formulate his ideas was important enough for the class to pause for a moment.

☐ **When a student raised a hand first in a discussion, the teacher rewarded that student's rapid thinking while increasing other pupils' time for reflection** by saying: "Great, [student's name]! I have one idea that is ready to be shared! As we give others a little more time to think, improve upon your idea and how you want to say it."

☐ **The teacher did not allow students to "piggy back" on someone else's comments without thinking.** As a result, students did not repeat the same concept over and over during classroom discussions (e.g., "Now, we are all stating sports ideas, so we know that we can add any sport we want to our stories. You can write 'They played football, they played soccer,' and so forth. So it's time to change our thinking. What other topics do you want in our stories?").

☐ **Whenever a student gave a partially correct answer, the teacher rewarded that student and enabled him or her to learn which aspects of the answer were correct** by immediately turning to the group and saying, "Tell me what [the student's name] did right in [his or her] thinking to come to that answer."

☐ **Whenever students noticed a discrepancy between themselves and other students' abilities. The teacher stated that the differences occurred because someone had had less practice with the concept to be learned**, and not that some were less able than others. The teacher assured this child that he or she could practice with the teacher and his or her classmates.

☐ **The teacher did not typically begin reading response sessions by posing his or her own questions to students**. After an oral or silent reading experience, the teacher waited and allowed students to be the first to make comments or ask questions about the material read. If no comments were made, the teacher would ask questions that enabled students to initiate their own relationships to the reading (e.g., "What question do you think I would ask about this book/story? Why?"; "Which of these words from this list on the board do you know, and how do you know it?").

Summary

This chapter presented the needs for differentiated comprehension lessons and the characteristics of Strand 1 lessons, as well as how they differed from the goals of Strands 2 and 3 lessons. Every comprehension process begins with a Strand 1 lesson, and several types of lesson formats are available for use in this direct instructional experience for students in grades K–3: (1) thinking guides, (2) CPMs, (3) think-alouds, (4) leading students to initiate the comprehension process, (5) respondent-centered questions, (6) direct instructional responses to incorrect answers, and (7) the use of three distinct examples, demonstrations, and/or models. In Chapter 3, the components of Strand 2 lessons are described as well as the basic steps in this lesson format.

Reflecting on What You Have Learned

1. **Interpreting (Summarizing) the Main Points.** When instruction is not differentiated, the multiple intelligences, varied personalities, and literacy needs of a full classroom of students cannot be met. The CPI Approach to literacy gives students a means of contributing to reading discussions at strategic points and applying multiple processes as they occur. These lessons provide instruction before, during, and after the point of need.

2. **Making Professional Decisions.** The first decision a teacher faces is integrating the research-based instruction with school-adopted literacy programs. The goal of our instruction is "teaching the right things" to students, not "teaching the things right." What is the first step necessary to integrate Strand 1 with your current curriculum? What resources and materials that you currently possess are necessary to aide in the implementation of this instruction?

3. **Making Field Applications and Observations.** Time for whole-group instruction, small-group reflection, and uninterrupted individual reading need to be scheduled. Solicit the expertise of fellow teachers. Divide the strands among these teachers and have each create a model Strand 1 lesson, appropriate for the grade level, that can be shared with interested colleagues. After the teachers implement the instruction in the classroom, consider holding a meeting to reflect on successes and areas that need improvement before planning the next group of lessons.

4. **Keeping a Professional Journal.** Record the research in this chapter that will make the greatest impact on your students. List the assets and challenges in implementing this research in the classroom. Create an outline of the steps required to overcome these challenges.

5. **Making Multicultural Applications.** Through the use of multicultural literature, students recognize cultural nuances. To improve the readers' comprehension of such texts, explore multicultural life through the use of cultural studies, guest speakers, and videos.

6. **Checking Key Terms.** Following is a list of concepts introduced in this chapter.

TABLE 2.3. Books That Are Successful in K–3 Strand 1 Lessons and as Content for Think-Alouds

Revise prior knowledge and predict
Adler, D. (2000). *Cam Jansen*. New York: Viking.
Allsburg, C. V. (1988). *Two Bad Ants*. New York: Houghton Mifflin.
Brown, M. (2000). *Arthur*. New York: Random House.
Mayer, M. (2000). *Just a Mess*. New York: Golden.
Parish, P. (1995). *Amelia Bedelia*. New York: HarperCollins.

Infer author's intentions and depth of writing-style
Grimm, J. (1997). *Rapunzel*. New York: Dutton Books.
Kimmel, E. A. (1993). *Anansi Goes Fishing*. Minneapolis: Holiday House.

Determine word meaning: Decode, use contest, and learn new vocabulary
Frasier, D. (2000). *Miss Alaineus: A Vocabulary Disaster*. San Diego, CA: Harcourt.
Scieszka, J. (2002). *The Stinky Cheese Man and Other Fairly Stupid Tales*. New York: Scholastic.

Think strategically: question, confirm, disconfirm, and reread
Greene, C. (2002). *Martin Luther King, Jr.: A Man Who Changed Things*. Chicago: Children's Press.
Muth, J. (1977). *The Three Questions: Based on a True Story by Leo Tolstoy*. New York: Penguin.
Scieszka, J. and Smith, L. (2001). *Baloney*. New York: Viking.

Think-aloud strategies after reading

Notice novelty in the structure of the text and converse with author
Gaines, E. (1982). *The Autobiography of Miss Jane Pittman*. New York: Bantam.
Pattou, E. (2001). *Mrs. Spitzer's Garden*. San Diego, CA: Harcourt.

Put the book in our life: Summarize evaluate reflect and paraphrase
Aaseng, N. (1980). *Winners Never Quit*. New York: Lerner.
Aesop. (1999). *The Hare and the Tortoise*. Minneapolis: Millbrook.
Bunting, E. (1989). *Wednesday Surprise*. Boston: Scott Foresman.
Milne, A. A. (1998). *Pooh Goes Visiting*. San Diego, CA: Trafalgar Square.
Monjo, F. N. (1993). *The Drinking Gourd*. New York: HarperTrophy.
Wiesner, D. (1997). *Tuesday*. Boston: Scott Foresman.

Anticipate the use of knowledge: Restating/reading ahead
Hilton, S. E. (1997). *The Outsiders*. Boston: Prentice Hall.
Ross, T. (1992). *The Boy Who Cried Wolf*. New York: Puffin.

Place a checkmark in the blank that precedes each concept you have learned on a first reading of this chapter. If you have learned eight of these, congratulations. You have comprehended most of the points concerning Strand 1 lessons already. For those you do not know, refer to the page listed here.

_____Differentiation (p. 19)

_____Thinking guides (p. 20)

____CPM (p. 21)

____Think-alouds (p. 22)

____Before point of need (p. 27)

____Scaffolding (p. 31)

Comprehension Process Lesson 1: Teaching Students to Think about Two Comprehension Processes While Reading

Design a lesson teaching two comprehension processes (other than predicting and inferencing using the steps in Strand 1 lessons). Scaffold the instruction as you model the process during whole-group read-alouds. The books listed in Table 2.3 are excellent to use when you perform think-alouds in Strand 1 lessons.

CHAPTER 3

Strand 2 of CPI in Grades K–3

Instruction *at* the Point of Student Need

"Apprehension was the feeling I first had as I began CPI Strands 1, 2, and 3. I started with the introduction of the first motion signal to my classroom of first graders. Prediction seemed the best way to start. Students were intent on listening as I modeled the CPM prediction motion, and suddenly they were joining to sign as we predicted together. At first, their attempts were gingerly made, as were mine. Then, as the first week of CPI sessions passed and turned into weeks, my students began to delve into each lesson with such enthusiasm that the introduction of a new motion was accepted immediately.

"The outcome was amazing. Students were intent on listening and participating at a level never witnessed previously. Students honored peers more easily, as they recognized their signals. This communication method improved our sharing time, since selection of respondents could be based on the signal indicated rather than on a random choice on my part. Students seemed to realize that before one could contribute, it was important to use one of the motions. Students now signal instead of waving their hands or speaking out. The highest merit was that students demonstrated an understanding of the comprehension process at a deeper level. Success! A fine example of the carryover effect occurred during our daily opening of predicting a *Family Circus* cartoon. Children were very eager to participate by using their motions. Additionally, parental feedback indicated a carryover effect to their at-home read-aloud times. As a result, parents learned the reading comprehension processes and motions through their children!"

—LETTER FROM DIANE E. VYHNALEK, *first-grade educator,*
Lois Lenski Elementary, Littleton, Colorado

Chapter Overview

As described in Chapter 1, the goal of Strand 2 lessons is to provide more time for students to practice comprehension processes independently as they read silently, under close teacher monitoring. At the same time, Strand 2 lessons create more opportunities for students to learn to experience the pleasure of "living within books." This chapter presents the following eight basic lesson formats that comprise CPI Strand 2 lessons: (1) student-share lessons, (2) stop-and-ask lessons, (3) praise–ask–raise (PAR), (4) pivotal point scaffolding, (5) think-aloud bookmark practice sessions, (6) think-aloud practice games, (7) adhesive note practice sessions, and (8) teacher and student sharing and storytelling at the end of silent reading periods. By the end of the chapter, you will realize how Strand 2 lessons differ from traditional sustained silent reading periods and how you can become a personal coach to a greater number of your students on a daily basis. You will also have answers to the following questions:

1. How can I increase the number of minutes that students actually spend *independently comprehending* during my reading classes?
2. How can I become more available to my students at the exact point in the reading process when their comprehension has been interrupted?
3. How can I increase the effectiveness of independent practice sessions in my classroom through the eight types of Strand 2 lessons?

The goal of Strand 2 lessons is to provide more time for students to enjoy and read books at school. Students practice using the comprehension processes independently and receive mini interventions one-on-one with teachers or peers whenever difficulties arise. As noted previously, Strand 2 lessons differ from traditional periods of sustained silent reading because students were instructed to raise their hands when they came to a point in a text when they are confused. Strand 2 lessons differ from independent practice sessions in which worksheets are used in that students select the books that they want to read, and written work relates to students' descriptions of how well they implemented the comprehension processes being practiced.

The eight basic types of Strand 2 lesson formats can be modified to meet your individual teaching style and student needs. You can use one or more as often as you desire. Unlike Strands 1 and 3, students often cycle through several Strand 2 lessons before they are ready to engage in a Strand 3 lesson. The eight types of Strand 2 lessons are described next.

Stop-and-Ask and Student-Share Lessons

Stop-and-ask and student-share lessons occur as short silent reading periods.

Stop-and-Ask Lessons

In stop-and-ask lessons you carry a notebook in which you record each student's questions in whichever format matches your teaching style (e.g., Excel grid sheet to check off type of comprehension process question asked; notes made on pages on which you record each students questions; forms for placing students in reteaching groups based on the types of questions asked, etc.). The two basic steps in stop-and-ask lessons and an example of a lesson conducted by Mrs. Vyhnalek in her first-grade classroom follow.

When students are involved in student-share Strand 2 lessons, they are so deeply engrossed in making meaning that they do not want to be disturbed, as Brooke, Juanita, and Marcus portray.

Basic Format of a Stop-and-Ask Lesson

Step 1. Have students select a book and read silently. (For this step, allow the students to self-select a book.) Tell them to raise their hands if they become confused.

Step 2. Assist students encountering confusion by giving a brief (about 30 seconds) response. Give a one-sentence answer containing the meaning needed by the student. Then, in a second sentence, state the comprehension processes used to gain that meaning.

Step 3. The student returns to independent, silent reading.

For example, from the classroom library Elisa chose the book *The Chick and the Duckling* by Mirra Ginsburg (1988). She raised her hand at the point where the chick jumps in the pond to swim, just like the duck.

ELISA: Mrs. Vyhnalek, I can't find the detail that explains why the chick isn't swimming?

MRS. VYHNALEK: Elisa, this author, like a lot of authors, puts details in her pictures. In this picture, we see that the duckling has webbed feet that help him swim. Look at the chick's toes—no webs, so he cannot swim.

Student-Share Lessons

Student-share lessons were described in Chapter 1. A sample student-share lesson conducted by Mrs. Vyhnalek is described next.

Earlier in the week, Mrs. Vyhnalek read the nonfiction book *Dinosaur Fossils* by Alvin Granowsky (1995). Today after she read the poem *Fossils* by Lilian Moore, Elisa said:

"In this poem, she's talking about how old fossils are; but they still tell us stuff. I just made a connection to the other story. Remember, he said that we didn't know that dinosaurs had ever lived until they found the fossils. Because I made that connection, I now understand that we know a lot about dinosaurs because of studying the fossils."

When you begin this lesson, list on a chart the comprehension processes that you have taught in prior Strand 1 lessons. Remind students to think about these as you read the book that they selected. Tell them that they can use CPMs to signal which of the comprehension processes on the chart they are using while you are reading; or they can wait until the story is over and discuss which process helped them the most to understand the book and why. After engaging in several student-share lessons, many classes enjoy voting to determine whether students will stop the story to share or whether this lesson will involve uninterrupted reading, followed by a discussion after the book is finished. If the latter format is chosen, one student can be selected to record the page number at which a peer signaled with a particular CPM, and upon the story's end, the entire class can return to that page while the student reports how that comprehension process helped him or her at that point in the text.

Basic Format of a Student-Share Lesson

Step 1. Read aloud to the whole class from a book that was selected by students.

Step 2. Students explain how they are comprehending or ask questions about what they do not understand. As you read, they make CPMs and you call on them to describe the comprehension process they are using. Alternatively, a recorder can list CPMs used beside students' names, so the story is read without interruption. After the oral reading is finished, the recorder can call on students to discuss how they used comprehension processes.

Step 3. Have a student lead a discussion about the book.

Step 4. Ask students to select which process they want to learn in the next Strand 1 lesson. This selection is based on the need to comprehend some aspect of the text they just heard (and others like it) more completely or at a deeper level.

For example, while Mrs. Vyhnalek was reading aloud from *Two Bad Ants* by Chris Van Allsburg (1988), Micah asked, "Why does it say, ". . . the lake tilted and began to empty into a cave?" Mrs. Vyhnalek explained: "The story is from the ants' point of view—the ants' perspective. You and I see someone drinking coffee, but to the ants, they're in a lake flowing into a cave. Perspective means seeing and understanding from another's point of view."

A completed lesson plan for a student-share lesson is provided at the end of this chapter.

Student Think-Aloud Bookmark and Game-Like Practice Sessions

Once students have learned a comprehension process through think-alouds that you have conducted in Strand 1 lessons (including those cited in Chapter 2), you can assist them to initiate these processes without your prompting in Strand 2 lessons that involve think-aloud bookmarks and games. The following game-like, instructional lessons have proven to be the most effective methods of doing so (Block & Israel, 2004).

Think-Aloud Flashcard Games

This activity begins with a review of the thinking processes depicted on the flashcards in Figure 2.1 (p. 24). Allow students to ask any questions they may have about each process. Next, hand out photocopies of Figure 2.1 and have students cut out the squares so that each student has his or her own set of flashcards. These cards can be used in a wide variety of game-like practice sessions; the basic think-aloud flashcard game is described next.

When you begin a book, hold up the flashcards on the top two rows of Figure 2.1 that have the number 1 in the upper left-hand corner. Ask students what they think when they perform each of these pictured think-alouds. Next, have one or two readers perform each think-aloud as they read the first few pages of a book or chapter to the class orally. Then shuffle the flashcards and pick two cards at random. Instruct students to read silently the first two pages of a new book or chapter and to look up when they have finished these pages. Ask them to hold up their copy of one or both the flashcards that depict the thinking they did while they read those pages. Have a few readers recount their thoughts before the group, holding up the flashcards that represent their thoughts. Repeat the process.

On the next day, shuffle the next four cards in Figure 2.1 (these cards contain the number 2 in the upper left-hand corner). Select one of them. Ask students to read the next two pages in the book used above and to perform the think-aloud depicted on the card you are holding, as soon as they have completed the passage. Students perform a think-aloud to describe their thinking processes as they attempt to model those depicted on that card.

Last, after students have finished a book (or a chapter from a longer fictional or nonfictional text), cut out the last five cards in Figure 2.1. These cards contain the number 3 in the upper left-hand corner. Ask students to hold up their copies of the flashcards that depict the comprehension processes that used most frequently as they ended their reading of that text.

You can create many variations of this think-aloud flashcard game. For instance, you can divide the class into teams and award points for teams whose representatives present effective think-alouds of the flashcards you hold up after reading a portion of a book. You can use think-aloud flashcard games in small-group lessons to reinforce the use of expert reading processes when students read text at their instructional levels. You can create think-aloud flashcard games to be used while you and the students read a common text together, performing various types of think-alouds before the class. You can ask students to hold up the flashcard that depicts the thinking process they heard you or their peers perform. You can break students into pairs and ask them to perform think-alouds together. Afterward, have them evaluate which were easiest and which processes need to be retaught.

Peer Think-Aloud Game

This fun-filled lesson is based on the principles of social learning (Vygotsky, 1962) and on scaffolded instruction (Bruner, 1978). In this activity, students perform think-alouds on their own (or in heterogeneous groups). Teach game rules by calling a student to the front of the class to perform a demonstration of the game with you. Classmates sit around the circle to watch the game's procedures. Tell the students that you and this student represent a pair of students. Then shuffle all the flashcards in Figure 2.1 that have the number 1 on them and place them face up on a table. Representing one of the students in the pair, you read orally from a text as students read along silently from their copy of this text with you. When you come to a point when you can perform one of the think-alouds reflected on the flashcards, do so. The other student holds up the flashcard that depicts that think-aloud so the class can see it. If your class agrees that the think-aloud you performed matched the thought process depicted on the card, the cardholder then describes how he or she knew that and receives 1 point. It is then the student's turn to repeat the process. You have the opportunity to select and describe how you knew if the think-aloud did or did not match the process depicted on the card held up by you. Continue in this rotating sequence.

Once you have completed this demonstration, pair students and allow them to begin a new book or chapter. First, they shuffle and turn up flashcards that are numbered 1 in the upper left-hand corner. After students have mastered the first set of thinking processes, repeat the game using flashcards numbered 2 as students read from pages 3–8 in a text. (See footnote on p. 24.) On a subsequent day, ask student pairs to shuffle the flashcards numbered 3 as they finish reading a chapter, book, or a large section of text. This game should be performed in 20-minute sessions so that you can call the class back together and ask students which strategies they performed independently. Conclude this game by asking which processes students would like for you to reteach before they play the peer think-aloud game again.

Think-Aloud Bookmarks

This activity is particularly useful when students read independently or take books home. Think-aloud bookmarks are inserted as markers in students' books to help them remember to think-aloud during reading and practice the thought processes that you have modeled in recent days.

To begin this activity, copy Figure 2.1 (p. 24) and cut the copies into three columns. Give each reader only the first column as a bookmark. After you have modeled the comprehension processes depicted on it, have students use it as a bookmark for 2 weeks each time they read silently at school or home. As they read, ask students to pause and write the page numbers from books in which they used each process in the square that depicts that process on the bookmark.

In week 3, after you have taught the think-alouds on the second column of Figure 2.1, repeat the above steps: Give each student a bookmark of that column to be used for 2 weeks at home. Again, students are to write the page numbers from books in which they used each process in the square that depicts that process on the bookmark, as described above. Similarly, after you have modeled the think-aloud in the last column in Figure 2.1, ask students to perform the same activities and allow them to take this last bookmark home.

To assess students' comprehension, use all three bookmarks in one book. Ask students to write the page and paragraph numbers from their books where they employed each thinking process. When students have finished a book, ask them to randomly select a page that was written on their bookmarks, and perform a think-aloud.

For instance, say you ask students to read *The True Story of the Three Little Pigs* (Farrell, 2002). In the first part students write what they thought as they overviewed the book, and they note on the bookmark at what page they performed the overviewing think-aloud. Then, after they finish reading the first two pages, they write down where they *looked for the author's important information, connected an author's big idea, activated their relevant knowledge,* and *put themselves in the book.* Students continue to read and complete the next five think-alouds on Figure 2.1 before they turn to the next page. At the end of the book, they write on their bookmark the page and paragraph numbers where they *noticed novelties in the text* that helped them to comprehend, how they *put the book into their lives* by summarizing, reflecting, and paraphrasing and how they *anticipated using the knowledge in the future.* Finally, ask each student to meet with you in a one-on-one or in small-group settings to perform a randomly selected think-aloud at a page that was noted on their bookmark.

Once this series of actions has been completed, the class continues to use Figure 2.1. These can then be evaluated to plan future individualized instruction for single or small groups of students.

Writing Think-Alouds on Thinking Guides

The fourth student think-aloud activity is to ask children to write the steps of their thinking (written think-alouds) on thinking guides. To create your thinking guides, use single sheets of paper that describe the steps that initiate and end a comprehension process. To begin this lesson, ask students to write a think-aloud on their thinking guide as you to describe how to use the comprehension process depicted (e.g., draw conclusions, infer, etc). Next, students discuss each step in the process. For example, students read a poem and write their inferences, following the steps in the inference thinking guide in each of the 3 columns after each stanza of that poem. They tell you how they inferred from stanza to stanza.

These innovative student think-aloud activities can be used in a wide variety of ways to increase students' amount of practice in thinking like expert readers. Table 2.3 lists books that have been used very successfully in these activities. Each book enables students to practice several comprehension processes before, during, and after they read.

Adhesive Notes Practice

Another individualized assessment involves think-aloud Post-it Notes. Photocopy Figure 3.1 (or the corresponding page in Appendix A), cut out each light bulb icon and place on a separate Post-it Note. Post-it Notes can be placed at strategic points within a text to remind students to think-aloud each time they see the think-aloud light bulb icon. Next, listen to each student's think aloud orally performed, or ask several students to write them on their Post-it Notes as they read silently. Make a grid that lists all the CPI think-alouds that you have taught, and check each one that students demonstrate without your prompting.

Praise–Ask–Raise Feedback during Strand 2 Lessons

Praise–ask–raise (PAR) is based on research confirming that exemplary teachers' actions contributed significantly to their students' exceptionally high comprehension abilities (Block,

FIGURE 3.1. **Light bulb think-aloud assessment strategy.**

Names of reading processes are written in blanks after student demonstrates an effective think-aloud.

1999; Block, Schaller, et al., 2002). PAR is an impromptu mini-intervention in which you give that child a three-pronged feedback statement after he or she has used a comprehension process correctly and without your prompting. You (1) praise the student for using the comprehension process independently, (2) ask how he or she was able to remember and employ it correctly at that point in the story, and (3) raise the challenge for that individual by teaching a mini-intervention lesson about a slightly harder but related process that you want the student to practice that day and during the next Strand 2 lesson. PAR has been demonstrated to build students' motivation and confidence in their independent comprehension abilities, their metacognitive skills (they must explain how they knew to use an appropriate process), and their courage to take the next step presented to them.

A slight modification of PAR involves students asking their teachers if they have done something correctly. Teachers respond by acknowledging a segment of the comprehension process that the student has executed well. Teachers *praise* (P) the student for the immediate growth he or she has accomplished. Then the teacher adds a separate statement, *ask*ing (A) the student what he or she was thinking to accurately complete that segment of the comprehension process. After the student answers this question, the student's abilities are *raised* (R) by posing a challenge that will assist that individual to use the comprehension process with more difficult texts in the future.

For example, Michelle asked Ms. Parks if she knew of any other books that had characters like Grace in *Amazing Grace* (Hoffman, 1991). In response, Ms. Parks *p*raised Michelle for finding so many good qualities in a character in a book. Then she *a*sked Michelle why she liked Grace. Michelle answered that she had imagined herself as Grace. Ms. Parks *r*aised the ante on Michelle's learning by asking why she thought she was able to connect so much with this book. Michelle answered that it was because the main character was her age and felt the same way as she herself did. Ms. Parks continued by asking which type of character she wanted to identify with next.

In summary, the purpose of the PAR method is to help students apply what they have learned about comprehension processes on their own examine. According to Alec MacKenzie, a prominent social psychologist, "Most problems result from actions taken without thought. Those who know what to do succeed once. Those who know why they succeeded will succeed again and again" (1972, p. 17). PAR enables students to tell you why they comprehended a book, and why they know that they can do equally well or better in the future.

Pivotal Point Scaffolding

Another Strand 2 action is that of pivotal point scaffolding: modeling a comprehension process at a specific point in a text where a child has difficulty. Employing pivotal point scaffolding enable you to personalize the comprehension process and introduce new processes when specific students need them. In this type of think-aloud, you describe a real-world analogy or visual image of a thinking process that a confused student(s) needs to make sense of a specific word, sentence, or paragraph in a text.

The power of pivotal point scaffolding is derived from its timeliness. Intervening in the moment of confusion can catapult students into significantly higher levels of understanding.

Your modeling of specific, relevant thinking process projects students' thought processes forward immediately to overcome the point of confusion and focus on all the other clues in that text.

An example of pivotal point scaffolding appears next, as Mrs. Vyhnalek describes how authors develop characters. Instead of asking, "Who was your favorite character and why?", she said "This character is the most important because [add pivotal point scaffolding here]. In your judgment, am I correct?" You can include how you selected the most important points that you liked about a character.

Once the pivotal point scaffolding is complete, you can ask students to paraphrase what they learned so that they can perform this (or these) comprehension process(es) in the future when a text requires them. The best books to use for this purpose are high-quality fiction and nonfiction works that present universal themes, real-world issues, and common, human conditions written at a student's instructional level (Galda, 1998; Pardo, 1997; Raphael & Au, 1997).

Monitoring Paired Reading in Strand 2 Lessons

Paired reading activities that are continuously monitored are among the most effective forms of Strand 2 lessons. One method of monitoring pairs of students as they tutor each other is that of the Book Buddy Comprehension Process Record. This form (shown in Figure 3.2) lists the comprehension processes that each pair used during that day's Strand 2 lesson. At the end of each book buddy session, pairs agree on a rating that they would give themselves for their ability to perform each process independently, without their partner's or teacher's prompting. This rating system is similar to that used by critics in their ranking of new movies. It reflects tutees' perception of their comprehension. These forms can help students and teachers select the appropriate CPI Strand 3 group for the students during each CPI lesson cycle.

Ms. Jennings is helping these fifth graders learn how to give mini-interventions. She is training them to spend one period a week in K–3 classes, where they will engage in stop-and-ask Strand 2 lessons. These students will work with teachers to ensure that young readers can address their comprehension challenges at their individual points of need.

FIGURE 3.2. **Book Buddy Comprehension Process Record Form.**

Name: _____

Date started	Title of CPI	Number of times used today	Name of person	Rating (1-5)
9-23	Draw Concl.	2	Brandon	1 ② 3 4 5
9-23	Drawing Concluson	3	Sean	1 2 3 ④ 5
9-23	Main Ideas	7	Brandon	1 2 3 4 ⑤
9-23	Reread	1	Sean	1 2 3 4 ⑤
				1 2 3 4 5
				1 2 3 4 5
				1 2 3 4 5
				1 2 3 4 5
				1 2 3 4 5
				1 2 3 4 5
				1 2 3 4 5
				1 2 3 4 5
				1 2 3 4 5
				1 2 3 4 5

Another method of closely monitoring paired students during Strand 2 lessons involves the use of a CPI Book Buddy Process Checklist (see Figure 3.3). This form encourages students to reference specific comprehension processes when confusion occurs while reading. With this record you can track the frequency and effectiveness with which students apply each CPI process. Whenever tutors prompt their tutees, they place a checkmark in the "yes" column of that process. Tutors enjoy this form because it provides a record of all the processes that were taught. Whenever their partner stops reading, they reference it and ask if the student has tried the first, second, third, etc., process on the list, until the student's difficulty has been overcome. Emergent readers profit by checking a sheet that lists numerous processes whenever they experience difficulties.

This form also adds variety to book buddy sessions. For example, tutors can ask tutees to read orally. As tutees read, tutors can check each process on the form that tutees demonstrate or report using. When used in this way, the form enables tutors to stay thoroughly engaged as young students read. Documenting how much their buddies' comprehension processes have improved sharpens tutors' reading and writing skills and comprehension abilities.

Equally effective in monitoring Strand 2 lessons are *book buddy, student-made goal books.* Book buddy teams design these booklets to depict progress on their own self-selected literacy goals. The booklets reflect students' creativity and personalities (e.g., Chan, an 8-

FIGURE 3.3. **CPI Book Buddy Process Checklist.**

Name: _Suzannah Ellen_   Buddy's name: _Mariah_

Directions: When your partner needs your help, suggest one of these processes. Check whether your suggestion worked.

	Yes	No
1. Think of what makes sense—context.	✓	
2. Reread.	✓	
3. Till the text.		✓
4. Set purpose.		✓
5. Predict.	✓	✓
6. Infer.	✓	
7. Main idea.	✓	

Comments on my buddy's retelling of the part that was read:

    Told main ideas without me saying them

Comments on my buddy's use of the processes:

    She used 3 today! more than yesterday

year-old, cut his goal book out in the shape of a football; Shandra, a 6-year-old, drew a picture of Clifford, the big red dog, her favorite book friend, on the cover of her goal book). Young readers note their daily progress, and tutors praise and validate the goal books when the self-designated goals are attained. Stickers can also be placed on daily sheets to denote the completion of each day's work and to enhance each tutee's sense of accomplishment.

Incorporating Strand 2 Lessons into a Weekly Reading Program

Strand 2 lessons usually occur as short silent reading periods that contain two steps.

Step 1. Have students select a book (and sometimes a book buddy) and read silently or orally.

Step 2. As you or a book buddy monitors every students' use of comprehension processes, note them on a written checklist. Assist students encountering confusion by providing a brief PAR or mini-intervention. If you do not use PAR, answer a reader's question immediately with a brief one or two sentence answer that tells the missed meaning and identifies the process the student can use in the future to deduce that meaning independently. An example follows.

Elisa chose the book *Our Eyes* by Vicki Robinson (2002). In this book there is a diagram of the eye that labels the names of the parts within an eyeball. The author poses the question, Why do our eyes water? The sentence beneath that question reads "Our eyes water to wash themselves clean." Elisa became confused.

ELISA: I don't understand. I don't cry to wash my eyes. I cry because I'm sad.

MRS. VYHNALEK: (*pointing to words in the diagram and reading aloud*) "When our eyes water, tears flow out of the tear glands (where tears are made). Some tears may flow down our cheeks. Some tears flow into little holes (called tear ducts) in the inner corners of our eyes. These tear ducts drain the tears into the nose." In the future when you see a chart like this, *till* the text inside the chart because it will usually tell you details that relate to the main idea that may not have been given in the paragraphs around it.

Summary

There are many types of Strand 2 lessons. They assist students to read books and see the world anew. The books act as mirrors by which students can quietly reflect and make new discoveries about themselves, as people, by reading someone else's insights about similar life experiences (Block & Mangieri, 1996a–c; Block & Cavanagh, 1998; Galda, 1998; Gaskins et al., 1991; Pressley et al., 1995). Students have a master reader (a teacher or an adult volunteer) at their side to coach them at points of need.

Reflecting on What You Have Learned

1. **Interpreting (Summarizing) the Main Points.** When instruction is not differentiated, the multiple intelligences, varied personalities, and literacy needs of a full classroom of students cannot be met. The Comprehension Process Approach to literacy provides students a means of contributing to reading discussions at strategic points and applying multiple processes as they occur. These lessons provide instruction before, during, and after the point of need.

2. **Making Professional Decisions.** The first decision a teacher faces is integrating the research-based instruction with school adopted literacy programs. The goal of our instruction is "teaching the right things" to students, not "teaching the things right." What is the first step necessary to integrate Strand 2 lessons with your

current curriculum? What resources and materials that you currently possess are necessary to aide in the implementation of this instruction?

3. **Making Field Applications and Observations.** Schedules will need to provide time for whole group instruction, small group reflection, and uninterrupted individual reading. Solicit the expertise of fellow teachers. Divide the strands among these teachers and have each create a model Strand 2 lesson appropriate for the grade level and share with interested colleagues. After the teachers implement the instruction in the classroom, a meeting to reflect on successes and areas of improvement before planning the next group of lessons greatly enhances the success of future lessons.

4. **Keeping a Professional Record-Keeping Journal.** Record the research in this chapter that will make the greatest impact on your students. List the assets and challenges in implementing this research in the classroom. Create an outline of the steps required to overcome these challenges.

5. **Making Multicultural Applications.** Through the use of multicultural literature, students recognize cultural nuances. Explore multicultural life through the use of cultural studies, guest speakers, and videos, to improve the readers' comprehension of such texts.

6. **Meeting Students' Special Needs.** Strand 1 lessons provide the modeling and scaffolding necessary for struggling readers. Strand 2 lessons allow students to work on an independent reading level, thereby meeting the needs of struggling as well as advanced readers. Describe why Strand 2 lessons are equally effective for above- and below-grade-level readers.

7. **Checking Key Terms.** Following is a list of concepts introduced in this chapter. Place a checkmark in the blanks preceding each concept that you have learned on a first reading of this chapter. For those that you do not know, refer back to the page where it is referenced.

   ____Think-aloud bookmarks (p. 45)

   ____Praise–ask–raise (p. 46)

   ____Pivotal point scaffolding (p. 48)

   ____Monitored paired reading (p. 49)

   ____Student-made goal books (p. 50)

8. **Design a Comprehension Process Lesson.** Design a lesson teaching two comprehension processes using the steps in the Strand 1, 2, and 3 lessons. The major purpose of Strand 1 is to scaffold the instruction as you model the process during whole group read-aloud. Strand 2 allows the students to self-select texts with assistance when necessary. The reader selects the process requiring additional explanation in Strand 3 lessons. Then conduct a discovery discussion as described in the following Comprehension Process Lesson 2, to determine a student's depth of leaning and ability to ask for help.

Comprehension Process Lesson 2:
Teaching the Process of Asking for Help—Conducting Discovery Discussions

1. Create a chart for students to sign up for discovery discussions with you.

2. Create a folder in which you can record the information revealed in the discovery discussions.

3. Explain to students how to sign up for a discovery discussion. Specify that they can sign up for one every week, if they want to discuss new discoveries that they are making about their reading abilities.

4. Hold no more than three discovery discussions a day so that you are not depleted of the energy to stay intensely focused on each student's story about his or her abilities and progress.

5. Allow the student to open the discovery discussion. If he or she does not begin with a question, consider asking of the following:

   • What have you discovered about your reading abilities?
   • What are you learning about comprehension?
   • What do you want to learn to comprehend better?
   • What bothers you about your reading abilities?
   • What do you need me to do to help you improve comprehension?

6. When students share an insight, paraphrase it and ask if you heard them accurately. If you observe that a student has increased his or her comprehension in a specific way, ask the student if your observation is accurate. Then ask the student to demonstrate that comprehension process and describe how he or she knows when to use it.

7. To become a trusted mentor, do not rush from one student to the next. Rather, provide undivided attention to each student. The most important part of discovery discussions often occurs at the end, when many students gain the confidence to risk asking a very important question and sharing an insight about their reading weaknesses. Discovery discussions provide a safe setting in which students feel free to describe their weaknesses, from their own perspectives, in a way they do not otherwise do.

CHAPTER 4

Strand 3 of CPI in Grades K–3

Instruction *after* Students Have Experienced
the Point of Need

Ms. Williams, a second-grade teacher, had implemented many of the lessons in this chapter. One day in early May, Conrad offered this feedback to his teacher: "Talking about what I read with my friends helps me comprehend. I know you have to do a lot of planning so we can work together with a work buddy. Today, in my buddy reading group, Connor told me that I was a good reader! Thank you for teaching us how to comprehend by giving us choices and teacher–reader groups."

Chapter Overview

Teachers and curricula perform two important functions in developing students' comprehension. Pupils' active engagement is the third component in effective comprehension development. This chapter explains how to teach Strand 3 lessons that boost students' engagement. By the end of this chapter, you will be able to answer the following questions:

1. How can you help children become active partners in the comprehension process?
2. How do Strand 3 lessons empower children to express their voices, make wise choices, and initiate their own higher-level comprehension abilities?
3. What methods enable children's voices to become more powerful?
4. Which choices can you offer students that will increase their comprehension?

Strand 3 Lessons: Students Choose What They Want to Learn (Instruction *after* Need Was Experienced in a Strand 2 Lesson)

If this type of lesson is neglected, students' own ideas about how they can become better readers are often disregarded. When these metacognitions are expressed, however, many students experience new insights that they discovered, by themselves, about the reading process. By participating in Strand 3 lessons, many students experience an increased desire to improve their comprehension because they learn new insights that help them meet more difficult comprehension challenges (Block, 2003). Several basic Strand 3 lesson plans follow.

Teacher–Reader Groups

In a *teacher–reader group*, a group of students choose a comprehension processes about which they want to learn more. All students who want to become better at using those processes meet together in a small group, which is called a teaching and reading group or teacher–reader group. A specific comprehension process is then taught and discussed in a more focused way than in any other strand of lessons. Teachers help by writing scripts for student leaders of teacher–reader groups. (See Table 4.1 for suggested groups of comprehension processes that can be taught in teacher–reader groups.)

During these group meetings, students discuss how they accomplish a particular aspect of the reading process. All students bring one of their favorite books to the group meeting and demonstrate how they make meaning, infer, draw a conclusion, etc. As they demonstrate, they also discuss and ask questions about how they can learn to overcome specific reading problems by applying that domain of comprehension. The suggestions for overcoming these problems are recorded on a Teacher–Reader Group Thinking Chart, which is later shared with the other groups (see Figure 4.1 and Appendix A). Students are required to stay with the same group for at least two meetings; however, most remain in the same group for four or more lessons, electing not to change after the mandatory time has elapsed.

Between teacher–reader group meeting times, students practice the suggestions they learned. In the next week's meeting, peers teach the new things that they have learned about the aspect of making meaning for which the group has been assembled. The teacher–reader leader of that group records students' findings on the group chart so that the teacher can

Ms. William's students enjoy Fridays best because they get to conduct their teacher–reader groups. Notice how intently students attend to their peer's descriptions of what they are doing, and need to perform better, about the comprehension process for which they choose to learn more.

TABLE 4.1. **Suggested Areas of Focus for Teacher–Reader Groups**

Meaning Makers. We want to learn how to understand better, make more in-depth connections in texts, and interrelate two or more comprehension processes.

Transformer Titans. We want to learn how we can more rapidly infer, predict, and apply what we read to our lives.

Word Wanters. We want to learn more decoding strategies. We will bring a book we are reading to group meetings to model how we decoded a difficult word. We will ask classmates to find similar words and try out these strategies in their books.

Speed Mongrels. We want to increase our speed of oral and silent reading by learning to use the comprehension processes of tilling the text, skimming, scanning, and text-feature analysis.

Memory Menders. We want to find ways to retain more of what we read by learning to use the comprehension processes of reflection, summary, and drawing conclusions.

Critical Analyzers. We want to learn how better to connect what we read to other readings. We also want to learn how to validate and extend what we read by learning to use cause-and-effect thinking, reasoning, facts, opinions, as well as to suspend judgment.

track each group's progress. A teacher meets with only one teacher–reader group at a time. At the beginning of the year, other teacher–reader groups either meet at a different time that day (so that the teacher will also be present) or on different days. By midyear, some teachers train students to lead these groups alone, so that all students can meet in different groups at the same time. The teacher can move from group to group to note progress being made in each group's understanding of the comprehension processes being discussed. Such lessons are conducted most effectively if no more than three teacher–reader groups meet each week, so that the students can have three choices of comprehension processes about which they can learn more.

In this teacher–reader group, Conrad is telling his friends what he has learned to summarize this week, and he prepared a sample fable, using **The Boy Who Cried Wolf**, to show his group how he does it.

FIGURE 4.1. **Teacher–Reader Group Thinking Chart.**

- -

Name of the group: _____

Members of the group are: _____

Comprehension process taught: _____

Where and how do you use this process?

1.

2.

3.

4.

5.

6.

What new things have you learned that help you use this comprehension process more easily and better?

1.

2.

3.

4.

5.

6.

- -

Incorporating Strand 3 Lessons into a Weekly Reading Program

In Strand 3 lessons, students choose what they want to learn (instruction after the point of need) and can form teacher–reader groups:

Step 1. Divide students into small groups based on their needs and interests.

Micah chose to join the Meaning Makers group for a more complete discussion of the process of *perspective.* She needed additional clarification of the process to enhance her understanding for future readings.

Step 2. Work with a small group. Allow each student to use his or her individual skills as assets for the entire group.

Mrs. Chester chose to work first with the Meaning Makers group, realizing that the process of gaining perspective involves an abstract concept that could prove difficult for young readers to grasp. She wants to ensure that the students' discussion provided an accurate definition and detailed examples of the process.

Step 3. The group reports what was learned to the class.

As the Meaning Makers group reported the points of their meeting, the Perspective process was clarified and reviewed for all the students. Several students had misunderstood the process, and the corrected information was added to their background knowledge. The group felt that performing an oral storytelling of a previously read book from a different perspective would contribute additional depth to their current understanding.

To review, Strand 3 teacher–reader groups improve students' abilities to diagnose and overcome their comprehension weaknesses (Block & Johnson, 2002). In these groups students discuss new methods they use to make meaning and to find out what they want to learn next to comprehend better. Students and teachers offer suggestions for overcoming specific reading problems. Teacher–reader groups allow students to choose what they want to learn about the reading process and to have choices in the reading class that extend beyond simply selecting a book that they want to read.

Discovery Discussions

Discovery Discussions are Strand 3 lessons that occur between you and a single student. Students meet alone with you to discuss how they improved their reading abilities, what they depend on to read well, and what they need to comprehend better. Such self-knowledge is essential because students themselves are the most aware of the level of effort and drive they are willing to expend to become more successful comprehenders.

Strand 3 discovery discussions are distinct from teacher one-on-one conferences in several ways. First, they can be scheduled by teachers or students. Second, their purpose is to discover something that is blocking a student's comprehension, rather than the teacher assuming beforehand that he or she is aware of any difficulties the child is having. Third, they provide individualized time for teachers to listen to students' stories about their comprehension, rather than the teacher repeating prior instruction to the student. Fourth, discovery discussions are not top-down interrogations (i.e., teachers do not ask all the questions). Students do most of the talking and ask most of the questions.

Discovery discussions are intended to increase the level of effort and drive that students expend to become better readers (Block & Mangieri, 2003). They are modeled on past traditions, when children gained knowledge through fireside family conversations and by-the-bench mentoring. During these conversations, teachers and students ask more questions of each other, and students tell specific stories about their reading abilities. They are then exposed to focused learning in their zones of proximal development and are encouraged to communicate the next step they want to take to become better readers. As a result, students can ensure that they do not have to spend much time in the zones of their already known.

Discovery discussions also enable teachers to consistently nurture characteristics that correlate with high student achievement. We conducted research on discovery discussions to determine their value in providing teachers with students' perspectives on what they deem to be the most important aspects of comprehension instruction, even if these ideas related to minor adaptations. For example, a second-grade student stated, "I wish my teacher would make different voices for characters in stories." Integrating students' concerns and ideas into your classroom instruction increases their achievement, self-efficacy, participation, and motivation because they realize that their teacher actually listens to them and implements their ideas.

The study included 141 kindergartners, 163 first graders, 138 second graders, and 253 third graders from Georgia, Texas, New Jersey, Maine, Illinois, and Florida. Students were given unlimited time to respond to the following questions:

What do you want your teacher to do to help you learn more than you are in reading now?

What can your teacher do to become a better literacy teacher?

Students were asked to think about what the "best teacher of literacy" would do that would make it possible for them to learn more at their specific grade level. The most frequently cited qualities/actions follow.

Instructionally

- "Please don't forget to have story time every day."
- "Try to help us a little more by pointing to the words in the big book while you read."
- "Try to explain things until we understand them."
- "When you are trying to teach and it gets real hard, act it out, or make what you want us to learn into a story."

Personally

- "Try to be sure that you can be seen clearly by every student."
- "Try to spend more time really talking with us about deep thoughts in books."
- "Try to wear different clothes every day."

When reading aloud

- "Try to make different voices for characters in the story."
- "Don't read too many elaborated books."
- "If you have to read a book that is complicated, try to explain it as you go. Try to use books that help us learn how to be kinder and fairer."

When we are telling you what we comprehended

- "Try to give us two chances to answer, and trust everyone equally."
- "Try not to assume we all misunderstand because one of us is having a problem. Help that one, but don't slow down and reteach the whole class.
- "Keep down the number of names that you write on the board."

Our goal was to collect research about what students want their teachers to do during literacy instruction. Apart from conducting formal research, we recommend that you implement comparable midterm surveys with your entire class in December and March of each year to collect students' feedback on what they would like you to do "more of" in class. The three groups of questions that comprise these surveys follow:

- What activity that we have done in class thus far this year helped you comprehend the most? What was it about this activity that helped you learn so much?
- To find time to do more of this activity in the future, what would you want us to *not* do any more? Why has this activity not helped you learn as much as others have?
- What do you want us to do that we have not had a chance to do this year? What would you change about our class? Why would this activity or change help you comprehend more?

The steps for discovery discussions appeared in Comprehension Process Lesson 2 (p. 54).

Structured Turn Taking

For more than 100 years, psychologists and educators have recognized the importance of experiential relevance to student learning. In the words of William James (1890), "millions of items of the outward order are presented to students' senses which never properly enter into their experiences. Why? Because they have no interest for students. Only those items which students notice will shape their mind" (p. 402). When you increase students' abilities to voice their interpretations of what they comprehended, they can more ably enter discussions of text. Structured turn taking is designed to accomplish this goal.

During a structured turn-taking lesson, students ask questions about problems they had as they read in a Strand 2 lesson. The process of identifying a problem and taking the risk to inquire into areas of comprehension weaknesses teaches younger readers to ask better questions of themselves when they read silently. Structured turn taking also empowers students to alter their energy allocations (e.g., shift their attention from one thing to another) and organize their metacognitions (e.g., "I'm clear about _____, but I don't understand _____") as they progress through a text (Ames, 1992; Wigfield, Eccles, & Rodrigues, 1999).

The basic lesson format and an example lesson conducted by Ms. Williams with her second graders are presented at the end of this chapter (Comprehension Process Lesson 3). In structured turn-taking lessons, kindergarten and first-grade students answer verbally, whereas second and third graders write the comprehension questions that arose while they read in a Strand 2 lessons. You can elicit these questions at the end of Strand 2 lessons in a wide variety of ways. For instance, you can introduce a new comprehension process (or processes) in a Strand 1 lesson. Then ask students to engage in a Strand 2 silent reading period for 5–10 minutes and use the process that you just taught. At the end of this lesson, have them ask a question about using the process on a piece of paper. Alternatively, ask students to pose questions orally to you as they arise while they read; compile a master list of these questions to be used on the following day in a Strand 3 structured turn-taking lesson.

Another option: Distribute note cards on which students write questions about how to overcome comprehension challenges as they read. Then, in small teacher- or student-led group discussions, students draw cards and relate the comprehension processes that they used to answer the question on that card for themselves as they read. At first students generally ask questions about content, such as "Why was the wolf mean?" after reading *The Three Little Pigs* (Scieszka, 1993). As they experience more structured turn-taking lessons, their questions become more sophisticated until they query into their own inabilities to understand—for example, "Why did I have trouble finding the main idea in this book?" Each time you begin this activity, first model the latter types of questions.

Strand 3 structured turn taking is a key component in comprehension development because it develops self-regulated readers. Such learners have three important characteristics. First, they regulate their comprehension processes and intertwine facts in the text with their own purposes. Second, the challenging choices that their teachers present to them lead them to believe that they are capable of deriving meaning from any text that interests them. Third, the challenging choices that their teachers present to them to question texts in their own unique manners enable them to set numerous goals for themselves before, during, and after reading. As a result, such students most often monitor their own comprehension, evaluate how well they perform compared to their own standards, and voice their understandings uninhibitedly (Zimmerman & Bonner, 2000).

Empowering Students' Choices: Strand 3 Book Buddy Lessons

It is equally important to provide students in K–3 with reading choices. Implementing a weekly Strand 3 book buddy program does so. Children make choices all day long about which of the multitudinous stimuli around them to attend. Using the book buddy format enables you to teach them how to *consciously* select the comprehension processes they need to use during reading. As a result, you can refrain from delivering too much direction. If we, as teachers, insist on doing all of the thinking for our students, and if they interpret this behavior as meaning that everything has to be done according to the teacher's way, then what have we left for our students to turn to with pride concerning their own comprehension?

In Strand 3 book buddy lessons, students are taught to commit themselves, to take chances, and to get involved in making meaning up to the limits of their capabilities.

Book buddy interactions can dispel students' fears that they are incapable of comprehending, and raise their levels of comprehension by helping them become internally guided readers. Over time, students come to understand that comprehension is not merely a matter of terminating confusion but also one of selecting appropriate thinking processes to remediate that confusion. Students participating in book buddy lessons ask their partners questions about the reading process, and learn how to detect when incoming stimuli are coherent or incoherent. Assuming this control rewards students by promoting deeper levels of personalized comprehension (Cameron & Pierce, 1994; Lion & Betsy, 1996). Students' efficacy can increase when they teach other students by becoming book buddies or the "reader of the day," which is described in a subsequent section of this chapter.

In a study of 637 children from grades K–3 who were asked what they do to improve their own comprehension, none cited any methods that they used to teach themselves. The only action they knew to take to boost their comprehension was "to read more" (Block, 2001d). We, as teachers, can develop students' self-efficacy as comprehenders by assisting them to work through the confusions of life with characters in books. When students are taught to understand how a character resolved matters of right and wrong, for instance, they augment their ability to comprehend what other characters do relative to other large issues and human conditions (Lehr & Thompson, 2000). Orellana (1995) reported that when students were allowed to collaborate and select their own book groups for reading, based on interest, their reading significantly improved at every grade level. We have found that when teachers continually allow students to group and regroup themselves—to lead their small-group discussions in teacher–reader groups and book buddy programs, students realize that they are more alike than different in their reading abilities—regardless of the reading level at which they entered the group.

Block (1997a) demonstrated a side benefit of this Strand 3 lesson. Students who became book buddies reported that they no longer felt a need to hide their faults from fellow group members. They more freely admitted their errors in comprehension because they were group officers, which meant they had the responsibility of telling their peers when they did not comprehend something well. This admission tended to increase students' abilities to diagnose their own comprehension problems.

Strand 3 Book Buddy Lessons

Buddy reading, or "book buddies," involves pairing underachieving readers with older, more advanced students from classes that are a few grade levels above their own. Book buddies can also be formed from among students of different reading levels in the same classroom. In the typical format, the more able students select books at their partner's readability level and share them with their "buddy" once a week for 30 minutes. Both book buddies share the same book and ask (and answer) each other's questions about the content. Primary-grade teachers meet with intermediate-grade teachers to schedule time for their teams of book buddies to read. They also identify locations on the school campus where buddy interactions can occur in a relaxed atmosphere.

The benefits of buddy reading are well documented (for a review of the research, see Block & Dellamura, 2000/2001; Johnston, Invernizzi, & Juel, 1998). The tutor, the early reader, and the teacher all benefit from this program. Even as early as grade 1, benefits are apparent. As Suzanna, a 6-year-old, wrote: "I liked it too day cus it was fun. I red One hole book I like my reader because She is nice and it is fun I lik reading with my reader She likes me and I like her."

In book buddy sessions, most often, two students are engaged in reading processes 100% of the time. Tutors also quickly develop dramatic modulations and inflections in their oral read abilities. They also learn to use other vocal qualities to sustain their younger readers' interests, such as pronouncing individual words with wide-ranging pitches, varying the pace, and creating distinct voices to depict different characters in a story.

In addition, by choosing a book to share, tutors gain a sense of accomplishment. They realize that their own reading ability has progressed when they choose books for their buddies and recognize how much easier it is for them to read the books than it was in their recent past. This value of realizing how far they have come as readers disperses positive effects and leads to growth in other subject areas, as has been documented through testimonials and retelling forms (Block, 2002a). Figure 4.2 presents a retelling form that can be distributed during paired second- and third-grade Strand 3 lessons so that students can record their comprehension strengths and weaknesses. It can also be used in kindergarten and grade 1 if these students' reading partners come from grades 3–5.

After several book buddy sessions have been initiated, you can lead a Strand 1 lesson in which you instruct tutors in how to select books for their tutees that will teach them how to apply specific comprehension processes. For instance, David, a fifth-grade student, contemplated and considered many books for his buddy before selecting *The Stinky Cheese Man* (Scieszka, 2002). This was his "all-time favorite book" and he was excited about his choice. Then he decided to search for a second book. The goal that his teacher had established for this particular book buddy session was to increase Sam's (his buddy's) prediction abilities. After carefully surveying several titles, David added *If You Give a Moose a Muffin* (Numeroff, 1991) to his buddy's reading plan. According to David, "For a kindergarten child, this book will be better for me to show how to make a prediction. That's what I want to teach today." After this book buddy lesson, David reported that being required to examine this process of prediction and apply it to *If You Give a Moose a Muffin* increased *his* abilities to make predictions when he read. Verbalizing the predictive thinking process by teaching with think-alouds and repeated examples made this expert reading process more automatic for him.

Tutees realize many benefits from buddy reading as well. First, they are assigned an older student in the school who befriends them. In Sam's case, he had come to enjoy David's visits almost as much as his recess periods. He would see David in the hall, wave, and proudly announce to anyone within earshot: "That's my buddy!" Not only did Sam's esteem,

FIGURE 4.2. **Retelling form for use in paired Strand 3 lessons (such as book buddy programs).**

Name ___*Mark Ethan*_____ Date _*2-16-04*___

I listened to _____*Jason*_____ retell the book ____*Enemy Pie*_____

1. Ask your partner to retell the book. As he or she talks, check what is said. Write one sentence after each comment. *He learned how to be a frend*

2. Check the comprehension process your partner did well and write a sample sentence he or she said after each process you checked.

   My partner told about:

   __✓__ The characters ___*of Dad, Stalney.*_____

   __✓__ The setting ___*Tree House and Houses*_____

   __✓__ The events in the story or several facts from the book ___*played basketball and cheeckers*

   __✓__ The beginning ___*was in the morning*_____

   __✓__ The ending ___*was happy*_____

   __✓__ Applied it to his/her life ___*Yes — will be a frend now*____

   __✓__ Told why he/she did or did not like it ___*to end — Want to do on and on*

   __✓__ The main ideas ___*were to try to like peopel*_____

   __✓__ The details ___*about the pie was real good*_____

Describe the process your partner did best.

___*Paused to apply to his life lots*_____

___*He reread when he didn't understand*_____

_____

Describe the process with which your partner needs more help.

___*Finding main ideas*_____

___*Infer*_____

_____

belongingness, and pride increase, his literacy abilities grew at a rapid pace. This acceleration was marked not only in measurable rises in readability levels but also in Sam's deep, internalized value for literacy in his life. One measure of the impact of the book buddy program on his affective literacy growth was evidenced when he presented David with a treasured Christmas present. Sam walked into the library with his beloved gift hidden behind his back in a paper sack that he had decorated. Before he handed it to David, he whispered in Ms. Carey's ear that he had selected this present with special care because he wanted David to have the very best present in the world. When David opened his package, he saw Sam's treasured gift: a book for David to keep forever! Having a book of one's own was something that Sam had come to value—a published goal that every reading program strives to achieve.

The third person to benefit from a Strand 3 buddy-reading program is you. Many young readers need a fair amount of one-on-one instructional time. Such tutoring would not be possible for you to deliver to all your students so frequently without a weekly Strand 3 book buddy program in action. For example, if you were to share a book for 30 minutes with every student (in your class of about 23 pupils), it would require that you do nothing else except "buddy read" *every minute of the school day* for *two full days* every week.

Book buddy activities enable you to provide less able readers with opportunities to receive the benefits of exclusive attention, interesting reading experiences, and personalized instruction from people other than yourself. Furthermore, book buddies enable younger readers to pose more questions and hear literacy strategies explained in words that are more closely attuned to their own oral vocabularies. Elementary-age tutors communicate difficult concepts through words that are part of the rapidly changing, colorful, everyday vernaculars of children.

Traditionally, individual book buddy sessions begin with a story read aloud by the tutor, who then asks questions in an oral format. Then, the younger buddy in the pair shares his or her thoughts and responses to the book. Most often, these exchanges are not documented with written records of the questions asked and answers given. As a result, it is difficult for teachers to chart the specific progress of each child. We recommend the following types of writing activities, which can eliminate these deficiencies and significantly increase the effects of buddy reading. The lessons are easy to implement—an important factor for teachers who manage buddy-reading programs.

Studies have shown that when buddy reading is coupled with writing activities, writing abilities, comprehension, and reading retention increase (Block & Dellamura, 2000/2001; Invenez, Mendon, & Juel, 1999). For this reason, book buddy sessions are more successful when journals are kept. A journal can be a file folder that contains single sheets of notebook paper. Each tutor's and tutee's name is written on the folder's label and cover. Prior to each book buddy session, tutors can record the date of the session on the notebook paper, titles of books to be read, and questions that they want to ask about the book, or activities they want to engage using the book. Following each question, the tutor leaves space to write the answers given by the tutee.

As a closing activity, on the back of each page, tutors can write the response their tutees gave to one or more of the following questions (or questions) that their teachers use to assess individual tutees' reading progress:

1. What did you learn today that helped you read better?
2. Is there anything else that you would like to share or say about this book?
3. What do you want to learn at the next book buddy session?

To sum up, a book buddy program encourages tutors and tutees to reach new heights in comprehension. By incorporating writing activities, you can significantly increase the program's benefits. Book buddy journals, buddy reading records, retelling forms, and goal books used in Strand 2 and 3 lessons (as described here and in Chapter 3) have been demonstrated to significantly increase tutees' and tutors' literacy abilities (Block, 2001b; Block, Schaller, et al., 2002).

Reader of the Day

A sixth basic Strand 3 lesson format is that of reader of the day. The reader of the day is a student who opens a full class meeting that is designed to discuss how well students have learned the comprehension process that was introduced in a prior Strand 1 lesson and practiced through several Strand 2 lessons. The child you select to be reader of the day must have demonstrated a mastery of the comprehension process being learned. Before the end of the school year, all students will have been a reader of the day at least once. Even your least able readers can lead discussions about how they selected a "good book" after you taught the Strand 1 lessons relative to that process (described in Chapter 2).

Before each Strand 3 lesson, you meet with the reader of the day to review the plans that the student has created for the class discussion and activity. Then, the reader of the day describes something important that he or she has learned about the comprehension process(es) the class has been studying. The student (1) demonstrates how he or she learned to initiate that comprehension process, (2) performs the process with a book before the class, and (3) invites classmates to ask questions about the process. The reader of the day can also assist peers as they engage in the planned activity. Afterward, hold a discovery discussion with the reader of the day and ask him or her to identify how the experience assisted his or her comprehension; then plan a higher comprehension goal for that student. This method of allowing each student to create comprehension activities that teach peers and to start the school day develops a sense of partnership and ownership between teacher and students (Block, 2001c; Horne, 2000).

After several reader-of-the-day Strand 3 lessons have occurred, many young readers become accustomed to the idea that their words can inaugurate the day's reading activities. They are more willing to pose questions at the beginning of reading classes about comprehension difficulties that they had during the prior day's Strand 2 lessons.

Summary

Your students' simplest requests about reading comprehension can be addressed using the various Strand 3 lesson formats presented in this chapter. The forms of Strand 3 lessons presented in this chapter can be adapted to provide tailored opportunities for students to diagnose and discuss their comprehension strengths and weaknesses. The basic Strand 3 lessons presented in this chapter were (1) teacher–reader groups, (2) discovery discussions, (3) midterm surveys, (4) structured turn taking, (5) book buddy reading programs, and (6) reader of the day.

When you implement Strand 3 lessons frequently, student-initiated comprehension processing becomes more commonplace. Students should meet together and decide the areas in which they need to learn more. Strand 3 lessons encourage young readers to teach others how they can boost their meaning making to higher levels, and enables them to learn how to increase their own comprehension abilities.

Reflecting on What You Have Learned

1. **Interpreting (Summarizing) the Main Points.** List five important principles you learned in Chapter 4.

2. **Making Professional Decisions.** In approximately one paragraph, describe your fondest memory of a comprehension lesson that was designed to (1) increase your students' voice, (2) increase your students' choice, and (3) enable students to hoist their own comprehension abilities higher. How did it increase your students' comprehension?

3. **Making Field Applications and Observations.** Interview students about choices, voices, and hoists that they have exerted in their own reading lessons. Compare these students' abilities with the benefits described as accruing from the lessons in this chapter.

4. **Keeping a Professional Journal.** Make a list of all activities in this chapter in one column. In a column to the right of that, note the titles of children's or adolescent literature you want to use to help students express their voices, choices, and decisions in each of these lessons. Fill in as many as possible, and add to it throughout your teaching career.

5. **Making Multicultural Applications.** Perform a case study by visiting with a student for an hour, during which he or she shares a favorite book, lesson, and writing sample. Choose a student from a heritage other than your own. After the visit, write about what you learned from the experience that will assist you in adapting the lessons in this chapter for students from that heritage to enhance their ability to make better choices, express more courageous voices, and hoist their comprehension abilities higher.

6. **Meeting Students' Special Needs.** Which activity would be best for students who do not speak English at home: structured turn taking or buddy reading? Defend your answer.

7. **Checking Key Terms.** Following is a list of concepts introduced in this chapter. If you have learned the meaning of a term, place a checkmark in the blank that precedes that term. If you are not sure of a term's definition, increase your retention by reviewing its definition. If you have learned four of these terms on your first reading of this chapter, you have constructed many meanings that are important for your work.

    ____Teacher–reader groups (p. 56)

    ____Thinking charts (p. 58)

    ____Structured turn taking (p. 61)

    ____Buddy reading (p. 62)

    ____Buddy reading retelling form (p. 65)

8. **Design a Comprehension Process Lesson.** Comprehension Process Lesson 3 can lead students out of passive decoding habits and into active, questioning, idea-seeking habits. This lesson contains two different methods, which you are to modify in two new ways. At its core is the principle that the more we ask students

to write and answer questions while they read, the more they will do so independently and metacognitively, without prompting. Structured turn taking assists students to become active participants in making their own meanings from text.

Comprehension Process Lesson 3:
Increasing Students' Abilities to Ask Questions through Structured Turn Taking

This CPI Strand 3 lesson encourages students to ask questions about what they need. The following procedures are basic steps that can be modified in a variety of ways to meet your students' needs.

1. Students read a story (either to themselves or aloud with the teacher).

2. Students are each given a note card with a number on one side. (Each student receives one note card, and all the note cards should have different numbers on them.)

3. Students are asked to write a question about the story just read or an idea they would like to discuss with the class. (This step should take only a few minutes.)

4. The note cards are retrieved and redistributed to different students who then take a few minutes to read their question/idea and think of a way to start a group discussion about the topic.

5. The student with the card numbered 1 reads his or her question or topic aloud and then begins the discussion for the class. Members of the class raise their hands and respond. This process continues until all the questions or topics on the cards have been discussed.

    There are many pros to this activity. Using note cards gives the students time to consider their answers and how they want to present them to the class without having to experience on-the-spot pressure. Students also know when they will be called on to answer their questions, so they are not taken by surprise and placed in situations in which they may feel embarrassed. The note cards also give students the ability to ask a question anonymously. Many times this is easier for children because they will not fear being ridiculed by their classmates.

    The note cards can also be used with partners or in small groups where a few children can discuss what they think and then share their discussion with the class by telling or writing their answers. The note cards can serve to encourage students to get to know one another and become comfortable speaking in front of other students, especially those they do not know well. Because this is a discussion session, children need not fear being wrong. They can freely express their feelings, and whether they agree or disagree with others.

CHAPTER 5

CPI Lessons That Increase Literal Comprehension of Fiction

With anticipation, the students watched for the reaction on Mr. Smith's face. Juan had responded to Mr. Smith's question about the story, and everyone seemed in agreement with the response. But now, Mr. Smith had asked him if he was sure his answer was correct and on what did he base his response. Neither Juan nor his classmates were as confident as they were a moment ago. Juan was confused!

Chapter Overview

Unfortunately, many reading classrooms look like this: Students sit patiently waiting for the teacher to guide them to the "correct" answer. They believe that everything they read should be interpreted literally. The students believe that teachers know all the answers, or if they do not, they can find them in the "teacher's manual." If students become confused, they try to "read" their teacher's expression and guess the correct answer. These behavior patterns, long supported by traditional teaching methods, limit students' comprehension in two ways: Students do not learn how to construct accurate literal interpretations, and they refrain from thinking beyond a literal level to apply what they read to their lives.

It is essential that students learn to be self-regulated readers. Teachers must guide readers through the process of constructing literal interpretations. Through the instruction in this chapter, K–3 students become motivated to read *through* the challenges, selecting more difficult books and extending the depth and breadth of their background knowledge. When young readers have gained the confidence to check their knowledge base for the accuracy of their understanding of a text, they no longer seek the knowing nod of the teacher.

In this chapter, you will learn about research and Strands 1, 2, and 3 lessons that facilitate students' abilities to construct accurate literal understandings. These procedures develop students' abilities to comprehend single sentences as well as interpret meaning between sentences, paragraphs, within a full text, and among multiple texts. The discussion includes methods that strengthen students' abilities to ask themselves questions while they read and bolster their recall. This chapter's goal is to ensure that students build accurate, factual bases from which they can draw inferences and images. Once students understand what an author intended, they are better able to make valid translations to their lives.

By the end of this chapter, you will be able to answer the following questions:

1. How can teachers instruct readers to move beyond "word calling"?
2. What strategies promote self-regulation by readers?
3. How can you successfully present decoding and comprehension instruction simultaneously?
4. How can you teach students to build their own background knowledge?
5. How can you assist students in setting their own purposes for reading so that goal setting becomes automatic?
6. How can you increase the number of questions that students ask of themselves and others as they read?
7. When is the best time for students to seek clarification and make connections while reading?

Successful understanding of a text—the ultimate aim of reading—is dependent upon several skills. As a result, many distinct sources of reading comprehension failure have been proposed, including phonological processing difficulties (Stahl, 1998; Stanovich, 1986), word-level deficits (Perfetti, 1998), sentence-level deficits (Kintsch, 2001; Miller, 1999), and higher-level deficits such as poor inference-making ability (Oakhill, 1993). Attention to gaining meaning at the word-level is intensifying and decoding processes cannot be ignored when discussing comprehension. Comprehension of text is logically impossible when a reader cannot read the words. Young readers must learn how to decode well, if they are to understand what they read. In CPI, comprehension and decoding instructional goals can exist side by side in single lessons.

Crafting Accurate Literal Understanding at the Word Level

Word calling is defined as reading every word accurately but not comprehending the meaning. This malady arises for many reasons. First, "word-callers" emerge early, often in kindergarten or first grade, partly because the principles in CPI were not taught. By second or third grade, many young readers become challenged by words for which they cannot merely guess meanings by using common sense or personal past experiences (Chall, 1998). Furthermore, because they have not been taught the textual differences between expository and narrative text, many content-area readings are too conceptually dense for them to comprehend. Third, because such readers tend to read infrequently, they need the literal comprehension processes presented in this chapter more than avid readers. Last, word calling most often decreases students' desire to self-select reading for leisure, which in turn, diminishes readers' knowledge about the world. Because they have a smaller knowledge base, they have less well-developed schema to apply to new text, which makes the comprehension of these books more difficult.

Although predictable ability-level or below-grade-level books are appropriate in the decoding portion of instruction, they should not be relied on to build comprehension abilities in students in K–3 grades. Exposure to these books alone will not eliminate word calling. These books reinforce young readers' ideas that reading should always be predictable (i.e., relatable to personal experiences) and that all words should be memorized.

In contrast to use if predictable texts, when students activate their schemas through reading more challenging and complex texts, they can learn how to decode new words and expand their vocabulary. The correlation between good reading and extensive vocabulary has been repeatedly verified through research and practice (see Blanchowicz & Fisher, 2002, for a review of these studies). Even more impressive is that teaching students vocabulary increases their comprehension skills, as was recently determined by the National Reading Panel (2000). A second research panel, sponsored by the RAND Corporation (RAND Reading Study Group, 2002), was convened to analyze research in the field of comprehension development. An effective instructional program includes vocabulary instruction. If readers cannot understand the individual words in text, they will not be able to understand the complex relationships specified by words in sentences, paragraphs, and passages. Students learn more new words through directed vocabulary instruction than when left alone to learn new terms in independent reading (Carver, 1994, 1995; Nagy & Herman, 1987). Without instruction, it would take most kindergarten readers about 12 years of reading, with exposure to 2,000 words daily and learning the meanings of at least seven new vocabulary words each day, to reach the level of reading vocabulary that fluent readers possess by fourth grade. Young students can learn how to ask themselves the following questions to learn new words:

How is this new word like/unlike the other words in the book?
What function does this word normally perform? (Is it a naming, describing, or action word?)
Where might I see this word outside of this book?

When, prior to reading, you say "This word is like _____" to introduce a new word in a Strand 1 lesson, during one-on-one sessions in Strand 2 lessons, or in the small-group reteaching sessions of Strand 3 lessons, you encourage students to volunteer answers to the above questions and to develop their automatic reference to context clues when they read silently. Moreover, through sharing one another's ideas and learning through child vernacular in Strand 3 lessons, students more aptly and rapidly apply new words to their lives. Because CPI lessons include words that readers want to learn and think are important (Adams, 1990), these words become permanent additions to young readers' speaking, listening, reading, and writing vocabularies.

Crafting Accurate Literal Understanding at the Sentence Level

One of the most difficult problems in teaching literal comprehension when reading fiction is to get past "skills, drills, and kill." For many years teachers have used a multitude of different methods to teach decoding but have not done so when helping students to comprehend. To increase decoding abilities, primary-level educators have taught students to use phonics, word meanings, context clues, syntax, semantics, picture clues, structural analysis, sentence meanings, word parts, sight words, rhythm and rhyme of the English language, as well as the flow of ideas within a paragraph.

Only in the 1990s did teachers begin to differentiate literal comprehension instruction for fictional text as a needed focus of instruction. They began to teach students (1) to use descriptive thinking guides (Block & Mangieri, 1996a–c); (2) to diagram thinking processes as a way to recognize relative levels of importance within sentences, between sentences, and within paragraphs; and (3) to recognize the different functions that paragraphs serve. Only then were young children able to comprehend at literal levels with less effort. By the turn of the century, teachers and researchers were beginning to design even more distinct methods by which children could be taught literal comprehension as a process and not as a product of individual skills or strategies.

Why is this evolution so important today? *Skill* can be defined as anything children can think of or do that, when asked if they have a particular skill, can be answered with yes or no. For example, being able to underline a main idea is a skill because students can simply be asked if a particular sentence is or is not the one that they think is most important. Yes, they can underline it correctly, or no, they cannot. *Strategies*, however, are defined by the state of ongoing mental processing, not by whether something can or cannot be done. For instance, decoding and comprehension strategies are tools that are used during the process of making meaning. Strategies construct processes that create something new. Thus, *strategic thinking initiates comprehension processes that make meaning.*

Students are either strategic in their reading, or not. For example, young readers can be taught to think strategically throughout the reading of a sentence or to form strategic decisions about how future events in a fictional plot are likely to unfold. Good young readers go beyond the use of strategies as they read, however, by regulating their strategic thinking and choosing how many strategies they apply at any point. Thus, critical comprehension processes of fictional text are comprised of self-initiated comprehension processes that transform the literal meaning of words describing characters and events into the reader's own mental images and lives.

Expert reading requires the coordination of many strategic processes while reading a single sentence (Bransford & Schwartz, 1998; Kintsch, 1994). Moreover, a comprehension process unlocks syntactical clues and identifies relationships among words in phrases and clauses. The most effective approach is to teach children to think to the end. When children overlook a clue or connection, and they do not know how to proceed in a sentence, they can be taught to say to themselves "Think to the end." By doing so, they can continue to hold the things they do not understand at bay until they accumulate more blocks of meaning and a complete structure of comprehension.

Crafting Accurate Literal Understanding at the Paragraph Level

Teaching students to paraphrase a paragraph as accurately as possible on the literal level helps them to retain new knowledge. Learning from that text, however, demands more. It requires "a good situational model linked with the reader's long term knowledge" (Kintsch,

1994, p. 321). Kintsch has designed a construction integration (CI) model that suggests that texts should induce students to form appropriate mental literal comprehension images. These images should include not only text-based representations but an active inferencing process in order to ignite young readers' prior knowledge (Kintsch, 1998).

These data demonstrate that literal comprehension is guided by a top-down understanding of the arguments in specific sentences. Young readers must be taught how to link arguments within sentences to subsequent sentences. In the process, they begin to understand that some arguments overlap and involve more than one sentence. Some propositions can be embedded within single sentences that relate to the larger theme conveyed in a paragraph. By learning to look for these ongoing interconnections in a text, young readers develop the flexibility to become textually bound (i.e., accurately interpret the author's message) as well as nontextually bound (i.e., apply new ideas that were triggered by a connection made by the reader and that were not written or inferred by the author). Simultaneously, Strand 1 lessons teach young readers to use other literal comprehension processes, such as detecting clues to meaning from signal words, using tilling-the-text thinking, and recognizing paragraph functions.

As students integrate these processes into their everyday practice of reading, they learn to let their own imaginations add to the images they form. This creative aspect of comprehension is a crucial element in literal interpretation because it assists students in understanding the author's intended messages. Creative process thinking allows readers to explore all possible knowledge links and choose how they can best tie together new pieces of knowledge as they unfold (Freire, 1999). The following CPI lessons develop these abilities.

CPI Literal Comprehension Lesson That Moves Beyond Building Background: Teach Students How Background Builds

It is advantageous to teach students how to build background rather than for teachers to build their background for them. This CPI lesson teaches students how to construct connections between the opening sentences in a text. It also builds their abilities to recognize the frameworks within which different genres exist (National Reading Panel, 1999). When students are able to recognize these frameworks, they can then initiate "genre-specific thinking" as they read. Students must be taught how to use these frameworks. The lessons presented in this chapter must be included more frequently in teacher's manuals of basal readers. Research by Wiley and Voss (1999) indicates that even good teacher preparation programs merely explain the nature of comprehension to educators, rather than teaching them how to teach comprehension processes for specific text genres.

In this CPI lesson, students learn that curriculum functions as a bridge. Each new section they read serves as a bridge that connects what they already know with what the authors want them to understand. Teachers must support students as they use their background knowledge as a means of moving across the bridge. As they read, students' thinking processes accompany the author across the bridge. The new knowledge created is more encompassing, and students experience fewer misunderstandings and omissions in the process. By using interactive links between sentences during the reading process, students create a dialogue with the author as they travel across the curriculum. The Strand 1 lesson you can use or adopt to introduce this process to young children appears below and on pages 85–88.

To sum up, we must no longer teach students to build background knowledge merely by giving instruction about *how* we want them to build that knowledge; students can be taught instead to let background knowledge build by learning to follow along in their curriculum, using it as a bridge to support the passage of relevant personal background experiences to mingle with the author's message. As young readers move along the curriculum bridge with their bank of background knowledge, their literal comprehension of specific sentences solidifies. Students must be taught to use the material that they just read (the single sentences) as new pieces of their background knowledge to apply to upcoming sentence comprehension. You can begin teaching this process by modeling how you connect facts from one sentence to another, until a complete mental image that is context bound is formed. In essence, it is not as important for us to build students' existing knowledge as it is for us to teach them how to mingle their relevant background knowledge with new information as it unfolds. This instruction can occur through a Strand 1 lesson that includes the following think-alouds:

Begin the first think-aloud by reading aloud and stopping after you have read the first four pages. Tell readers that they have a choice when they reach the third or fourth page of a book:

> "You can continue to read carefully and think about experiences you have had that are *very similar* to the experiences in the book. Or you can begin to let your mind wonder and think about things that you want to think about, rather than to concentrate on the words in the book. Good readers follow along with the words in the book, pausing briefly to recall background knowledge that they have read before or identical experiences that they have had in their lives. Let me show you how I activate relevant knowledge as we continue to read the next page in this book."

Now, using an overhead transparency of a single page of text, point to specific sentences to which you are connecting relevant prior knowledge. Demonstrate how you activated your similar personal experiences and how you eliminated inaccurate prior knowledge. Read a sentence and describe an event from your personal experience that contributed knowledge to that statement. For example, after reading the first sentence from *The Three Little Pigs* (Scieszka, 1993), "Once upon a time, there were three little pigs"—you might say:

> "I really can picture these three little pigs in my mind because I went to a state fair and saw three pigs that looked just like the ones described in this sentence. I can remember exactly how they smelt, felt, and sounded. Now I am ready to understand the next sentence about these three little pigs. I have activated my prior knowledge rapidly, and it will assist me in understanding the most important points in the next sentence."

Then, read the next sentence in the book—"The three little pigs lived in a forest."
You might say:

> "As I was reading, if I started thinking about the last time I went on a picnic in the forest, my mind would have been distracted by a minor detail ('in a forest') and wandered away

from the words in the book. I would not be attending to what the author said, because the picture in my mind would not contain three pigs. Also, I should not think about a picnic because the author did not say that the pigs went on a picnic. By eliminating these thoughts, I can return to the words in the book and more accurately understand how the next sentence adds to the fact that the pigs lived in a forest. Returning to think about the exact words in the book, I can concentrate on what the author is going to say next about the pigs' lives."

Ask the class to practice building relevant background knowledge in a Strand 2 lesson. As you are monitoring their reading, have each student perform a think-aloud with you in a one-on-one conference to evaluate how well he or she is building background knowledge. After an appropriate amount of practice has occurred through Strand 2 lessons, convene Strand 3 groups for students to discuss what they want to learn to improve their abilities to implement this process.

CPI Literal Comprehension Lesson That Teaches Students to Establish a Purpose

Among the most important actions you can take as a teacher is *to refrain from giving students the purpose for reading* and instead teach them how to set their own purposes. When you establish readers' purposes too often, they will not learn to do so themselves; once accustomed to being told the purpose, students often need repeated trials before they trust themselves enough to decide what is important to comprehend. Typically, students are taught how to set a purpose for reading or are asked to predict what a text is about merely by looking at a book's cover. CPI lessons, in contrast, help students to think about the direction the author's thoughts are taking before they set their purposes for reading on in a book. You can remind them of these thought processes by conducting a Strand 1 lesson, the outline of which appears in Figure 5.1.

In this lesson ask them to read the first two page of a big book with you or to read silently from the opening of a text they selected to discern which parts capture their interest and attention. When students are taught to read the first two pages *before* they set their reading purpose, they are more likely to (1) apply relevant background knowledge to that text, (2) follow the author's train of thought, and (3) depend on that genre's style to infer meaning.

The increased pleasure that arises from using this CPI lesson to develop young readers' process for setting their own reading purpose is three-pronged. First, when students set a purpose after having read two pages, they are less likely to be disappointed that the author did not answer a question they posed. The purpose for reading further remains in line with the author's train of thought. Second, if teachers ask students to set a purpose without reading the first two or so pages, young readers are likely to set a purpose that they think their teachers want them to set. As a result, they learn to sacrifice their free choice for the stronger motivator of wanting to please the teacher. Reading for someone else's purpose is less pleasurable than reading for one's own goals. Third, if teachers ask students to set a purpose before they have read the first few pages, they inadvertently force students to give the most general answer as their purpose. No students wants to give a wrong answer before peers, so

FIGURE 5.1. Lesson 3 (summary): Teaching students to think about two comprehension processes while they read.

- -

Helping students "set their own purpose prior to reading" and to "infer" while they read

Step 1: Explain to the students how to set their own purpose prior to reading, how to make inferences while they read, and how the processes will help them become better readers.

Step 2: Read two pages and do a think-aloud that shows how you set your own purpose for reading. Ask students to state their purposes.

Step 3: Put an adhesive note on the bottom of page 3 of the text and describe the inferencing process to students. Demonstrate how to infer. Explain that you were able to infer things because you recognized clues in the way the author wrote the first three pages. Tell the students what these clues were. Pick up the adhesive note and turn to page 4. Put the adhesive note on the bottom of page 4.

Step 4: Repeat the think-aloud and move the adhesive note of step 3 two more times (for pages 4 and 5).

Step 5: Place the adhesive note on the bottom of page 6. After reading page 6 together, ask students to make their own inferences and tell you how they did so.

adhesive note

- -

to save face, students tend to give a safe answer: a basic but bland purpose. The effects of this CPI lesson are listed in Table 5.1. Second graders were asked to set their purposes prior to and following instruction. Notice the increased specificity and depth of purpose set after CPI instruction.

CPI Literal Comprehension Lesson That Develops Young Readers' Abilities to Ask Questions and Seek Clarification as They Read

The following excerpts from a Strand 1 CPM lesson of asking questions (Figure 5.2), the Asking Questions thinking guide (Figure 5.3), and the CPM for clarifying (Figure 5.4) demonstrate the value of these two processes for readers in grades K–3. Both of these Strand 1 lessons are learned rapidly by most students. To teach them, follow the basic steps of a Strand 1 lesson but add the information from Step 2 on Figures 5.2 and 5.4 at the appropriate point in the lesson. When you are teaching the CPM for asking questions, it is helpful to focus on only one question from the thinking guide (Figure 5.3) at a time. By writing it on a chart and ask-

TABLE 5.1. Examples of the Effects of Teaching Students How to Set Their Own Purpose for Reading: Pre and Post Responses

Oh, What a Thanksgiving
by Steven Kroll
Illustrated by S. D. Schindler

Purposes set by second graders
before they were taught CPI Strand 1 Purpose-Setting Lesson

MICHELLE: I will learn about being in school.

ALLIE, CJ, AND NATHAN: I will learn about Thanksgiving.

SAM: I will learn about Christmas.

NICOLE: I will learn about fall.

SHYLA: I will learn about turkey dinner.

STEPHANIE: I will learn about how to fold the American flag.

ALLIE: How to make the turkey.

CASSIDY: America.

Posttest results after students were taught the purpose-setting process
"What do you want to learn in this book?" (after having read a few pages)

KYLE: I want to learn about the Mayflower.

SHYLA: I want to learn about the veterans.

STEPHANIE: I want to learn about the pilgrims.

ALLIE: I want to learn about where the boat stopped and how to make buildings out of bricks.

MICHELLE: I want to learn about the people when the pilgrims came.

SHYLA: I want to learn about where the people lived.

NATHAN: I want to learn about how to make the boats.

NICK: I want to learn about how to make the U.S.

CJ: I want to learn about how the pilgrims survived with no food.

"Why do you want to continue reading?"

NICK: I'm learning about how they made beds.

CJ: I'm learning a lot about the first Thanksgiving.

SAM: I'm learning about getting turkeys at the store.

NATHAN: To learn.

ALLIE: I'm learning about the pilgrims, and I want to learn more.

MICHELLE: I want to learn more because it looks like the boy is thanking the pilgrims.

Designed by Rachel R. Escamilla, School of Education, Texas Christian University, Fort Worth, TX, and used here by permission.

FIGURE 5.2. Excerpts from a Strand 1 CPM lesson on asking questions.

Strand 1: Teach How to Ask Questions of Yourself While Reading

Explain and model this process three times in action (i.e., use thinking guides, examples, models, and think-alouds as you read a book orally).

Explain Asking questions permits the student to check his or her comprehension of the author's train of thought. As events that provide comprehension challenges occur, the reader must ask, "Do I understand the author?" The reader then elicits the reading processes necessary to bring greater meaning to the text.

1. **Thinking Guides**. Display the CPM chart for asking questions. Highlight the words **understand the author** to remind the students of the importance of understanding the author's message. (Adding pictures to the chart assists students with the steps that accompany this CPM. Select a permanent spot on which to display the motion chart and highlighted comprehension process sentence for students to reference in future lessons.)

2. **Model**. Demonstrate the motion for asking questions. Have the students practice the motion with you as you model it three times. As you begin the motion, tell the students that placing the finger to the forehead above the eyebrow is sign language for thinking. When readers encounter confusions in the text, it is necessary to "stop: think: ask questions." If readers fail to stop at points of confusion, then complete comprehension of the text stops.

3. **Think-Alouds**. Read the first two pages of text and stop. (Readers set purpose themselves.) Ask students to use the CPM when they have questions during your reading of the book.

FIGURE 5.3. **Asking Questions Thinking Guide.**

Thinking Guide

Asking Questions to Clarify

1. Why?

2. Is the most important point _____ or _____?

3. What do you mean by "_____"?

4. If I understand, you mean _____. Is that right?

5. Where will the point you are making not apply? How does _____ relate to _____?

6. If your idea is accepted, what is the greatest change that will occur?

7. Would you say more about _____?

8. What is the difference between _____ and _____?

9. Would this be an example?

10. Is it possible that _____? What else could we do?

11. If _____ happened, what would be the result?

FIGURE 5.4. Excerpts from a Strand 1 CPM lesson on clarifying.

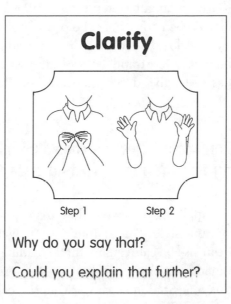

Clarify

Step 1   Step 2

Why do you say that?

Could you explain that further?

Strand 1: Teach Clarifying

Explain and model this process three times in action (i.e., use thinking guides, examples, models, and think-alouds as you read a book orally).

Explain. The comprehension process of clarifying assists the reader when encountering challenging reading material. When vocabulary, phrases, or sentences cause comprehension difficulties, the reader must pause to seek clarification through the use of multiple processes, such as decoding, checking context clues, and so forth.

1. **Thinking Guides**. Display the CPM chart for clarifying. Highlight the words **Why**, **explain**, and **further** to cue the students when forming clarifying questions. (Adding pictures to the chart assists students in performing the thoughts depicted by the motions. Select a permanent spot on which to display the motion chart and highlighted comprehension process sentence for students to use in future lessons.)

2. **Model**. Demonstrate the motion for clarifying. Have the students practice the motion with you as you model it three times. As you begin the motion, tell the students to think of the first step of the motion. The fingertips together represent closely connected information where it is difficult to "see" the meaning. At Step 2 the fingertips separate and the hands open, revealing the palms of the hands, to convey that now the meaning of the reading has been revealed.

3. **Think-Alouds**. Tell students to show you this motion any time they are confused. You will stop to clarify and answer their question when you see this motion.

ing it repeatedly for a week, young readers begin to model your questioning behavior as they read.

In like manner, once you have taught students the CPM for clarify, young readers of all ability levels willingly signal when they need help discerning a meaning (as shown in the photograph below). They will do so (1) during shared readings, (2) while you are providing instruction to the whole class in Strand 1 lessons, (3) when they are reading silently in Strand 2 lessons, and (4) as peers give descriptions of their thinking processes in Strand 3 lessons.

CPI Literal Comprehension Lesson That Teaches Students to Make Connections by Attending to an Author's Writing Style

Young students increase their application of what they read to their lives when they know how to attend to an author's writing style. That is, they learn how to transfer emotions to literary characters. This strategy can also be called empathetic reading. Students can learn how to breathe life, feelings, and human emotions into characters that exist ephemerally, only as figments of an author's imagination. Students who are more reality bound than internally guided by imagination have greater difficulty understanding characters (Culp, 1985; Hunt & Vipond, 1985); they find it difficult to become personally involved in the story.

Students' inability to connect emotionally with characters can be compounded by a tendency to select texts that do not have any characters they would like to know; thus these students spend more time reading boring books and do not learn how to select really good books. In addition, many of these students fail to understand characters' motives because most authors leave character motivation to be inferred—a process that students must engage simultaneously with empathetic reading. Still another barrier is that these students rarely stick with a book long enough to get to know the characters. Without intervention, students

Maria initiated the CPM for **clarify** when Mr. Smith read the word **donkey** in a big book version of **Sylvester and the Magic Pebble**. At that point, her teacher stopped, defined donkey, Maria nodded with a smile, and Mr. Smith continued reading.

Jennifer made a connection between the book that Mr. Smith was reading, so she signaled with the CPM (shown on the next page) to indicate that she knew she had executed the comprehension process of making connections and she wanted her teacher to know that she had. Often, teachers do not interrupt the lesson to call upon students when they motion. Through these motions, students can practice becoming aware of the types of processing they are engaging as they comprehend text.

are less likely to vary their reading rates in order to savor descriptions of characters in a selection. Hence, they do not become captivated by the characters or the events (Nell, 1988), and their comprehension difficulties increase. Follow the basic steps of a Strand 1 lesson. Students will become automatic in their performance of the connecting motion as their comprehension processes mature (see lesson in Figure 5.5).

Strand 1 CPI Lesson for Developing Students' Comprehension Process for Building Background Knowledge

For this lesson plan, we chose *Don't Fidget a Feather* (Silverman, 1999). This story is about Duck and Gander, two friends wanting to impress each other—but how far will they go before the friendship is tested?

- *Genre: Fiction.* Help the students build background in fiction. Remind them that in a fictional story, characters are introduced in a specific setting. Furthermore, there is a sequence of events, constituting the plot, usually focused on a problem, and a climax that presents a successful solution.
- *Topic: Friendship.* Select students to define friendship. How do they know if someone is being a friend? What are some examples of friendly behaviors? Unfriendly behaviors?
- *Self: Friends.* Ask students to answer these questions silently: What things do you like to do with your friends? How do you feel when you are playing with friends? Do you ever become angry with your friends? Do they ever become angry with you? How does that feel?
- *Author.* Ask questions about how this book compares to other books this author has written.
- *Theme: Friendship.* Ask questions to help students deduce that friendships (1) are a vital part of life; (2) are based on similar interests, activities, and environments; (3) change; and (4) endure through fun and sad times.

FIGURE 5.5. Excerpts from a Strand 1 CPM lesson on making connections.

Strand 1: Teach How the Mind Makes Connections

Explain and model this process three times in action (i.e., use thinking guides, examples, models, and think-alouds as you read a book orally).

Explain. Making Connections is a comprehension process that brings the text alive for the reader. It provides a personal experience to the story that increases comprehension, giving the reader the opportunity to relive the experience through the story characters.

1. **Thinking Guides**. Display the CPM chart for making connections. Write "Make Connections" on a chart and record answers to "What does this remind me of?" Highlight the word **remind** to remind students that their minds use their past experiences to make connections. (Adding pictures to the chart assists students with the steps that accompany this CPM. Select a permanent spot on which to display the motion chart and highlighted comprehension process sentence for students to reference in future lessons.)

2. **Model**. Demonstrate the motion for making connections. Have the students practice the motion with you as you model it three times. As you begin the motion, tell the students to think of connecting the information in the book to the information in their minds, like connecting the links of a chain. Their fingers hook together, link-to-link, to create the chain.

3. **Think-Alouds**. Read the first two pages of text and stop. (Readers set purpose themselves.) Ask students to signal and describe connections they make as you read the rest of the book.

Summary

As students learn to apply the appropriate comprehension processes to aid in decoding and comprehension at multiple levels of the text, they become self-regulated readers. They gain the confidence to select more challenging reading material, which in turn improves their vocabulary and broadens the depth and breadth of their cognitive schema. With this new-found confidence, the reader is motivated to attend to the strategies applied by expert readers. The reader now reads with a new sense of purpose: the ability to build bridges in fiction through knowledge of genre, topic, and author style. The application of the processes in this chapter develops a more accurate literal interpretation of this genre.

Reflecting on What You Have Learned

1. **Interpreting (Summarizing) the Main Points.** For students to truly comprehend texts, they must apply multiple processes simultaneously. Comprehension occurs at many levels as readers engage a text. Comprehension processes must be taught with an emphasis on understanding the process itself. Students are thereby enabled to apply processes independently as they encounter the challenges of reading. Gaining self-regulatory abilities is of utmost importance to young readers. Through this self-regulation, they develop confidence and motivation to spend a lifetime "living within the books."

2. **Making Professional Decisions.** Implementing a lesson, as described in this chapter, is a lengthy process. Reflect upon your motivation to assure that lessons of this type are integrated into your daily schedule.

3. **Making Field Applications and Observations.** Share this knowledge with supportive teachers and enlist their assistance in implementing these lessons with their students. Brainstorm ideas to fine-tune the lessons and the daily schedule to allow maximum opportunity for making these lessons a part of everyday instruction. Discuss with your principal the possibility of creating opportunities for teachers learning CPI to observe a colleague experiencing success in the implementation of these lessons.

4. **Keeping a Professional Journal.** Record the key points of this chapter to present to the principal in establishing a need for observation of a mentor teacher. In addition, use this information to motivate fellow teachers to join the effort to implement these lessons.

5. **Making Multicultural Applications.** Include multiple fictional texts to motivate and expand students' background knowledge of various cultures. Guest speakers and videos can provide additional experiences with different cultures. Design a 1-week plan that you could use in a K–3 classroom with children of many cultural backgrounds.

6. **Meeting Students' Special Needs.** When teachers incorporate CPMs into their comprehension lessons, young struggling readers have an additional visual and kinesthetic clue to increase their comprehension. Visual learners can see a

graphic depiction of the mental actions they should engage in while they read. Other struggling readers benefit from the kinesthetic motions that they are asked to perform when they demonstrate the specific CPM they are being taught, such as drawing conclusions, asking questions, summarizing, and the like. Visual or kinesthetic depictions of the silent mental processes that occur when meaning is obtained can assist young struggling readers to increase the levels of comprehension achievements. Alternatively, CPMs assist advanced students by increasing their ability to reflect upon the types of thinking that they did while they read. Specifically, advanced students increase their metacognitive processing before, during, and after their reading because they are taught the CPM motions (Block & Rodgers, 2004). This expanded level of comprehension is the result of advanced students' abilities to more rapidly understand the mental processes that they have learned through rote memory. By obtaining this deeper understanding, advanced students become more self-regulated readers.

7. **Checking Key Terms.** Following is a list of concepts introduced in this chapter. If you have learned the meaning of a term, place a checkmark in the blank that precedes that term. If you are not sure of a term's definition, increase your retention by reviewing its definition. The retention of these definitions constructs meanings that are important for your teaching.

> ____Word calling (p. 71)
> ____Skill (p. 73)
> ____Strategy (p. 73)
> ____Building bridges (p. 74)
> ____Setting purpose (p. 76)
> ____Empathetic reader (p. 82)

8. **Design a Comprehension Process Lesson.** In the previous lessons, the particular selection of the two processes was deliberate. Choose two processes from Appendix B that exemplify the thought processes at two different levels: one in concrete terms and the other in abstract terms. Design a lesson that includes (1) background knowledge, (2) setting purpose, (3) attending to author's style, or (4) making connections.

Comprehension Process Lesson 4: Teaching Perspective and Identifying with Characters—Strand 1, 2, and 3 Lessons for Fiction

Steps in Strand 1 Lessons for Fiction

There are six steps in a Strand 1 lesson of integrating comprehension process lessons (instruction before point of need, including the use of thinking guides, models, examples, and think-alouds):

Step 1

Identify that students need to learn to understand the main characters' feelings and perspectives to obtain a deeper meaning from fictional text.

Objective: The student can define and successfully apply the comprehension processes of feeling and perspective.

Step 2

Explain and model each process three times in action.

"For a reader to truly understand a story, he or she must be able to feel the joys and disappointments of the characters. These feelings are the motivation for the characters' statements and behaviors. To help you better understand the feelings of a character, you must be able to pretend that you are the character in the story, so that you may view the story through the character's eyes. This is called *perspective*. Perspective is the ability to see, hear, and feel as another person."

Thinking Guides

Display the motion chart for feeling (see Appendix B). Write *Feeling* on a chart and record "How are the characters feeling?" and "What are my feelings about what I read?" Highlight the words *characters feeling* and *my feelings* as well as the picture clues to remind the students to use this information when they want to describe their feelings about the story.

Now display the motion chart for perspective (see Appendix B). Write *Perspective* on a chart and record "Pretend you are them" and "My eyes seeing through someone else's eyes." Highlight the words *Pretend* and *My eyes seeing through someone else's eyes*. Remind the students that perspective is trying to understand someone else's point of view.

Model

Demonstrate the process motion for feeling. Have the students practice the feeling motion with you as you model it three times. Comprehending the feelings of the characters as well as our own feelings as we encounter similar experiences are the focus of this comprehension process. As you discuss feelings, place your fingertips to your chest and stroke upward several times. To truly understand a character's feelings, you must try to place yourself in the character's "shoes," to experience his or her perspective. Demonstrate the perspective process motion. Have the students practice with you as you model it three times. Perspective gives the reader the opportunity to become the character in the story. When you have perspective, your eyes (place your fingers in a v-shape to the corner of your eye) can see through someone else's eyes (hold your other hand with fingers in a v-shape to represent someone else's eyes and turn and "walk" your fingertips from your eyes toward the other fingertips).

Think-Alouds

Use the think-aloud to establish the purpose for reading. Read the first two pages of text and then stop. (Readers set purpose themselves.)

> "One day, Duck went swimming in the lake. What a great swimmer I am, she thought. Just then, she heard a big splash. 'Greetings, Duck,' said Gander. 'Hi, Gander. Watch me swim.' Duck paddled as fast as she could. 'Not bad,' said Gander. 'But I'm faster.' "

Stop and notice the students' expressions of eagerness for the reading to continue. Next, let the students speak. Give the students the opportunity to ask questions and make predictions. Continue the reading. After reading page 3, demonstrate the feeling process motion and state, "I think Duck is feeling proud of himself that he won the race, because that's how I feel when I win a contest." Continue reading through page 5. Stop here. Now Gander has won and declared himself the champion. Demonstrate the feeling process motion as you state:

> "Now Gander is feeling proud. But I think Duck must be disappointed because he lost, and he wanted to prove to Gander that he was the champion I know I feel disappointed when I want something and I don't get it."

After reading page 9, motion the perspective process as you state:

> "Now I understand how important winning is to Duck and Gander. Duck was just watching Gander as the bee buzzed around him, and he didn't even try to help him. The only thing he was thinking was that now he was the winner. And Gander did the same thing."

Step 3

Read-aloud and ask several students to perform a think-aloud to demonstrate each comprehension process.

After reading page 11, have the students discuss the feelings of Duck and Gander. Remind the students to motion the feeling process as they begin their contribution to the discussion: "How does this understanding of their feelings improve your understanding of the story?" As you continue reading the story, tell the students to signal when they would like to express feelings by motioning the feeling process. Pages 18 and 19 are written from Fox's perspective. After reading these pages, ask the students to retell that event from Duck or Gander's perspective. Remind the students to motion the perspective process as they begin the retelling. Encourage the students to motion the feeling and perspective processes to signal a desire to contribute to the story discussion through the remainder of the book.

Step 4

Ask students to read silently for 10–20 minutes and when they use feel or gain a perspective of a main character. Mark the location in the text. As they read, move from desk to desk asking each student to tell you where in the book they felt as if they were the main character and what they were thinking when they used these comprehension processes to make meaning. For this step, have the students choose from a group of books previously selected by you that will give the students numerous opportunities to feel as if they were the main character.

Step 5

Ask how the processes helped the students to comprehend better. Inquire into the following areas:

• How did these two processes help you as you read? "Feelings help me understand the character's actions and motives and help me predict future actions better. When I can understand the character's feelings, then I begin to put myself in the book. My feelings about the characters make me feel as if they are my friends. I felt like I was right beside him when he was glad and sad. I stopped to ask myself questions when I became confused."

• How did these two processes help you think ahead, clarify, remember? "Feelings and perspective clarified why the main characters were so serious about the competition. Their feelings about winning were so strong that they allowed themselves to be in a dangerous situation."

• How did these two processes help you stay involved in the story? "Even though I was able to better understand the feelings of the main characters, I still could see the story as someone watching. This story created feelings in me that were different than the characters' feelings. They were going to let each other get hurt. I had to finish the story to make sure everyone was OK."

• How did these two processes help you overcome distractions in the room? "The use of feeling and perspective made the story seem like it was really happening. It was more exciting than anything happening in the room."

• How did these two processes help you overcome confusion in the text? "At first, I thought the characters were being silly. But after I saw the story from their perspective and understood their feelings, I knew they were very serious."

Step 6

Develop a plan with the students for using these processes together as they read in the future.

How can the feeling and perspective processes help you when you read? "Feelings and perspective help me to understand the motives behind the characters' actions. You have to really feel what the character is feeling to understand how they see things and to understand their perspective in the story. When I apply feeling and perspective, it's like I become the main character and I'm living the story."

Steps in Strand 2 Lessons for Fiction

Strand 2 lessons can occur as short, silent reading periods that contain two steps.

> *Step 1.* Have students select a book and read silently. For this step, allow the students to self-select a book.
>
> *Step 2.* Assist students encountering confusion with a brief response.

Steps in a Student-Share Lesson

> *Step 1.* Read a book selected by students aloud to the whole class.
>
> *Step 2.* Stop to allow students to make comments about what they are comprehending or to ask questions about what they do not understand as they arise (or make a list of them for later discussion).
>
> *Step 3.* Have a student lead a discussion about the book.
>
> *Step 4.* Ask students to select what process they want to learn next about crafting comprehension.

Steps in a Stop-and-Ask Lesson

> *Step 1.* Have students select a book and read silently.
>
> *Step 2.* Aid each student who raises his or her hand when encountering a comprehension problem by providing a two-sentence response, when possible.
>
> *Step 3.* Then the student returns to independent, silent reading.

Steps in Strand 3 Lessons for Fiction: Students Choose What They Want to Learn (Instruction after Point of Need: Teacher–Reader Groups)

Step 1

Divide students into small groups based on needs and interests.

In the above example, several students demonstrated an adequate understanding of feeling and perspective, but either the "tugs at your heart" or the "jumping for joy" emotion was missing. The teacher suggested the Memory Menders group for these students, because it could increase their processes of reflection.

Step 2

Work with a small group and allow each student to use individual skills as assets for the entire group.

Encourage the students to discuss the comprehension processes and how they help them to understand the story better than if they simply discuss the story's events. Using generic terms in the discussion enables the students to apply this new understanding to future texts. For example, every student in the Memory Menders groups talked about how they stop to think about what they have read. The group listed all the methods they use, the chart was posted, and students referred to it later when they read other books.

Step 3

Report to the class what the group learned.

For example, as the Memory Menders group reported the points of their meeting, all the students gained a review of the processes of reflection, drawing conclusions, and summarizing. Students gained additional insight into these processes because the points were presented in the language of their peers.

CHAPTER 6

CPI Lessons That Increase Literal Comprehension of Nonfiction

"Dr. Block, would you please tell teachers something for me? Tell them that whenever they ask us to read nonfiction, let us please have a friend right beside us as we read. We need someone with us at all times not just to help us figure out words, but we need them so we'll have someone to say 'Wow!' to when we read all the real cool parts."

—RENALDO, *grade 3*

Chapter Overview

Many children come to school already having an internal representation of the concept of story, and are thus able to comprehend and retell basic story elements quite easily. The same is not true for nonfiction text. Most young students must be taught how to read from many different nonfictional texts that address specific domains of knowledge before they develop the organizational system of expository text and the accompanying metacognitive processes (Taylor, Graves, & van den Brock, 2000). Because CPI lessons are genre-specific, they provide these new awarenesses and abilities. The more experiences students accumulate with nonfiction text, the better their nonfiction genre-specific road markers become (Ambruster, 1991; Block, 1993; Meyer, 1975; Taylor & Beach, 1984). Unfortunately, in prior years, most students in grades K–3 were not taught genre-specific comprehension lessons (Duke, 2000). An objective of this chapter is to assist teachers in filling this instructional void.

As early as grade 3, most children have developed either a positive or negative attitude toward expository text. Many pupils have also deduced, incorrectly, that comprehending is all one basic, generic process. They approach every book with the same set of "before-reading" expectations, metacognitions, and meaning making actions. It is important to teach students that recognizing and removing comprehension obstacles is a genre-specific task. When students learn to use different comprehension processes with different genres, their overall comprehension increases, and they rate themselves as more competent readers (Block & Johnson, 2002; Smolkin, 2002).

The Importance of Teaching Genre-Specific Comprehension Processes

Many students choose nonfiction texts without teacher prompting. This willingness occurs, in part, because informational books provide them with more detailed vocabulary. Such texts also satisfy pupils' innate curiosities and present vivid facts about topics of personal interest. Moreover, when teachers of students as young as 5 years of age read nonfiction books aloud, children's problem-solving abilities may improve (Duke & Kay, 1998).

The CPI lessons in this chapter are important because expository texts are the primary means by which students in grades K–3 acquire academic knowledge. Students' failure to comprehend these texts amasses an increasingly cumulative knowledge deficit as children progress through the grades. Furthermore, the ability to comprehend nonfiction books enhances readers' self-efficacy as well as the value they place on learning to read a broad range of expository texts.

Self-efficacy refers to young readers' beliefs about their own abilities to learn and perform a given task at a specified, desired, or designated level of proficiency (Bandura, 1986; Paris & Winograd, 2001; Schunk & Zimmerman, 1997). Previous research has clearly demonstrated correlations among learners' self-efficacy, motivation, and self-regulatory mental processing (Schunk, 1990). Students who read expository text with ease and pleasure augment their self-efficacy and enjoy reading a wider variety of genres. This increased pleasure, in turn, motivates them to choose books from a wider spectrum of interest areas. This self-initiated exposure to many types of text not only helps children grow as readers (because it develops higher-level thinking processes), but also to think more precisely and specifically. By contrast, students who do not read expository text well have fewer experiences of success, most often because they have not had adequate exposure to diverse genres. This void in experiences not only reduces their opportunities to learn how to comprehend genre-specific text but also reduces their experiences in engaging and exercising their own genre-specific reading comprehension processes. This deficit pattern is a cyclical one. The absence of many genre-specific lessons in a curriculum significantly decreases self-efficacy in the ability to make meaning from expository texts in grades K–3 students (Lysaker, 1997).

Expository texts are presumed to be more difficult than narratives because both their structure and content are less familiar to students. Hence, such texts present additional comprehension obstacles for struggling comprehenders. The presentation of new ideas, information, and the patterns in which authors organize their ideas all differ markedly from narrative text (Alexander & Jetton, 2000). Furthermore, many younger, less able readers fail to identify and follow the explicit expository cues and access features (table of contents, text in graphs, bold-face terms, glossary, subheadings, etc.) without specific instruction in these areas. As a result, the tasks of identifying main ideas, distinguishing important from less important facts, noticing inconsistencies, recalling, summarizing information, and monitoring comprehension become extremely difficult in expository texts.

Genre-specific comprehension instruction is important for another reason. Once students enter the work force, the majority of their reading will involve expository text. Moreover, more than 60% of the passages in standardized state or national reading comprehension tests are expository, genre-specific texts (Alverman & Mosie, 1991). When the comprehension features of expository text are taught, all levels of comprehension increase—literal, inferential, and applied—because students learn how to bridge the inferential gaps that nonfiction writers leave to readers' meaning-making processes more accurately. Moreover, when students are taught how to create mental images from nonfiction text, the resultant pictures are mental representations of realities in their world. These representations resemble a network, with nodes that depict individual text elements and connections that focus on meaningful relationships.

For all of these reasons, it is becoming increasingly more important that we help students acquire the comprehension processes necessary to obtain knowledge and pleasure from reading nonfiction material. Through the CPI lessons in this chapter, young students engage their knowledge of genre-specific text features rather than merely insert their own background experiences into the informational topics.

Informational texts do not end in the traditional fictional mode of "happy ever after." Too frequently in the past, teachers were asked to present expository text with methods that were similar to those used to teach narratives (e.g., begin on page 1 and read continuously, at the same speed and with one continuous purpose to the end). Readers cannot build momentum in nonfiction books by applying this tool of story grammar. *Story grammar* refers to the predicable sequence of events that occurs in narrative text *only*: (1) the setting, characters, and problem are introduced; (2) attempts to solve the problem occur; (3) the climax occurs; and (4) the sequence ends in a resolution. Because expository text contains none of these elements, we need to develop new methods by which students can build the momentum and motivation to reading nonfiction books. Recent research suggests that students as young as 3 years old can learn how to comprehend informational text (Hapgood, Palincsar, & Magnusson, 2000; Moss, 1989; Pappas, 1991, 1993). With CPI lessons, we are now prepared to teach them how to proceed.

Nonfiction comprehension instruction must develop students' understanding of the distinct structures that frame the writing styles in each genre and content area. For example, pictures, tables, figures, graphs, diagrams, maps, cartoons, and photographs communicate different information if they appear in historical, scientific, or artistic texts. Such books also have specific access features that signal important features of exposition, such as tables of content, graphic captions, glossaries, and indexes that do not appear in fictional texts. Psychologists agree that these language features emerge because they represent different methods of thinking and writing that characterize each discipline of knowledge (Weaver & Kintsch, 1996).

To review, understanding nonfiction content requires the ability to (1) recognize textual features used to convey meaning in a content area (e.g., cross-sections superimposed on photographs of trees to show growth band rings in scientific textbooks); (2) create a coherent mental representation of many facts in a paragraph (e.g., the procedure for computing carbon dating that appears in anthropology texts); and (3) understand the chain of logic and deliberate thinking that characterizes different disciplines (e.g., mathematics vs. history). The CPI lessons in this chapter also show how nonfiction texts share similar features with each other and fiction (e.g., temporal order, hierarchies of ideas within single paragraphs, analogous and metaphorical references, figures of speech, as well as details and main ideas that revolve around a central theme).

CPI Genre-Specific Lessons

CPI Genre-Specific Lesson 1: Teaching Nonfiction by Reading Two Texts Consecutively

CPI methods that have been proven to increase students' comprehension of content disciplines include (1) reading two or more nonfiction texts about the same topic consecutively, (2) teaching students to think about two comprehension processes as they read, (3) reminding them that using genre-specific comprehension process at particular points in a text enriches their understanding, and (4) teaching the genre-specific lessons in this chapter (Block & Rodgers, in press).

Research has demonstrated that teaching two nonfiction texts about the same subject one after another increases students' comprehension by 33% above what they experience after reading only a single fiction or nonfiction book about the same topic (Block & Reed, 2003). In this daily 20-minute lesson, you explain the reasons why you want students to develop the habit of reading two books on the same topic before they switch interest areas, then model what you think as you compare two nonfiction books on the same topic (Strand 1). Ask students to select two books related to their own personal interest. Begin the Strand 2 portion of the lesson by asking them to scan and read silently for 10–15 minutes. Then ask students to share something they learned from reading two books on a single subject that they would not have known if they had read only one book. A recent research study (Block & Reed, 2003) demonstrated that this CPI lesson significantly increased young readers' comprehension more than use of basal texts, workbooks, or teacher-chosen fictional book reading that were used for the same length of time.

CPI Genre-Specific Lesson 2: "Skim and Scan Until I Choose to Stop and Savor"

This CPI lesson is designed to (1) motivate students to explore a broad base of genres, and (2) help them learn how to respond emotionally and cognitively to nonfiction material. One of the traits of high-quality expository text is that the contents are so reader friendly that students want to pause and reflect as they read. In this lesson, students learn how to skim and scan through a nonfiction selection until they choose to stop and savor, carefully reading a section of personal interest. This Strand 1 lesson begins by demonstrating how you normally skim and scan a newspaper or magazine, until you find a section that you really want to stop and learn more about. Repeat this demonstration with two other types of nonfiction.

Skimming and scanning a nonfiction text can build motivation because students learn that they do not have to read every word, as they often do in reading fiction. They can stop to savor pieces of information that are of particular interest to them, and glance over sections of facts that they already know. Skimming and scanning also develop the momentum that leads to an enjoyment of reading nonfiction material; the speed of reading increases each time students skim over pages when they already know the content. Then, when a section of a text becomes interesting or contains new information, students can stop for extra time to ponder. In doing so, momentum and motivation to keep on reading nonfiction mounts, because students are in charge of, and enjoy, varying the rate at which they read.

Moreover, by teaching students about these two reading speeds, they can establish a pace for reading nonfiction that is distinctive from the mental ebb-and-flow patterns created when they read fiction. Specifically, when students learn that they can control their own nonfiction reading speed, they appreciate this genre more. For example, they appreciate that expository texts do not demand a careful attention to setting, plot, characterization, climaxes, and resolutions to be comprehended, as do fictional texts. When students choose which part they want to read first, they engage their metacognitive processes—a very satisfying, self-esteem building activity (especially for less able readers). They begin to ponder:

- "Which problem about _____ do I want to learn more?"
- "Where would I like to start really reading in depth?"
- "What question do I want this book to answer?"

CPI Genre-Specific Lesson 3: "Tilling the Text"

Tilling the text refers to reading with the goal of obtaining the gist of the content and structure of a nonfiction selection. Students can be taught to "till a text," just as farmers till the soil before they plant. Students who learn to till a text increase their understanding of informational text significantly above students who do not do so (Block, 2001c). Tilling the text enables students to (1) better predict the facts that will appear on future pages, (2) build more accurate pictures in their minds when photographs are absent, and (3) maintain their motivation to keep on reading.

Previewing is also part of tilling a text. It teaches students how to (1) use content, authorial, and textual clues to discover meaning; (2) become aware of subtleties in authors' choices of words and writing styles to increase comprehension; (3) use subheadings, print features, paragraph lengths, and amount of white space to establish reading goals and determine a text's conceptual density; and (4) use background knowledge so as to expand (rather than interfere with) understanding. In CPI, students learn how to prepare their minds before they read (just as farmers fertilize and plow the soil before they plant).

To teach students to till a text, you teach them to skim the entirety of a nonfiction selection. With this information, students can establish the rate of reading speed and depth of thinking that they want to use with each text. Students can also identify which sections they will skim and scan for the gist of the content, and which specific selection they will want to slowly digest and savor. While you teach these tilling-the-text processes, model how it is useful to stop reading from time to time to process meaning. Pause at difficult points in a text where children could have problems interpreting an author's writing or the textual features.

The tilling process enables students to vary the pace, breadth, and depth of their interrelated thought processes, which in turn increases the joy they experience when reading. The tilling processes make textual features of specific genres salient to students. Furthermore, as Blair-Larson and Williams (1999) demonstrated, tilling-the-text activities can become increasingly advanced as students mature. Schmitt (1988) was among the first to document the effects of tilling a text on students' comprehension. When taught how to till a text, third graders gradually assumed responsibility for previewing textual features without prompting. In so doing, they activated their prior knowledge. Blair-Larson and Williams (1999) and Block (1999) also found that when students were taught to make connections between their tilling of texts and the knowledge gained from immediately preceding sentences, they comprehended texts more completely. Teaching context clue usage at this point in the curriculum has been proven to be especially effective, using the CPM and sample lesson illustrated in Figure 6.1. Tilling the text also helped students interpret subtle symbolisms, images, and foreshadowing.

Once you have completed a tilling-the-text lesson, you can ask students to practice using this process with fictional genre through series books (i.e., *Clifford, Frog and Toad)*. In this way, the same authorial writing styles can be reread. The similarities found in series books reduce the difficulty of tilling a text and increase the speed with which such comprehension processes become automatic. Using this method of instruction, each student has an increased chance of successful comprehension.

CPI Genre-Specific Lesson 4: Attending to Authors' Writing Styles

To help readers recognize the logic that an author followed when he or she divided the text into subtopics, show pupils how to skim a text and identify dense sections that may require more concentrated thinking. You can teach the skill of attending to an author's writing style by showing students how to skim or scan a full text for 1–3 minutes before beginning a more focused reading. During this scanning, show students (by talking aloud) how they can think silently to themselves, before they read, about the connections between subheadings that they think the author is making. For example, you might say: "I see that the author is beginning with the history of San Antonio, then moving to the present activities, and concluding the chapter with a description of three major tourist attractions."

You can conclude the think-aloud by teaching students that such an overview (or tilling of the text) can establish a mental framework of the book's main ideas; in other words, the overview tells them where they are going as they read. It also enables students to adhere closely to the main idea track created by the author—a process demonstrated to increase retention (Beck & Dole, 1992; Mangieri & Block, 1994). Such think-alouds show students how to think while they read. Knowing how to think is as powerful an instructional tool for building comprehension abilities as storytelling and sharing examples that tie the text to students' life experiences.

Outlines of the connections between subsections in a text are called *story frames*. This teaching tool can be used in tilling-the-text lessons. In teaching a Strand 1 lesson about story frames, you can provide partial outlines of a chapter's key points and tell students how you recognized that these were the main points. Then ask the students to complete the remainder of the outlines as they read. Students share their outlines, the rationales for the key points they chose, and the connections between key points they made after the story has been completed. A sample story frame appears in Figure 6.2; a blank story frame to photocopy and use in your classroom appears in Appendix A.

CPI Genre-Specific Lesson 5: Predicting the Functions of Paragraphs

When students anticipate the likely function of upcoming paragraphs, they can initiate valuable thinking processes that assist them in making meaning (Kintsch, 2001). You can help students remember these functions by using the acronym *IDEAL* (although authors do not always order their paragraphs "ideally"). In an ideal piece of writing, the order of paragraph

FIGURE 6.1. **CPM to use in Strand 1 CPM lessons on identifying context clues.**

Context Clues

What context clues give the words a bigger leap forward in meaning?

Strand 1: Teach How the Mind Uses Context Clues

Explain and model this process three times in action (i.e., use thinking guides, examples, models, and think-alouds as you read a book orally).

Explain. Applying the comprehension process of context clues supports the reader in making use of evidence found in the text to continue comprehending the material. When comprehension breaks down, the reader must implement a search of the context clues to bring meaning to the reading material. Context clues for building a meaning range from the initial sounds of words, illustrations, and the words in proximity to the challenging text, to the information learned through the previously read sections.

1. **Thinking Guides**. Display the CPM chart for **context clues**. Highlight the words **bigger leap forward in the meaning** to remind the students that context clues add depth to their comprehension of the reading material. (Adding pictures to the chart assists students in performing the thoughts depicted on this CPM. Select a permanent spot on which to display the motion chart and highlighted comprehension process sentence for students to use in future lessons.)

2. **Model**. Demonstrate the motion for context clues. Have the students practice the motion with you as you model it three times. The context clues motion begins by forming a letter **c** with one hand (the **c** stands for clues) and holding the other hand flat, palm up, touching the bottom of the hand making the letter **c**. Then move both hands upward together. This motion is similar to the sign for **help**. This motion signals a recognition of words that help to improve text comprehension.

3. **Think-Alouds**. Read the first two pages of text and stop. Signal with the motion and ask students which context clue could be used to increase comprehension. Repeat this process on each page.

functions is (1) introductory, (2) descriptive, (3) evaluative, (4) assessing, and (5) last (concluding summary). To teach these functions, show sample paragraphs from a text that students are about to read on an overhead projector. Demonstrate how you recognize the function of a few paragraphs. Then ask students to perform think-alouds to demonstrate how they recognized the functions of subsequent paragraphs. At this point, the Strand 1 lesson ends, and you cycle through Strand 2 lessons several times as students write the functions of paragraphs within different genre as they read silently. Last, convene Strand 3 CPI groups so that students can decide which types of paragraphs are still causing them comprehension difficulties.

CPI Genre-Specific Lesson 6: Comprehension Motions That Can Be Introduced Best through Nonfictional Texts

Strand 1 lessons that teach the comprehension processes and motions of (1) summing up, (2) using context clues to learn new concepts and vocabulary, (3) building to a main idea, (4) drawing conclusions, and (5) determining causes and effects are best used when reading two nonfiction texts on the same topic as the agenda. These five processes are also used to understand fictional text, but they are altered when applied to different genres. In the next few pages you will learn how to teach the CPMs for each of these mental processes. In addition, CPMs that can be incorporated into Strands 1, 2, and 3 lessons to develop young readers' abilities in these five essential, genre-specific processes are suggested.

With each CPM depicted in Figures 6.1, 6.3, 6.4, 6.5, and 6.7, introduce the process by using the basic steps of a Strand 1 lesson (described in Chapter 2) and add the information contained at Step 2 for each (as shown in the figures listed above). (See also the Practice Sheets for Strand 2 lessons on main ideas that appear in Appendix A.)

In summary, you can combine CPI Genre-Specific Lessons 3, 4, and 5 and show how, before beginning reading, you (1) till a text by identifying difficult sections, (2) attend to authors' writing styles, and (3) consider the functions of paragraphs. In the future, each time students read independently, monitor them and ask them to describe how they are using these sets of comprehension processes with specific texts.

Summary

By teaching the genre-specific processes in this chapter, nonfiction reading becomes more pleasant and distinct from fictional reading. As a result, students spend more time reading expository text (Block, 2001d). As their experiences with pleasurable, nonfictional text accumulate, students choose to read more complex expositions containing more new information. With all that is demanded of today's students, it is imperative that they master larger bodies of such new knowledge more efficiently and independently. When students in grades K–3 know how to (1) read two texts on the same topic consecutively, (2) skim/scan and savor, (3) till the text, (4) predict paragraph functions, (5) attend to authors' writing styles, (6) sum up, (7) use context clues, (8) identify main ideas, (9) draw conclusions, and (10) recognize causes as well as effects, they are well equipped to enjoy and gain meaning from a wide variety of expository text.

FIGURE 6.2. **Sample story frame completed by Renaldo while he read the nonfictional text An Invisible World by Jan Reynolds and Ed Reynolds.**

Story Frame Form _for Invisible World by Jan Reynolds & Ed Reynolds_

Setting: (When and where does the story take place?) _Above and below a pond_

I know this because the author uses these words: _Above and below underwater_

Main characters: (Who are the most important people in the story?) _birds, insects, people_

I know they are important because: _They have names by their pictures_

The problem starts when: _A girl wants to make a pond at school_

or

The main character's goal is: _to learn about life in water_

The plot: (What happened?)
Event 1: _Get water in bucket_

After that . . .
Event 2: _Put wood in so animels can float on it_

Next . . .
Event 3: _watch animals play_

Then . . .
Event 4: _Return watar and animels to pond_

Turning point: (How I know the plot is reaching a solution)
The resolution: (How did it end?) _Study hard but return animels to their home_

I know this because the author uses these words: _"animals are important in the environment where they live"_

Author's moral or purpose (or, purpose for me): _All animals need each other_

I think this is the moral because: _The author ended the book by telling us this and the animels ended happy._

Many teachers allow students to make poster-size thinking guides in groups so that classmates can see the different thoughts that can occur while everyone reads nonfiction text. Also, many teachers in CPI research classrooms group children's nonfiction trade books into boxes that are labeled by the comprehension process that is most required to understand that text. In this way, students can select valuable books to practice these processes in Strand 2 lessons, and to demonstrate their strengths and weaknesses relative to them in Strand 3 lessons.

Reflecting on What You Have Learned

1. **Interpreting (Summarizing) the Main Points.** Summarize this chapter's key points, making a graphic to depict your thought processes. The summary and graphic combined must be only one page.

2. **Making Professional Decisions.** Select an activity in this chapter. Design a method to evaluate an individual's success, and compare your assessment to those presented in Chapter 10. How many principles did you deduce, before you read them, to be important in evaluating comprehension?

3. **Making Field Applications and Observations.** Using one of the CPI lessons in this chapter, create a lesson for your class and assess its effectiveness. Discuss its strengths and weaknesses with your colleagues by describing your objective, the steps you took in implementing the lesson, and the materials. If you are not pres-

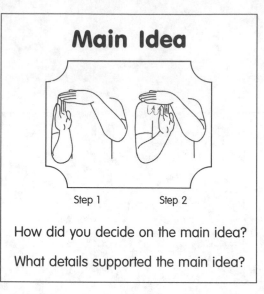

Main Idea

Step 1   Step 2

How did you decide on the main idea?

What details supported the main idea?

Strand 1: Teach How to Identify the Main Idea

Explain and model this process three times in action (i.e., use thinking guides, examples, models, and think-alouds as you read a book orally).

Explain. The comprehension process of identifying the main idea teaches readers to develop a main idea by joining the supporting details. The main idea is the sum of the parts of a selection. To identify the main idea entails interpretation and prioritization of the details.

1. **Thinking Guides**. Display the CPM chart for identifying the main idea. Highlight the words **details supported** to remind the students to accumulate the supporting details, then selectively determine the level of importance to disclose the main idea. (Adding pictures to the chart assists students with the steps that accompany this CPM. Select a permanent spot on which to display the motion chart and highlighted comprehension process sentence for students to use in future lessons.)

2. **Model**. Demonstrate the motion for identifying the main idea. Have the students practice the motion with you as you model it three times. To create the main idea motion, place your left hand, palm down, at eye level. This hand represents the main idea of a selection. Place the fingertips of your right hand to the fingertips of your left hand, with your arm remaining in a vertical position. Move your right hand to the left, touching the palm of your left several times. These movements of your right hand are the details that support the main idea. It is important that your right hand moves from right to left. From the students' perspective, the movement is the same as the direction of reading text.

3. **Think-Alouds**. Read the first two pages of text. (Readers set purpose themselves.) Next, stop at the end of each paragraph. Ask students to perform the CPM and identify the main idea.

Once students learn CPI motions, they initiate them throughout the day without prompting. In these photos, Ms. Cummins's students are delivering paired social studies reports. On their own volition, Jason and Elizabeth used the main idea CPM as they gave the main ideas from their reports. Notice that left-handed students make this motion as a mirror image.

ently teaching, design an ideal program that would systematically incorporate all CPI lessons into the comprehension instruction that you want to deliver, in the order you deem best. Defend your ordering.

4. **Keeping a Professional Journal.** Philosophical Journals. In approximately one paragraph, write a concise description of your philosophy for instructing and assessing genre-specific comprehension. This description will help you verbalize to students, colleagues, parents, and administrators how you make your instructional assessment decisions concerning the use of nonfiction in your classroom. Before you write this description, write a one-sentence reflection concerning the following: What type of teacher did you do best with, when you were a young student, in learning to comprehend nonfiction and why?

5. **Making Multicultural Applications.** Select a book that contains main characters from a culture that is different from those of the students in your class. Use that book as you teach one of the lessons from this chapter to students from a minority cultural background. After you complete the lesson, write about the adaptations that you had to make, or will make in the future, to meet the special needs of students from minority cultures.

6. **Meeting Students' Special Needs.** Based on the information in this chapter, project how the education field in the future will use more technology and nonfictional reading to advance the comprehension abilities of more students. In this projection, include a forecast of the percentage of comprehension instructional time that will be linked to technology by the year 2010. Be prepared to defend your projection and compare it with your colleagues.

7. **Checking Key Terms.** Following is a list of concepts introduced in this chapter. If you have learned the meaning of a term, place a checkmark in the blank that precedes that term. If you are not sure of a term's definition, increase your retention by reviewing its definition. If you have learned all of these terms on your first

FIGURE 6.4. CPM for a Strand 1 CPM lesson on drawing conclusions.

Within the figure:

Draw Conclusions

Step 1   Step 2

The author's words tell me _____,
but the idea is _____.

What idea is the author trying to give me?

Strand 1: Teach How the Mind Draws Conclusions

Explain and model this process three times in action (i.e., use thinking guides, examples, models, and think-alouds as you read a book orally).

Explain. Drawing conclusions is the process of interpreting the author's information in relation to the judgments made by the reader. Conclusions drawn from a text are a subjective combination of readers' background knowledge, personal perspective on the topic, and the author's expected outcomes.

1. **Thinking Guides**. Display the CPM chart for drawing conclusions. Highlight the words **author trying to tell me, author's words**, and **idea** so that students remember to base their conclusion on the author's text **in relation to** their own perspective. (Adding pictures to the chart assists students with the steps that accompany this CPM. Select a permanent spot on which to display the motion chart and highlighted comprehension process sentence for students to use in future lessons.)

2. **Model**. Demonstrate the motion for drawing conclusions. Have the students practice the motion with you as you model it three times. As you begin the motion, tell the students to think of a funnel. Begin with hands apart at shoulder height; this is where the information enters the funnel. Then, as readers continue to condense the information, the diameter of the funnel narrows until a conclusion can be drawn. Your hands move downward to convey the narrowing of the funnel until they meet in a V-shape to form a point—the conclusion.

3. **Think-Alouds**. Read the text. Ask students to perform the CPM for drawing conclusions and tell you what they did to draw a conclusion.

FIGURE 6.5. **CPM for a Strand 1 CPM lesson on summing up information.**

Strand 1: Teach How the Mind Summarizes

Explain and model this process three times in action (i.e., use thinking guides, examples, models, and think-alouds as you read a book orally).

Explain. The comprehension process of summing up involves a condensing of the information provided by the author, **exclusive of reader judgment**. The reader must collect and compact the main ideas of a selection to sum up the text.

1. **Thinking Guides**. Display the CPM chart for summing up. Highlight the words **What** and **if I look back.** (Adding pictures to the chart assists students with the steps that accompany this CPM. Select a permanent spot on which to display the motion chart and highlighted comprehension process sentence for students to use in future lessons.)

2. **Model**. Demonstrate the motion for summing up. Have the students practice the motion with you as you model it three times. To demonstrate summing up information, place your right hand at shoulder height, your hand open with palm toward the students. As you move your right hand downward, move your left hand up to meet the right hand and form a closed circle with all fingers together. This movement, similar to the funnel, shows a gradual condensing of the information into a summary.

3. **Think-Alouds**. Read the first two pages of text and stop. (Readers set purpose themselves.) Ask students to sum up and use the CPM. Ask them to describe how they did so. Repeat this process throughout the book.

An example of the summary that Summer, a first grader, wrote following this CPI lesson on summing up appears in Figure 6.6.

FIGURE 6.6. **Effects of teaching the CPI sum-up lesson: A first grader's summary following instruction.**

♡   Corduroy   ♡

I'v felt like Lisa before because I realy wanted that two hedded Stroller for my stufft dolls but wene my parants said no I felled very sad. Because I could't buy it.

Renaldo was so excited that he had reached a summary of his social studies chapter that he made an large CPI sum-up motion. He wanted Ms. Cummins, his third-grade teacher, to realize that he was among the first to do so for this chapter. Marguette, seated beside him, had just reached a summary also!

FIGURE 6.7. **CPM for a Strand 1 CPM lesson on identifying causes and effects.**

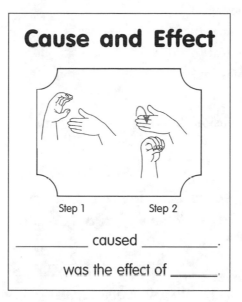

Strand 1: Teach How to Identify Cause and Effect

Explain and model this process three times in action (i.e., use thinking guides, examples, models, and think-alouds as you read a book orally).

Explain. The comprehension process of identifying cause and effect aids readers in understanding how one event is the cause, or is caused by, another event. Readers learn how motives can cause or affect characters' behaviors, or how natural phenomena can affect characters' behaviors as well as natural events. This process also connects the impact of one event on another.

1. **Thinking Guides**. Display the CPM chart for identifying cause and effect. Highlight the words **caused** and **effect** to trigger a search for the cause or effect of an event. (Adding pictures to the chart assists students with the steps that accompany this CPM. Select a permanent spot on which to display the motion chart and highlighted comprehension process sentence for students to use in future lessons.)

2. **Model**. Demonstrate the motion for cause and effect. Have the students practice the motion with you as you model it three times. Cup your right hand in a **c** shape (cause) and place your left hand parallel to your body with your palm facing toward you. Move the **c**-shaped hand forward and over the left hand, representing moving forward in time. As the right hand moves forward, change the **c**-shape into the sign language letter for **e** (effect) by drawing in your thumb to your palm and placing your fingertips along it. This motion exhibits a cause bringing about an effect.

3. **Think-Alouds**. Read the first two pages of text and then stop. Ask students to signal with the CPM and describe the cause and effect. Continue in this manner.

reading of this chapter, you have constructed many meanings that are important for your teaching.

> ____Self-efficacy (p. 93)
>
> ____Story grammar (p. 94)
>
> ____Tilling the text (p. 96)
>
> ____Story frames (p. 97)
>
> ____IDEAL (p. 99)

8. **Design a Comprehension Process Lesson.** Modify the following lesson.

Comprehension Process Lesson 5: Building Bridges—Strand 1, 2, and 3 Lessons for Nonfiction

Genre: Nonfiction

Explore the differences and similarities in fiction and nonfiction texts. Introduce the topic of eggs. Activate students' prior knowledge with a K-W-L chart: *K* (what I know), *W* (what I want to know), *L* (what I want to learn). Select fiction and nonfiction texts on eggs. Read a nonfiction text first. After the students are given the opportunity to share all new knowledge and questions, review the book by identifying text features (i.e., fonts and special effects, textual cues, illustrations and paragraphs, graphics, and text organizers). Using a Venn diagram, compare and contrast fiction and nonfiction texts and return to the K-W-L chart after each nonfiction reading to add new knowledge, insights, and questions. The students may also have information to add to the Venn diagram, as well as new comparisons to fiction material. Additionally, the text should be studied to decide the text structure. The text structures more commonly applied to nonfiction texts include cause and effect, problem and solution, question and answer, comparison and contrast, description and sequence of events.

Topic: Established through genre study

Self:

Eggs are a common item in the students' refrigerators. In addition, some students will have experiences with watching eggs in incubators or finding a bird's egg that has fallen from the nest. List all facts about eggs from students' prior experiences on a chart.

Author:

An author study can further develop the students' schema of genre and topic. Select several nonfiction authors so that the variety in writing styles clarifies the students' knowledge of the topic. Update the K-W-L chart and Venn diagram after each reading.

Theme: Establishing a Purpose

Read first two pages of text and stop. (Readers set purpose themselves.) There are three steps in this Strand 1 lesson of integrating comprehension process lessons before the point of need. The genre-specific comprehension processes used in nonfiction reading usually include clarifying, questioning, determining important ideas and main idea, monitoring and repairing comprehension, using context clues, synthesizing causes or effects, and drawing conclusions.

Step 1. Identify Two Genre-Specific Comprehension Processes That Students Need

In this lesson we will focus on clarifying (specifically to address unknown content-related vocabulary) and drawing conclusions (in particular, how these texts relate to the egg theme).

Step 2. Explain and Model Each Process Three Times in Action

> "The comprehension process of clarifying helps you when you encounter unknown vocabulary or have difficulty understanding text. Without getting a clarification, your comprehension of the information will be disrupted. The comprehension process of drawing conclusions identifies the idea the author wants the reader to understand."

Thinking Guides

Display the CPM chart for prediction (see Appendix B). Write *Prediction* on a chart and record "Which picture helped me predict?" and "What did I already know that helped me predict?" Highlight the words *picture, I already know*, and the picture clues to remind the students to use this information when forming predictions. (Adding pictures to the chart assists students with the steps that accompany each CPM. Display the motion charts and highlighted comprehension process chart for the students to use in future lessons.)

Display the CPM chart for inference (see Appendix B). Inferences are my understanding of what the author wants me to know but does not state directly. (Remember to highlight the word and picture clues for displaying in the classroom for future lessons.)

Model

Demonstrate the prediction motion. Have the students practice the prediction motion with you as you model it three times. Explain:

"Predictions utilize known information that I 'see' in the text [fingertips to eyes] to envision what will happen in the future [fingertips turn to look and move through time]. Predictions and inferences are similar in that they explore the unknown."

Demonstrate the inference motion. Have the students practice the inference motion with you as you model it three times. Explain:

"Inferences begin with the author's train of thought and move to the unstated. As the reader, I incorporate what the author said [hand stationary to left of body] and what I know [move the hand in an arching motion to the right of body] to infer the meaning."

Think-Alouds

Using *Alexander and the Terrible, Horrible, No Good, Very Bad Day* by Judith Viorst (1998), read the first two pages of text and then stop to let students set the purpose for themselves. After reading the first five pages, turn the page and discuss the illustration. While demonstrating the prediction motion, state, "I predict that Anthony's mother forgot to put dessert in his lunch because things keep happening that make Anthony sad."

On page 13, after Anthony says that next week he's going to Australia, demonstrate the inference motion and state, "I infer that Anthony wants to go to Australia because he thinks sad things would stop happening if he were in a different place far, far away."

Step 3. Read Aloud and Ask Several Students to Perform a Think-Aloud to Demonstrate Each Comprehension Process

Steps in a Strand 2 Lesson (Instruction *at* Point of Need)

Ask students to read silently for 10–20 minutes, marking the location in the text when they apply a comprehension process. As they read, move from desk to desk asking each student to tell you where in the book he or she used one or both comprehension processes and what he or she was thinking as he or she used these processes to make meaning. Repeat this strand as many times as necessary, until most students can use the comprehension processes without prompting. All the steps in Strands 1, 2, and 3 lessons can be reviewed by referring to Table 1.2 (pp. 9–10).

CHAPTER 7

Teaching Students to Infer, Predict, and Interpret Fiction and Nonfiction

Julianna, a vibrant third grader, listened intently as Ms. Escamilla taught a Strand 1 lesson on how to infer. Ms. Escamilla told the class to take what they know and add to it what they read together. Then they pull their thoughts ahead to think about what would most likely be described in the next sentence in the new book *The Three Questions* (Muth, 2002). Julianna looked at her thinking guide to reread each of the steps in inference. She thought for a moment, then she made the inference motion. Ms. Escamilla called on her first, and she got it right!! She was so happy. She was learning so much!

Chapter Overview

Recently, state legislatures have passed laws that require the assessment of inference, predicting, and interpreting processes on statewide, criterion-referenced literacy tests. The questions on these tests are intended to assess the depth of students' understanding. In part, these laws were passed to address the reality that many children arrive at school unprepared to think deeply about texts that adults read aloud. Inference-based instruction teaches students to process and integrate text-based ideas into their background knowledge significantly more rapidly than literal-based instruction (Hansen, 1980; Pearson & Fielding, 1996). In particular, prediction questions assist readers in grades K–3 to stay actively engaged in reading (Hansen, 1980; Hansen & Pearson, 1983).

This chapter describes research-based CPI lessons that teach inference, prediction, and interpretation processes. By the end of this chapter you will have answers to the following questions:

1. How can inferencing, predicting, and interpreting processes be developed in Strands 1, 2, and 3 lessons?
2. How can you assess students' inference, prediction, and interpretative abilities?

Theories of Inferencing, Predicting, and Interpreting Processes

Inferencing is the ability to conclude or predict something that is implied but not stated explicitly. Inferencing is one of the most complex and unique human cognitive activities (Taylor et al., 2000). When inferencing, a successful comprehender connects previous experiences, persons, events, and objects encountered so that

> text becomes a coherent whole rather than a random list of facts and events. If all goes well, the result of inferential processing is a mental representation of a text that is relatively stable and can be accessed at a later point in time to answer questions and retell the story. (p. 165)

There are 10 major types of inferences that students can learn (Johnson & Johnson, 1986):

1. *Location inferences.* "After check-in, the bellhop helped us carry luggage to our room." Where are we?
2. *Agent inferences.* "With clippers in one hand and scissors in the other, Chris approached the chair." What is Chris?
3. *Time inferences.* "When the porch light burned out, the darkness was total." When did this occur?
4. *Action inferences.* "George arched his body and sliced into the water; his form was perfect." What is George doing?
5. *Instrument inferences.* "With a steady hand, Dr. Hoff put the buzzing device on my tooth." Which tool is Dr. Hoff using? (*Instrument* is defined as a "tool or device.")
6. *Category inferences.* "The Saab and Volvo were in the garage, and the Audi was out front." These three are members of what category?
7. *Object inferences.* "The gleaming giant had 18 wheels, and it towered above lesser vehicles on the turnpike." What is the "gleaming giant"?
8. *Cause–effect inferences.* "In the morning, we noticed that the trees were uprooted, and some homes had lost their roofs." What caused this situation? (In this example, the cause needs to be inferred. Often, a cause is stated and the effect must be inferred.)
9. *Problem–solution inferences.* "The side of Ken's face was swollen, and his tooth throbbed." What should Ken do about this problem? (In this example, the solution must be inferred. Sometimes a solution is stated and the problem must be inferred.)
10. *Feelings–attitude inferences.* "While I marched past in the junior high band, my dad cheered, and his eyes filled with tears." What was my dad feeling?

Predicting is a type of inference in which readers deduce the next event, action, or idea. Weaver and Kintsch (1996) analyzed more than 100 textbooks and found that as many as 12–15 inferences were embedded in a single sentence. Such density demands that inference processes becomes automatic. *Interpreting* refers to accurately processing and integrating textual information.

Before students can draw an inference, they must (1) place facts into categories, (2) frame these categories in relation to a goal, and (3) maintain a focus on an author's writing goals

(Haenggi, Kintsch, & Gernsbacher, 1995). Although some weaker readers can learn to image without instruction, most must be taught how to engage the specific inferences listed previously. When they are taught through the CPI lessons in this chapter, they become aware of, and use, the arcs of inferred information that authors depend on readers to make. They also score significantly higher on main idea questions covering previously read material (Block & Stanley, 2004).

This finding also explains why weaker readers must be taught to think about what a text means to them as they make literal sense of printed words. If the lessons in this chapter are not taught, students in grade K–3 are likely to be unable to interpret pronouns and connectors. Some will not even realize that stories consist of a series of connected, related events. Others will not discern how soon an author is likely to change topics, and how specific that author's word choices are. Many young readers fail to realize that texts have overarching main ideas, messages, and themes (Yuill & Oakhill, 1991). To make these connections, young readers need more than simply to be asked inference questions after they have read (Cornoldi & Oakhill, 1998).

Other studies have demonstrated that students must be taught Strand 1 lessons in a personally contextualized instructional milieu (Fitzgerald & Spiegel, 1983). Such lessons should provide training on (1) identifying various features of a story or exposition, and (2) how to infer by categorizing single facts (Kintsch, 1998; Long, 1994).

The Difficulty of Inferencing, Predicting, and Interpreting Processes

There are many reasons why young students have difficulty learning how to infer, predict, and interpret (Piaget, 1963; Singer & Ritchot, 1996). First, many young readers believe so strongly in a personally constructed, nontextually based interpretation that they simply overlook the facts and cause–effect patterns that would more closely align their thoughts with the author's. These students may blatantly reject printed evidence that contradicts their interpretations. Students must learn how to dispel their own desires to move material in a certain direction when their interpretation of facts in a book is inconsistent with the author's train of thought (Otero & Kintsch, 1992).

Another difficulty in learning to infer stems from the fact that many primary students have not been taught how to comprehend a broad range of rhetorical structures and authorial writing patterns (Chambliss, 1993; Kintsch, 1991). When readers recognize a text's macropropositions, generalizations, and themes, independent inferencing can be engaged. When young readers practice and master the signal clues described in Chapter 5, they can more rapidly infer the links that an author makes between propositions within sentences, as well as the implied logical connections between sentences and paragraphs.

Most young readers must be taught how to interpret. Contemporary society has conditioned students to expect immediate answers; rather than to patiently interpret. For instance, today's unit of impact is only 6 minutes in length—meaning that young readers expect to have inferred or identified the most important point in a story within the first 5–6 minutes of reading.

Fortunately, students' inferential, predictive, and interpretive abilities can be improved when they are (1) exposed to these processes in Strand 1 lessons, (2) taught to reread in

Strand 2 lessons, and (3) taught to pause and reflect in Strand 3 lessons (Block & Stanley, 2004). Students who had trouble inferencing and predicting, but who were taught to talk about their comprehension processes, remembered more about the information from the text than did students in a control group (Pressley et al., 1995). Discussions of comprehension processes (as occur in CPI Strand 3 lessons) are powerful because they enable students to *close gaps in coherence* (sections of text that depend on a reader's inference to achieve connection). When coherence gaps are closed, students do not stray too far from an author's specific, intended *arcs of information* (i.e., those links between propositions that connect the text's macrostructure). Moreover, such discussions enable young readers to (1) express their ill-conceived overreliance on their own knowledge and belief systems, and (2) explain difficulties that they had as they tried to infer, interpret, or predict at various points. Young readers who were taught to infer (using the lessons in this chapter) generated significantly more solutions to the problems about which they read in fictional and nonfictional text (Block & Stanley, 2004).

Finally, young readers need to exert more effort to infer, interpret, or predict when reading nonfiction than fiction. When reading expository text, students must anticipate how a particular system of thought will unfold; they also must use the text structures of that text's discipline (as described in Chapter 6). Drawing inferences from nonfiction text also requires more links to memory than inferring points in fiction. Information retrieved from long-term memory must be added instantly to the newly constructed facts learned from that book. By contrast, fictional plots depend more on a reader's ability to keep track of the location and movement of actors—which is easier to visualize than the more abstract quality of nonfiction material. Imagery can thereby play a larger role in drawing inferences from fictional text than is possible when reading nonfiction (Block, 2001a; Keene & Zimmerman, 1997; Kintsch, 1998).

Teaching Inference through CPI Hypothesis Testing

One of the new approaches to instruction on inferencing involves teaching young students to infer by testing hypotheses. Good readers have many ways of forming sophisticated hypotheses (Carr, 1998; Frederiksen, 1981; Stanovich, 1986), including using the information they have comprehended at this point in a text, combining this knowledge with what they know about the topic, and predicting the next points that will be made in the text. They confirm or disconfirm their hypotheses by finding the correct answer in the material being read, not by guessing or using only one salient word or detail (Brown, 2002; Mackey, 1998). Students who are unable to infer cannot create a mental map of "where the author is going" or identify the body of thought the author is creating. As a result, they cannot use this body of thought to set hypotheses, seek answers to personal queries, or infer. Alternatively, students who make good inferences are able to (1) express meaning, (2) refer to individual facts, (3) follow the author's writing style and body of thought, (4) interpret figures of speech, (5) identify the macrostructures on which arguments are built, (6) unite all this information, and then draw inferences based on it (van Dijk & Kintsch, 1983).

Another aspect that distinguishes valid from shallow inferences is the degree to which certainty is developed by using multiple facts. Whenever young students do not spend enough time acquiring information before making inferences, their resultant interpretations and predictions are likely to be inaccurate (Fisher, Schumaker, & Deshler, 2002). If these students are to learn how to inference by creating hypotheses, they must be taught how to do so. The Strand 1 lessons that follow significantly increase students' reading achievement and the amount of time they spend collecting and reflecting on details, main ideas, and authors' themes while they read (Block & Reed, 2003).

CPI Inference Lesson I: Writing Hypotheses or Predictions

This Strand 1 lesson begins by teaching the Comprehension Process Motion for predicting, as shown in Figure 7.1. This motion shows what the mind does to make a prediction. Hold up the left arm horizontally in front of the upper chest to signify the horizon in view. Form a V shape with the index and middle finger of the right hand and point to the right eye to signify that readers have to mentally understand the ideas they see. Then move the right hand forward and beyond the left arm to convey how the mind makes predictions by moving beyond the known into unseen territory. Obtaining an accurate comprehension of all the information provided by the author equips the reader to make interpretations and predictions.

As you teach the basic steps in this Strand 1 lesson, add the information described in Figure 7.1. When you have modeled how to make a prediction process motion, ask students to signal you that they have made a prediction. When you see a child making the prediction motion, ask him or her to describe what he or she predicts and why he or she made that prediction. For example, teach them the sentence stem: "I predict _____ because _____." (You can reference and use the sample Strand 1 predication and inference lesson at the end of this chapter as you teach.)

Ask students to make hypotheses as they read and to write them down. Regarding weaker comprehenders, content for this lesson should be well structured and coherent so that the hypotheses that authors' are depending upon readers' to make are easier for students to recognize (Fisher & Trabasso, 2001; Kintsch & van Dijk, 1978). In this lesson, place Post-it Notes at points in a text where an author is depending upon readers to infer, predict, or interpret. (An example of this Post-it Note appears on p. 131.) Then instruct students to stop whenever they come to such a place and write a hypothesis about the inference that they think the author is expecting. Taking time to write this educated guess increases the amount of time that students' minds are engaged in synthesizing facts. When this lesson is repeated, students become more comfortable with the experience of inferring and reflecting as they read.

CPI Inference Lesson 2: Diagramming the Inference Process

The purpose of diagramming is to demonstrate graphically how students can make hypotheses that become valid inferences, predictions, and interpretations. In this lesson, teach students the three-part thought process involved in making inferences that is depicted in Figure 7.2. This process is based on inferences that students are likely to have already made in their lives. Hold up the thinking guide in Figure 7.2 and say:

FIGURE 7.1. **CPM for a Strand 1 CPM lesson on making predictions.**

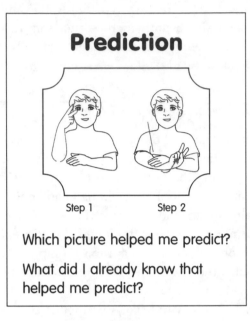

Strand 1: Teach How the Mind Makes Predictions

Explain.

"The comprehension process of prediction helps you, the reader, connect story events to your personal knowledge and experiences. This connection provides a thorough understanding of the author's train of thought and the ability to forecast events. Your prediction is based on actual story knowledge supplied by the author."

1. **Thinking Guides**. Display the CPM chart for prediction. Highlight the words **picture** and **I already know** and the picture clues to remind students to use this information when forming predictions. (Adding pictures to the chart assists students with the steps that accompany this CPM. Select a permanent spot on which to display the motion chart and highlighted comprehension process sentence for students to use in future lessons.)

2. **Model**. Demonstrate the motion for prediction. Have the students practice the motion with you as you model it three times. Explain:

"Predictions utilize known information that I "see" in the text (**fingertips to eyes**) to envision what will happen in the future (**fingertips turn to look and move through time**). Predictions and inferences are similar in that they explore the unknown."

3. **Think-Alouds**. Read the first two pages of text and stop. (Readers set purpose themselves.) Ask students to signal with the CPM and describe how they made a prediction by saying "I predict _____ because _____."

Ms. Escamilla enlarged each thinking guide that she taught, laminated them, and allowed students to write on them during Strands 2 and 3 lessons. Her class made the Prediction Thinking Guide to depict the comprehension processes they used to make predictions.

"If your mother, father, grandmother, or grandfather told you to take your umbrella to school, your brain would automatically think of rain, although no one has said that word. This is an inference, a comprehension process you use to make meaning, called *inferring,* and you can do this when you read and listen. To infer, you think about what the author wrote."

At this point, fold the thinking guide to show only the first column on that sheet. Read the first stanza of a poem, for example, and ask students to write down the thoughts they had about that first verse in column one. Then describe how the thinking process of inferring continues by suggesting that they think about prior knowledge they have of similar experiences that have occurred in their lives.

At this point, make this aspect of the process visible by unfolding the thinking guide to display the second column. Refold and reopen this second column as you tell them that their minds process information in a similar fashion when they infer as they read. Now write the thoughts about similar prior experiences in your life you had in relation to the first stanza of the poem. Then ask your students to record their thoughts on the second column of their thinking guide. Finally, unfold the last column of the thinking guide and explain that when they combine the information in the first two columns, they can generate a hypothesis that is likely to be what the author wanted them to infer.

Next, distribute copies of Figure 7.2 (also in Appendix A) to students and ask them to fold it along the two vertical dashed lines, as indicated. Then ask them to read the following sentence (which you will have written on the chalkboard, chart pad, or overhead acetate) and

FIGURE 7.2. **Teaching students the inference process.**

Thinking Guide: Drawing Inferences

Name: _____ Date: _____

What is said or read	+ What you know	= What is meant
1.		
2.		
3.		
4.		
5.		

write it on their thinking guide in the first column. "Nibbsie came running with the stick in his mouth." Have students unfold the second column on their page. Explain:

> "As you read, your mind added a few things based on what you know. You came up with an entirely new thought as you read that sentence. Write what your mind added, based on what you know about names like 'Nibbsie,' and about living things that run with sticks in their mouths."

Ask students to write their thoughts in the middle column of the guide.

Finally, ask students to unfold the third column and tell them that this next mental process is similar to what their minds do each time they infer as they read. The mind moves from the words read, to retrieving things already stored in it, to combining the two sources of data to generate a hypothesis about the author's implied meanings. Have students write their hypothesis in the third column.

Discuss with students what they have learned about the inferencing process. Note that the author does not tell readers that Nibbsie is a dog. They know that Nibbsie is a dog, however, because the author gives enough clues for readers to infer that it is one. Tell students that as they read, they should look for more than one clue to generate hypotheses about what an author means. When they do so, they are inferring. Now provide the students with practice activities. Use the "power of three" at this point in the lesson: Show one picture and ask students to unfold their thinking process guide as they write their three steps in making an inference. Then show a second and then a third picture. Continue by reading three poems and having students write their three steps in the inferencing process on their thinking guides for each poem. (They will write after each verse.) Last, ask students to read silently a text from selection of their choice and to write the three steps of the inferencing process in the same manner. (See Comprehension Process Lesson 6 for the materials you can use to teach this lesson.)

Teaching Inferencing by Using Text Structure and Writing Styles

Another method of increasing children's inferencing ability involves *spreading activation* (Britton & Graesser, 1996), a comprehension process in which concepts from one body of knowledge are dispersed to related concepts, causing the related concepts to become more activated in the brain. This spread of activation continues as long as readers continuously think about the material being read. Three types of "spreading" can be taught: (1) making strong application of knowledge to students' lives, (2) having positive emotional responses to the information, and (3) identifying when negative inhibitory connections occur between two ideas.

Knowledge spreads more rapidly when areas of personal interest are included; students are more motivated to read, and they hold their purposes more strongly in mind. As a result, they connect concepts to the author's overarching goals far more rapidly. When students prejudge a text to be important, the relationships between knowledge structures and literal arcs

When CPI lessons use personally relevant stories, many students experience several comprehension processes. As shown above, almost every student learned how to make predictions when Ms. Escamilla read **Will You Be My Friend?** by Eric Carle in this Strand 1 lesson.

of information are not as difficult to make. Because literal comprehension then requires less energy, students can pay greater attention to inferring, predicting, and interpreting.

CPI Inference Lesson 3: Explaining the Reasons behind Inferences

Most young readers must be taught how to explain their predictions and their inference (Block, 1996). Among the most effective methods is to perform a Strand 1 lesson that describes how specific traits of literary characters are combined by an author so that readers can infer whether a character is a hero or villain. You can also describe how characters' traits can be inferred by noting details about relationships they form with other characters. Books that students in grades K–3 enjoy discussing and reading to practice inferring include *Goodbye* (Arnold, 2002), *Aesop's Fables* (Pinkney, 2000), *One-Eyed Cat* (Fox, 1984), *Sea Glass* (Shreve, 2002), and *Enemy Pie* (Munson, 2000).

The Comprehension Process Motion for reasons and evidence can be taught to open this Strand 1 lesson. To do so, select one of the books cited above (or another), in which students must recognize several pieces of evidence to reach the correct interpretation or inference. Use this book throughout the regular steps in a Strand 1 lesson, but insert the content in the steps from Figure 7.3 when you reach Step 2 in the lesson.

CPI Inference Lesson 4: Using Photographs and Cartoons to Teach Inferencing

You can ask readers to make inferences from pictures in Strand 1 and 2 lessons. Beal (1990) and Holmes (1987) have reported that less able readers who were taught to infer an artist's message from photographs rather than having to make an inference based on text demonstrated that they could infer as well as expert readers do. Similarly, if you remove the dialogue from the last two sections of a cartoon and ask readers to write their inferences about them, you can teach many less able readers to infer with less difficulty than if you asked them to read from text alone. Then ask students to explain how what they inferred would make sense in the last two cartoon captions.

FIGURE 7.3. CPM for a Strand 1 lesson on identifying reasons and finding evidence.

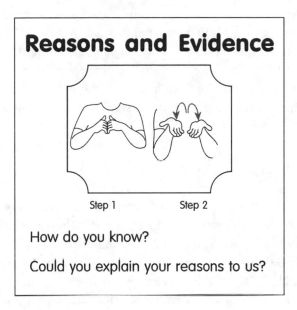

Reasons and Evidence

Step 1   Step 2

How do you know?

Could you explain your reasons to us?

Strand 1: Teach How the Mind Reasons and Finds Evidence

Explain. The reasons and evidence comprehension process requires readers to substantiate their beliefs and theories about the text by providing a text-based connection to the author's meaning. Reader interpretations that cannot be integrated in the author's message interfere with the story comprehension.

1. **Thinking Guides**. Display the CPM chart for reasons and evidence. Highlight the words **How do you know** and **explain your reasons** and the picture clues to remind students that random responses disrupt the comprehension of a text.

2. **Model**. Demonstrate the motion for reasons and evidence. Have the students practice the motion with you as you model it three times. The reasons and evidence comprehension process requires readers to explain **how** they arrived at their inferences; hence, the sign language for "how" is used as the CPM. Begin by placing the backs of your fingers on both hands together. Unfold your fingertips while rotating hands outward to reveal palms, as if presenting something. This motion demonstrates providing reasons for the reader's inferences.

3. **Think-Alouds**. Read the first two pages of text and stop. (Readers set purpose themselves.) Read two more pages and ask students to give reasons or evidence for their inferences, interpretations, or predictions and use this CPM.

Teaching an Author's Macrostructures

One of the most longstanding bodies of research about inferencing includes information about the role that reader-friendly ("considerate") and reader-unfriendly ("inconsiderate") texts play in the process (Beck, McKeown, Hamilton, & Kucan, 1997; Beck & Dole, 1992). Reader-friendly texts are well organized, contain familiar content, and have well-marked macrostructures. Recently, it has been established that when children in grades K–3 read texts that are inconsiderate, it is very difficult for them to make inferences (Britton & Graesser, 1996). For this reason, the following lessons have been developed to assist students when they have to read such text.

CPI Inference Lesson 5: Paraphrasing

Considerate text is coherent and contains supports for comprehension. We must teach children not to respond to inconsiderate texts in kind but rather in kindness. In other words, whenever children are reading a text in which it seems particularly difficult to make connections between individual sentences, they must be taught how to do so by extending kindness to the author (Beck et al., 1997). Kindness can be shown by allowing students to paraphrase what they would anticipate the author could have used to make a connection between sentences. This same instructional direction could be given to assist students in making probable connections between paragraphs. After students have created four paraphrases, they should be able to identify the author's macrostructure and writing style, which they can then follow throughout the remainder of the text.

CPI Inference Lesson 6: Teaching Inferencing with a First-Person Narrative

This Strand 1 lesson begins by providing students with instruction concerning the CPM for inferencing, shown in Figure 7.4. This CPI motion is taught by following the basic steps in a Strand 1 lesson, inserting the motion for inferencing wherever appropriate, and using the information from Figure 7.4 at Step 2 in the lesson. Next, give young students a first-person story in which the narrator is identified only as "I," and students must infer who "I" is.

Divide the story into paragraphs and tell readers to look for their first inferring clue in the first paragraph. Call on students who give the inference motion and discuss what they thought as they read: How did they predict or interpret? Continue to discuss subsequent inferences in this manner, one paragraph at a time, until the correct narrator is identified and readers explain the inferences they made to arrive at this identity. In a similar exercise, you can place pages with separate paragraphs (each with clues as to the narrator's identity) on a table and ask readers to select the first one, to begin. When they have finished the first section, they retrieve the next paragraph, working at their own pace and thinking about the information they read in each successive paragraph. When they are ready to predict the identity of the narrator, they should signal the inference motion and then, once you have arrived at their seat, whisper it in your ear. You record the amount of time it took each student to make a particular inference. Allow them to change their minds if they wish and to choose whether to read on or reread previous paragraphs after their first inference. When all stu-

FIGURE 7.4. **CPM for a Strand 1 lesson on making inferences.**

Inference

Step 1   Step 2

Take what the author says, add
what you know, and end up with
what was meant.

Strand 1: Teach How the Mind Makes Inferences

Explain. Inferences are statements of implied meanings. These meanings are derived from personal knowledge: they are not stated explicitly in the story. The reader must discern the author's meaning by accumulating clues as the story progresses.

1. **Thinking Guides**. Display the CPM chart for inference. Write **inference** on a chart and record "What I read plus (+) What I know equals (=) Inference." Inferences are my understanding of what the author wants me to know without directly stating it.

2. **Model**. Demonstrate the motion for inference. Have the student practice the motion with you as you model it three times. Explain:

"Inferences begin with the author's train of thought and move to the unstated. As the reader, I incorporate what the author said [**hand stationary to left of body**] and add it to what I know [**move the hand in an arching motion to the right of body**] to infer the meaning."

(Adding pictures to the chart assists students with the steps that accompany this CPM. Select a permanent spot on which to display the motion chart and comprehension process sentence for students to use in future lessons.)

3. **Think-Alouds**. Read the first two pages of text and stop. (Readers set purpose themselves.) Read the next two pages. Ask students to signal with the CPM when they have inferenced and describe the thinking processes they used to do so. Repeat this process.

dents have made at least one inference, ask the first few who accurately identified the narrator to explain the inference process they used.

After students have practiced their inferring skills for a week, you can reinitiate this activity by presenting a second set of paragraphs on the table for students to read in the same manner. When they have identified the correct narrator, record their times again, so that they can see tangible evidence of the improvements they have made in inferring. Figure 7.5 contains a story that can be used in grades 2 and 3 for this lesson.

CPI Inference Lesson 7: Think-Alouds That Model How to Gain Another Person's Perspective and Identify Gaps in Knowledge to Infer

As students retell a story, gaps in their understanding of the macrostructure of a selection will become clear. As Galda (1998) discovered, "It is easier to continue crafting a story alone when the reading is about people, especially people that have experiences that are similar to us. When there are big differences between the experiences and ourselves or the decoding demand is too large, the characters and events in the story push readers out of the book" (p. 123). Therefore, instead of pushing different cultures onto students, we must first mentor them in the process of attaining a new or different perspective, understanding divergent ideas and unfamiliar words, and closing gaps within texts. This mentoring process occurs through think-alouds that model how to fill gaps in knowledge with text-bound inferences. First teach the CPM for gaining a new perspective, depicted in Figure 7.6 by following the regular procedures for a Strand 1 lesson, inserting the information in Step 2 into the lesson, calling upon students who use this process motion to signal that they have obtained a new perspective, and asking them to describe how they gained it. Figure 4.2 (p. 65), the buddy retelling evaluation form, is an excellent teaching aid for a Strand 3 lesson on gaining perspective. It keeps students engaged because it breaks into steps the predicting, inferencing, and interpreting processes that pairs can discuss.

CPI Inference Lesson 8: Continuous Checks

After describing how to discern facts from concluding statements, students make checkmarks in the left margin of their paper to denote how many sentences an author takes to reach a concluding thought or goal. Continuous checks is a Strand 2 lesson. Afterward, students meet to conduct a small-group, Strand 3 lesson, discussing what they have learned and what they want to learn next.

CPI Inference Lesson 9: Round-Table Inference Group

The goals and objectives for this Strand 1 lesson are that young readers will learn to:

1. Distinguish between literal and inferential questions and be able to compose their own questions.
2. Answer an inferential question by using both obvious and "between-the-lines" clues.
3. Transfer what they have learned in round-table discussions by answering questions in the group and using constant self-questioning when reading independently.

FIGURE 7.5. **First-person narrative.**

- -

CLUE #1

Lunch made me sleepy, so I curled up to take a nap. With sleep came a wonderful dream. I was stretched out on a lovely green lawn with the sun warming my body. Birds were singing gaily overhead, and little yellow daffodils peeked out through the grass. I reached out to touch one—and suddenly there was no sun.

A heavy shadow had shut out the light. Something grabbed me and I cried out, fighting to get free. It was no use; I was traveling through space. This was no dream. It was real. I had been captured, and there was nothing I could do about it.

CLUE #2

Soon I felt something solid at my feet. I could move, but it was hard to stand. My legs felt limber. Where was I?

Cautiously, I stepped forward. OUCH! I bumped into a wall and went in the other direction, but every time there was a wall. Four walls and no door. I'm in a cell!

All of a sudden there was a blast of cold air from above. I looked up but could see nothing. Where was the air coming from? Suddenly I knew. there was no roof on my cell! I had discovered a way out.

CLUE #3

Creeping carefully toward a wall, I attempted to reach the opening. I wasn't big enough, so I curled up and began to think. The cell was still rocking. Maybe I could throw myself against one of the walls and tip the cell over. Again and again I rushed at the wall, but I finally gave up, defeated.

I tried to gather the energy for one more try. If that didn't work—wait, the movement stopped!

A minute later I heard an earthshaking bang as I felt a different motion. My cell was moving up and down, not back and forth. I couldn't keep my balance. I said to myself I'd swat whatever it was. I'd be ready. In an instant there was a horrible crunch, and the wall nearest me was ripped away. Beyond the opening I could see a dazzling light.

CLUE #4

"Now's your chance," I told myself, cautiously crawling to the opening. At first, I saw nothing but a shiny wood floor. Then I saw **them**!

Feet! Giant feet! They seemed about to surround me, so I quickly retreated. I could be ground to smithereens out there! Of course, that's what they were planning—that's why they made it easy for me to escape! Well, I'd fool them; I wouldn't move.

CLUE #5

No, I couldn't stay. I had to try to get out.

Once again I crept to the opening, but the feet were still there. Then I noticed something else. Near two of the feet, four round posts rose from the floor. The posts were topped by a thick, low roof. I could easily crawl under it, but those giant feet couldn't.

I took a deep breath and moved quickly. Racing out of my cell, I pranced rapidly until I was under the thick roof. I made it! My legs felt like rubber again, but I was safe for the moment.

CLUE #6

What would happen next? I wondered. I didn't have long to wait, however, for I heard voices high above the roof.

"Oh, Donald, she's afraid of us!"

"Well, naturally," came the reply. "That must have been a very frightening trip for such a little _____."

[Answer: kitten]

- -

FIGURE 7.6. **CPM for a Strand 1 lesson on how to gain a new perspective.**

Perspective

Step 1   Step 2

My eyes are seeing through someone else's eyes because I pretend I am that person.

Did this change your understanding of the character? of the story?

Strand 1: Step 2 of Perspective

Explain.

"To truly understand a story, we must be able to feel the joys and disappointments of the characters. These feelings are the motivation for the characters' voices and behaviors. To help you better understand the feelings of an author is portraying, you must be able to pretend that you **are** the character in the story, so that you can view the story through the character's eyes. This is called **perspective**. Perspective is the ability to see, hear, and feel as another person."

1. **Thinking Guides**. Display the CPM chart for perspective. Highlight the words **My eyes seeing through someone else's eyes** and **pretend**. Remind the students that perspective involves trying to understand someone else's point of view.

2. **Model**. Demonstrate the motion for feeling (see Appendix B). Have the students practice the feeling motion with you as you model it three times. Explain:

"Here we explore the feelings of the characters as well as our own feelings as we encounter similar experiences [**place fingertips to your chest and stroke upward several times**]. To truly understand a character's feelings, you must try to place yourself in the character's 'shoes.' This is called Perspective."

Demonstrate the motion for perspective. Have the students practice with you as you model it three times. Explain:

"Perspective gives you, as the reader, the opportunity to be the character. Perspective is the ability for your eyes [**place your fingers in a V-shape to the corner of your eye**] to see through someone else's eyes [**hold your other hand with fingers in a V-shape to represent someone else's eyes and turn and move your fingertips from your eyes toward the other fingertips**]."

3. **Think-Alouds**. Read the first two pages of text and stop. (Readers set purpose themselves.) Ask students to use the CPM to signal and explain when their minds have taken on a new perspective.

Building Background: Step 1 of This Strand 1 Lesson

Before round-table discussions begin, teach the difference between literal and inferential questions by sharing several whole-group stories, such as *Empty Pot* (Demi, 1990), *Turkey's Gift to the People* (Ricki, 1992), and *Annie and the Old One* (Miles, 1985). Begin by asking *why* (the first question in Figure 5.3, the Asking Questions Thinking Guide, p. 80) after each statement, so that students have to discern if that sentence is literal or inferential. They can generate their own definitions for literal and inferential statements or use the following ones that Ms. Johnson's third graders created:

- *Literal*: The answer is "right there" in the text. Everyone's answer should be the same to a literal question.
- *Inferential*: The answer comes from you. It is found by "reading between the lines." It is something the author *doesn't* tell you. It could be told to you by the words, or by your mind thinking about the details and clues that you put together from several sentences, or from pictures. Your answer could be different from the answers of others. If you answer with "I think," you have to tell *why*.

Round-Table Technique: Step 2 of This Strand 1 or Strand 3 Lesson

For homework the preceding night, have students write "Why?" questions based on the whole-group story. Encourage them to write inferential questions, in particular. In their groups the next day, have students read their questions to their teammates and together decide whether each question is literal or inferential and what comprehension processes a student would have to use to answer it. Using the idea of a round-table discussion, students recognize that everyone's questions and answers are equally important. By rotating through the Strand 3 groups, you can listen, question, explain, take notes, and determine which students have learned how to gain a new perspective.

Next, ask each team to choose its "best question." Have teams record questions in their learning logs, crediting the student who came up with each one. Students then answer each question by writing for about 10 minutes and discussing their answers. Later, come back together as a whole class and listen to each team's questions and answers.

"Roving" Teacher–Reader Groups: Strand 3 Lesson for Teaching Inferencing

In this Strand 3 lesson, each team comes up with its own "Why?" question to present to the whole class. (Students could also use different questions from the thinking guide in Figure 5.3, p. 80, after those have been modeled several times.) This question does not have to come from a group story; it could come from a weekly reader, social studies, current events article, a science textbook, a classroom issue, or a personal interest area. Collect all teams' questions and post them on the board. Rather than stay at their own tables, students choose the question they would like to respond to, and move to that table with their learning logs. Everyone writes for about 10 minutes as they answer the question. Then each table has its own discussion. Finally, the whole class comes together and students share thoughts about each question and what they want to learn next to become better inferers.

Two-Column Notes: Strand 2 Inference Lesson

Students can use two-column notes to record their thinking and the questions they generate from their reading. Again, students could pose several questions to be answered individually, in teams, or using the roving teacher–reader groups.

CPI Inference Lesson 10: Theatre Storytelling

This lesson enables students to learn how to make inferences from one large event to another. It is easier for young children to infer if they are presented with smaller units of information.

Activity 1

Read a story or nonfiction text to students, but do not read the climax or concluding section of the text. Divide the portions of the text that you read into chunks of information that can be enacted by small groups of students. Give a different section of text to each small group to reread as a group.

Activity 2

On the next day, each group practices enacting its section of text and then performs it, in order, before the class.

Activity 3

On the next day, Strand 3 groups meet to decide what prediction they want to make as to how the story or nonfiction text ends. Each group writes an ending, and members describe how they made their predictions.

Activity 4

On the next day, each Strand 3 group practices enacting its predicted ending. Then the students perform these endings. Last, they describe the comprehension processes they used to envision the ending they presented, and what they want to learn next to become better inferers.

Activity 5

Read the author's ending and discuss how students' predictive and inferential abilities could be improved.

Activity 6

Present a short passage that requires students to make an inference. Highlight the important words in the passage and describe how they contribute to discerning the correct inference.

Then give students a short passage and ask them to determine the important words in it and describe the contributions of these words to making the correct inference about the material.

Activity 7

Students are shown another passage one sentence at a time. Their task is to make an initial inference and then confirm, reject, or modify it as more text is exposed (via an overhead projector or a microcomputer). Again, students identify important words and demonstrate the words' usefulness in forming the inference.

Summary

This chapter presented 10 CPI lessons and the CPMs for predicting, reasons and evidence, and inferencing. To make valid inferences, readers must (1) fill gaps in textual coherence, (2) complete arcs of literal information, (3) engage domain knowledge, and (4) activate the spreading of knowledge thinking process. These lessons can be used with confidence to develop and significantly increase young students' inferencing, interpreting, and predicting abilities: (1) writing hypotheses and predicting, (2) diagramming the inference process, (3) explaining the reasons behind inferences, (4) using photographs and cartoons to teach inferencing, (5) paraphrasing, (6) teaching inferencing with a first-person narrative, (7) think-alouds that model how to gain a perspective and identify gaps in knowledge, (8) continuous checks, (9) round-table inferencing groups, (10) theatre storytelling, and (11) CPI Comprehension Process Lesson 6 (pp. 130–131). Once students have become proficient inferers, you can spend more time on developing their imagery abilities. Methods of doing so are presented in Chapter 8.

Reflecting on What You Have Learned

1. **Interpreting (Summarizing) the Main Points.** How could you fit these lessons into your current reading program, especially in programs and organizational plans such as Success for All, block schedules, integrated approaches, and departmental settings?

2. **Making Professional Decisions.** What advice will you give to fellow educators concerning the most important steps that they can take to teach young readers to infer and predict?

3. **Making Field Applications and Observations.** Implement one of the lessons from this chapter. Evaluate its effectiveness and describe to colleagues how you determined its level of success.

4. **Keeping a Professional Journal.** In one paragraph write a concise lesson on teaching inferential comprehension. Describe your instruction and assessment plans. This description will help you describe to students, parents, and colleagues

how you are helping students overcome any difficulties they may be having in inferential comprehension.

5. **Making Multicultural Applications.** Which of the basic approaches to teaching inferencing would be most appropriate for students from minority cultures? Answer and then check your response. The first approach should be to teach English-language learners more background knowledge to profit from the lessons on hypothesis generation and knowledge structure.

6. **Meeting Students' Special Needs.** How can you use audio books and interactive computer based books to meet special students' needs? How could you adapt the 10 lessons in this chapter to meet the special needs of below-grade-level comprehenders?

7. **Checking Key Terms.** Following is a list of concepts introduced in this chapter. If you have learned the meaning of a term, place a checkmark in the blank that precedes it. If you are not sure of a term's definition, increase your retention by reviewing its definition. If you have learned five of these terms on your first reading of this chapter, then you have already constructed many meanings that are important for your work.

    ____Inferring (p. 112)

    ____Predicting (p. 112)

    ____Interpreting (p. 112)

    ____Gaps in coherence (p. 114)

    ____Arcs of information (p. 114)

    ____Spreading knowledge activation process (p. 119)

    ____Gap-filling inferences (p. 124)

8. **Design a Comprehension Process Lesson.** Comprehension Process Lesson 6 contains a thinking guide that you can use to build this comprehension process. The thinking guide can be used as (1) an overhead transparency during Strand 1 lessons, (2) a graphic that students write on as they read silently in Strand 2 lessons, or (3) an image that is reproduced on Post-it Notes for use in Strands 1–3 lesson discussions. Try one, as delineated in Comprehension Process Lesson 6.

Comprehension Process Lesson 6: Teaching Students the Inference Process

Directions: Make photocopies of Figure 7.2 and fold them on the dashed lines along the three columns for this lesson. Students are to use the sheet each time they read in Strand 2 lessons. First, provide a Strand 1 lesson: Model the thoughts you have as you read a stanza from a poem or paragraph or page from a text by writing in each section of the trifold. Teach students the three-step process they can use to make inferences: (1) look for clues while reading, (2) identify more than one clue, and (3) put the clues together with what they already know to draw an inference. Modeling five examples from a text completes this Strand 1 lesson.

Instruct students to generate five examples on their own as you closely monitor them and deliver mini-interventions during silent reading activities in Strand 2 lessons. After they have completed several Strand 2 lessons, students can meet in student-selected groups to learn more about inferencing by addressing the step on the thinking guide and text that caused them the greatest difficulty.

Place adhesive notes on crucial pages to remind students that they should either make an inference or deduce reasons and evidence at this point to gain the greatest level of understanding. These Post-it Notes may contain (1) the steps in each of these comprehension processes, (2) a line drawing, or (3) the CPM that depicts the process needed at that particular place. Remind students to set their own purpose prior to reading, and to write their inference or reasons and evidence on each Post-it Note before they turn the page.

- *Step 1.* Explain to the students how to set their own purposes prior to reading and to use inferencing while they read. Explain how the processes will help them become better readers.
- *Step 2.* Read two pages and do a think-aloud that shows how you set your own purpose for reading. Ask students to explain what their purposes are.
- *Step 3.* Put an adhesive note (see accompanying diagram) at the bottom right side of the next page of the book. Describe the inference you wrote on the Post-it Note lines and talk about how to inference. Explain that you were able to inference because you recognized clues in the way the author wrote the first three pages. Tell the students what these clues were. Move the adhesive note to the book's next page (the fourth page of text).
- *Step 4.* Repeat the think-aloud and move the adhesive note of Step 3 but now, having made an inference, use the reasons and evidence graphic (i.e., the CPM drawing) on this Post-it Note for two additional times (e.g., on pp. 5 and 6 of a text).
- *Step 5.* After reading page 6 of the text together, ask students to make an inference and tell you how they did so a second time.

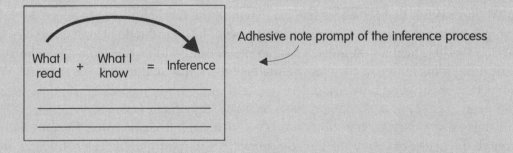

Adhesive note prompt of the inference process

CHAPTER 8

Teaching Imagery

Looking Up and Away
without Moving Too Far from the Text

Paige, a below-grade-level second-grade reader, was unable to image. However, after using audio books with texts for 20 minutes a week for 12 weeks (during Strand 2 lessons), she began to change. In a Strand 3 lesson, Mr. Stanley asked her to explain this change. She said: "I read really, really good now! The words just hop off the page and pop into my head. I can't stop the pictures they make, no matter what I do." Soon after that, Paige began reading chapter books that were written at a third-grade readability level.

Chapter Overview

Imaging is defined as learning how to form pictures in one's mind—that is, to visualize—while reading. Before mental images can emerge, young readers must have an accurate literal understanding of details and sense an author's purpose. They must also recognize the arcs of literal information that flow from one paragraph to the next, and be able to predict information that is likely to appear in upcoming sentences. They must understand an author's writing style so that the next arc of unknown information can be inferred. Although some students learn how to image when they are young, for others this skill is difficult to learn. Without instruction, many struggling readers create significantly fewer mental images than their more able peers (Gambrell & Koskinen, 2001; Sadoski, 1985; Sadoski & Paivio, 1994).

Today's students have a vast store of vivid images from real-world events they view through the media of television, film, e-commerce, and the Internet. They also have continuous access to rapid-paced images that convey information through music videos and advertisements. As a result, their minds have adapted to absorb rapid-paced images in microseconds, even when these scenes appear in a dense, highly stimulating, thematically linked visual array (Block, 2001c; van Dijk, 1980). To teach students how to use these same mental processes to create accurate images from print, it is useful to capitalize on the mental agility gained by today's students' in their real-world experiences. You can also implement the CPI lessons in this chapter. By the end of the chapter, you will be able to answer the following questions:

1. How can you improve your comprehension instruction so that less able readers become able, active imagers?
2. How can you teach students to add their imagination to the information they encounter while reading so that imagery becomes an automatic comprehension process?
3. How can you assist young students to generate more vivid images so that they can receive maximum pleasure and benefit from independent, silent reading?

Research on Imagery

The easiest image to create from text is a depiction of an explicitly stated spatial relationship (Haenggi et al., 1995). For example, when a story describes the actions of a main character moving through a building, many students can picture every arc of information between sentences because each one describes an object or event that they have experienced in their lives. Thus, when a literary character climbs from a house's basement to its top floor, the familiar descriptions of objects on each floor can evoke vivid images for readers. These mental pictures can also be easily stored in long-term memory. By constructing such cognitive representations, students can retain significantly more facts because numerous details are almost effortlessly inserted into an almost automatic image that their brains construct to complete a text-generated pattern or gestalt (Block & Stanley, 2004; Britton & Graesser, 1996).

A second condition that makes it easier for students to image is when a text contains vivid verbs and explicit nouns. For instance, it is easier to picture the action described by the word *screamed* than that of the word *said*. In a related finding, elementary students taught to picture the outlines for each of the United States as they memorized the capitals of those states remembered significantly more capital cities than a comparable group who were given an equal amount of time to learn without being taught how to image each state's outline (Levin, Barry, Miller, & Bartel, 1982).

External conditions also contribute to imagery formation (Torrance, 1981; Torrance & Sisk, 2001). Readers need freedom to form random, often unrelated, insights from text. Students must associate facts that, on the surface, appear to be unrelated. This condition explains why students remember items on a list better when each listing is associated with an unrelated but familiar object in a room (e.g., the subject remembered to include milk on their grocery list by creating a mental image of a milk carton being placed on the table in the entry of the home because the table is the first piece of furniture the person sees on entering the home [Beyer, 1986]). Furthermore, a large body of evidence indicates that a reader's degree of extroversion on the Myers–Briggs Personality Scale (Myers, 2001), as well as their maturity level enhance imagery abilities (Block & Reed, 2003).

Another factor that increases young readers' ease and effectiveness in developing imagery abilities is being taught how to recognize *when they misunderstand a sentence* in a text (Baker, 2002; Baker & Anderson, 1982; Ruffman, 2000). Such instruction can occur as early as 4 years of age (Perfetti, Marron, & Foltz, 1999; Piaget & Inhelder, 1971). However, when such instruction is not provided, even adults can have difficulty imaging when the decoding demands or idea density in a text is too taxing (Sadoski & Paivio, 1994). The readability level of a text and the degree of students' imaginative capacities also contribute to imagery ability. The CPI lessons in this chapter are designed to overcome these difficulties and enhance young readers' abilities to ignite their own creative thinking processes during comprehension of text (Levin, 1991; Perfetti et al., 1999).

Imagery behaviors can be learned (Block, 1993; Block & Mangieri, 1996a–c), and teachers rank imagery as one of the most important comprehension processes that should be taught to less able readers (Block & Mangieri, 2003; Block, Oaker, et al., 2002; Cazden, 1991). For some, the imagery lessons in this chapter will be the first instruction they will have received in this area. These CPI lessons are also likely to enable many readers to become so immersed in the reading experience itself, and in creating images evoked by the language process, that for the first time their minds will no longer be consumed only by the task of decoding language (Fleckenstein, 1991). Moreover, because imaging evokes readers' personal emotions, it is the best comprehension process for increasing students' positive, aesthetic responses to text. In the following excerpt, Reid, a third grader who was in a classroom in which CPI research was conducted, describes this power:

> "As I read, the scenery came back as it was all suppose to be, and emotions started pouring in. When I got to the part about turning around, I lost the fact that I was reading and I started reliving the whole thing in my mind. Right when I read the word *mom*, I could picture my own mother. A feeling of warmth gushed over me. What power a single word has when I picture it in my mind!"

The most important first step in all CPI imagery lessons is to ensure that students first have information on the subject about which they are to read. A second step is to teach imagery through concrete words and short instructional sentences. For instance, you can begin an imagery lesson by asking students to use a CPM signal when they have pictured the words *leaf, red leaf, green leaf*, and so on (Poltrock & Brown, 1984). A third step is to teach children to construct relationships among their prior knowledge, experiences, and the literal facts they are reading (Au, 1993; Wittrock & Alesandrini, 1990; Wittrock, 1998). Familiar words in stories can also be used at the early stages of teaching imagery. Such words, because they occur in a familiar context, make the unit to be pictured small enough so that not only can single words be imaged but also the contextual sentence in which they appear. As a result, students can predict the next sentence and describe the image they created that linked the two sentences together in their minds.

Last, each of the CPI imagery lessons in this chapter are more effective when you teach students to underline main ideas as they read (Chi, Slotta, & deLeeuw, 1994; Locken, 1981; Pearson, Hansen, & Gordon, 1979). When these steps are included in the following Strand 1 imagery lessons, young students learn how to generate images more rapidly (Koslyn, Brunn, Cave, & Wallach, 1984; Poltrock & Brown, 1984).

Teaching Students to Image with Fiction and Nonfiction

Imagery can be taught by asking students to (1) look up and away, (2) create similes and idioms, (3) create mental stories, and (4) create mental transformations. These CPI lessons follow. They increase students' generation of imagery when reading fiction and nonfiction.

CPI Imagery Lesson 1: Look Up and Away

To begin this Strand 1 lesson, model how you image concrete nouns such as *tree*, *house*, *school*. Next, ask students to read a list of these types of nouns and describe to you the images the words evoke (Miller, 1987). Then ask pupils to turn to a partner and describe each image that these words produced. When students can do this task well, move to a Strand 2 lesson and have partnered teams read an entire paragraph and write one sentence together about how their images changed as they read each successive sentence.

Once students feel comfortable and competent in making images, you change to a different Strand 2 lesson format. Instruct students to read silently and stop whenever they have created a vivid mental image that they want to share. Evaluate whether student images contain sufficient sensory information and prior personal experience to indicate that they have made an emotional connection to the text. If either of these components (i.e., sensory information, prior experience) is not present, conduct a mini-intervention for that student about how to add these thinking processes to image making. Subsequently, schedule two or more periods of intensely monitored, silent reading practice with particular texts and include mini-interventions for making mental images, as needed, so that pupils can improve and solidify their imagery skills. A lesson format, sample curricula, and student examples to use with this lesson appear in the Comprehension Process Lesson 7 at the end of this chapter. This lesson also illustrates how you can use the power of the three-pronged strands of CPI to teach imagery.

Finally, teach students to look within, to their own experiences, and then up and away from the text so they can pause to synthesize what they read with what they know in an image. Follow the CPI Imagery Lesson 1 steps, and explain that expert readers often look up when they build images or project into the future (Caine & Caine, 1997).

CPI Imagery Lesson 2: Create Similes and Idioms

Another instructional method is to teach young students how to create similes to describe the main ideas they are reading. A *simile* is a figure of speech that likens one thing to another by the use of *like*, *as*, and so on (for example: "The icing on the cake was *as* light *as* a feather"). An *idiom* is an accepted phrase, construction, or expression contrary to the usual pattern of the language or having a meaning different from the literal meaning of each word (for example: "I'm so hungry I could eat a horse").

Natalie, a first-grade student, wanted to describe how she had arranged all the snowballs in the story that she wrote. She wanted to communicate the splendor of this final product, which had taken her an hour to create. Ms. Armstrong, her teacher, took this opportunity to teach the entire class a CPI Imagery Lesson 2 on how to write similes. Ms. Armstrong wrote three examples on the chalkboard and performed a think-aloud to illustrate how the similes helped her to form images. The examples she used in this Strand 1 lesson were:

> This paper is *as light as a feather*.
> My heart is *fluttering like a butterfly*.
> My head is *spinning like a top*.

Next, students engaged in a Strand 2 lesson in which, in pairs, they discussed and created as many similes as they could. Ms. Armstrong described how these figures of speech could help them to image and remember text. On the next day Natalie recalled this lesson immediately after she wrote: "I formed 25 snowballs. I put them side-by-side in a perfect half circle. It glistened in the sun. It was beautiful." Natalie was not satisfied with this description, however, so she went back to work on her composition.

When finished, she raised her paper for Ms. Armstrong to read, explaining: "I wanted people to really see it, so I added 'It looked like a huge diamond necklace for a giant princess.'" By using the word *like* and knowing how to use similes to create effective mental images, Natalie concluded this writing experience with strong feelings of accomplishment and pride. Ms. Armstrong felt equally fulfilled because she had increased her students' abilities to image.

Idioms can be taught in the same manner. A list of idiomatic expressions that have been used successfully in grades K–3 CPI lessons follow:

A bird in hand is worth two in the bush.	For the birds
A bird's-eye view	Get all your ducks in a row.
A feather in your cap	Getting off the ground
A fly in the ointment	Giving someone the cold shoulder
A leg to stand on	Got a bee in your bonnet
A pat on the back	Half a loaf is better than none.
A rotten egg	Have other fish to fry
A snake in the grass	His bark is worse than his bite.
Actions speak louder than words.	Hitting the bull's eye
As plain as the nose on your face	In the dog house
As the crow flies	In the hot seat
Badgering someone	It's in the ballpark.
Barking up the wrong tree	Keep a straight face.
Be an eager beaver.	Lightning never strikes twice.
Beating around the bush	Make ends meet.
Beauty is in the eye of the beholder.	On your last legs
Beauty is only skin deep.	Opening a can of worms
Birds of a feather flock together.	Out of the frying pay and into the fire
By a long shot	Playing cat and mouse
By the skin of your teeth	Putting the cart before the horse
Catching 40 winks	Show her the ropes.

Chip on your shoulder	Sitting on the fence
Clamming up	Sticking your head in the sand
Cutting off your nose to spite your face	Take the bull by the horns.
Don't bite the hand that feeds you.	The apple of his eye
Eating crow	The last straw
Eating like a bird	The straw that broke the camel's back
Egg on your face	When it rains, it pours.

CPI Imagery Lesson 3: Create Mental Stories before Students Write Them

A third CPI Strand 2 lesson that develops imaging involves asking students to tell you about the events before they write their stories. The process of orally describing an unfolding event often stimulates images in students' minds. For instance, Cedric, a kindergartner, described the following image when his teacher asked him to first talk about what he wanted to write: "The second time Michael Jordan shot from the foul line, he missed the basket. Patrick Ewing jumped up and wrestled it away from everyone else!" Following his oral description, Cedric wrote about this scene and included even more details from the mental images that his conversation had stimulated.

CPI Imagery Lesson 4: Create Mental Transformations

Barrows (1985) was the first to suggest that teachers use guided imaging in a game-like activity. In this Strand 1 lesson, small groups of students assign human traits to an animal or inanimate object. Doing so builds mental agility and, as Barrows demonstrated, increases the speed and vividness with which students image. For example, one student might say, "An elephant is riding a bike." Then a second student would explain why that image "works" by adding a statement for the class to imagine. For example, "That's a good idea because then the elephant can get around faster."

Next, a third student would depict another trait the elephant possesses, saying, for example, "The elephant can talk, and he says, 'What's for lunch?'" Then, a fourth student would explain why this trait is a good idea: "That's a good idea because the elephant can communicate with people and other elephants as he rides past them on his bike." The next student would add another trait to the visualization: "He flies kites as he rides his bike." While this process is engaged, one student would write all of them on a chart for the class to see. After all students have contributed, they would orally read the chart. Last, students would be asked to write their own paragraphs using a different subject. When each student has finished his or her paragraph, a peer would read it and then write about the image that friend's paragraph created in him or her.

Teaching Imagery by Inducing and Invoking Images

Another method of teaching imagery is to invoke images through the use of beautiful language. These lessons are enjoyable and easy to implement. Ask students to image before, during, and after they read. Research has documented that only a few lessons are necessary for most students to increase the quantity and quality of their imagery (Gambrell & Koskinen, 2001; Pressley, 1976).

Imagery Lesson 5: Paint Mental Pictures, Learn CPI Visualizing, and Visualize the CPM Motions

Bales and Gambrell (1985) asked fourth and fifth graders to "make pictures in their minds to help them understand"; a control group was instructed to "do whatever you can to help yourself understand and remember what you are about to read" (p. 136). Students told to construct images found more inconsistencies in the material, and 70% of them used imagery to retain information, compared to only 1% of the control group. This lesson also increased these students' comprehension and retention (Bales & Gambrell, 1985). The full description of how to teach students to "paint mental pictures" appears as Steps 1 through 3 of Comprehension Process Lesson 7 at the end of this chapter. In this lesson, first teach students the CPM for feelings, shown in Figure 8.1, and for visualizing in Figure 8.2. The motion for feelings is to take the right hand and move it up and down vertically about 6 inches over the heart. The motion for visualization is to create a thought bubble above one's head. Place one hand on each temple at the forehead. Move hands above the head in a circle as if to make a big cloud. Hands end by touching in the middle about 1 foot above the top of the head.

Imagery Lesson 6: Translate Audiotapes into Print

Instruct them to image as they listen to a tape of a book. (Follow the basic steps in a Strand 1 lesson, inserting Step 2, as described in Figure 8.1.) Next, move into a CPI Strand 2 lesson and ask students to listen to books from five different genres on five consecutive days. Students are told to stop the tape after 15 minutes and write a description of the next image that is likely to occur in the story. Then they turn the tape back on to find out if their images were correct.

Young students read from a print version of the text being read on tape, and they are told not to turn book pages ahead of the taped narration. The use of audiotapes has been found to significantly increase imagery in students in grades K–6 because it stimulates main idea retention and inference abilities (Block & Stanley, 2004).

Teaching Imagery Using Poetry and Art*

Poetry and art are important resources to use in CPI imagery lessons. Both of these venues stimulate visual, audio, kinesthetic, and tactile input systems. Poetry draws the reading into a union of sound and descriptive word play in which the rhythm of our language is added to literal and inferential comprehension processes to increase understanding. The magnetism of poetry arises because "poetry becomes new experiences that readers create out of this memory, thoughts, feelings, and by paying attention to the ordered symbols of text" (Elster, 2000,

---

*This section was written in collaboration with Dionne Adkinson.

FIGURE 8.1. **CPM motion for a Strand 1 lesson on how to feel like a character feels.**

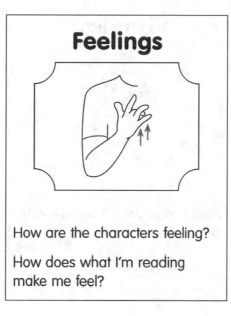

How are the characters feeling?

How does what I'm reading make me feel?

Strand 1: Teach How Imagery Evokes Feelings

Explain. The feeling comprehension process ignites the capacity of the reader to feel, and understand the causes of, the characters' feelings. The feelings experienced by the reader make the story come alive and provide a deeper connection to the characters and story line. The reader is then able to feel the joys and disappointments encountered by the characters. This connection creates an understanding of the motivation for the characters' voices and behaviors.

1. **Thinking Guides**. Display the CPM chart for feelings. Highlight the words **characters feeling** and **me feeling** and the picture clues to remind the students to attend to the feelings of the characters as well as the feelings provoked within them by the story.

2. **Model**. Demonstrate the motion for feelings. Have the students practice the motion with you as you model it three times. As you discuss feelings, place your fingertips to your chest and stroke upward and downward several times over the heart.

3. **Think-Alouds**. Read the first two pages of text and stop. (Readers set purpose themselves.) Have students signal when they want to express a feeling evoked by the images in their minds.

FIGURE 8.2. **CPM for a Strand 1 CPM lesson on visualizing while reading.**

Strand 1: Teach How the Mind Visualizes

Explain. When using the comprehension process of visualizing, readers create mental images of the reading material, thereby breathing life into the text. Students who successfully visualize the reading material later tend to question if they had read the book or watched the movie. Strong visualization of a text is similar to watching a good movie.

1. **Thinking Guides**. Display the CPM chart for visualizing. Highlight the words **image** and **mind** and the picture clues to remind the students that visualization is a process of creating a movie in the mind of the text being read.

2. **Model**. Demonstrate the motion for visualizing. Have the students practice the motion with you as you model it three times. To demonstrate the visualization CPM, place cupped hands at your temple, then move hands forward in arced motions, gradually bringing them together. This cloud-like motion reminds the students of "thinking clouds" or bubbles, as seen in cartoons and other texts.

3. **Think-Alouds**. Read the first two pages of text and stop. (Readers set purpose themselves.) Continue reading, stopping each time a child shows the CPM for visualizing. Ask that child to explain his image and how it was created.

p. 7). In like manner, art involves the use of one's hands to build a new concept or object, which can then be more readily visualized when only the words in a text are used to describe it.

Imagery Lesson 7: Write Poems with Vivid Words and Phrases

Poem writing begins by reading a few poems filled with descriptive words to students. As you read, do not show pictures. Excellent poets to select include Douglas Florian (1998, 1999), Shel Silverstein, Judy Viorst, and Eloise Greenfield (1978), whose works, such as *Insectopedia, Laugh-eteria, I Hate School* (Grant, 1997), and *Honey I Love*, respectively, contain vivid words and images. After reading, perform a think-aloud in which you ask students to signal when they have completed their visual image by making the visualization CPM. Then have them describe the images or pictures that occurred in their minds. Explain to students that they were able to imagine those pictures because the words selected by the author were very descriptive and guided them to see with their mind's eye. Each time they read, they are to attend to the vivid words authors use; those words were chosen with care to generate mental images. In turn, those vivid words can help readers to image when they as authors select equally vivid words and phrases for their own compositions.

Next, read poetry selections from three different formats, such as haiku, diamante, and free verse. Brainstorm topics for the poems with students. Themes valued by younger children describe best friends, pets, favorite foods, toys, or events such as going to theme parks, zoos, and shopping centers. Model for students how they can write many descriptive words on the top of the sheet of paper on which they will write their poem. These words can stimulate mental images while they are writing their first drafts. Ask students to write a poem in one of the types of *format poetry* (i.e., poems that follow a distinct rhyming scheme) that you have read to them. To end this Strand 1 lesson, demonstrate how you inserted the words that you wrote on your paper into sample poems that the class creates with you and displays.

At this point in the CPI cycle, students move into one of the Strand 2 lesson formats. Ask students to write and share poems that they wrote individually. In the discussion, peers describe the images that each poem elicited in them as they listened to it. Following this lesson, members of the class who choose to do so can enter into a small Strand 3 group of writers who wish to learn more about imagery. They can become the class's poet laureates for that week, writing poems to be read at the end of the week. After each of these poems is written, authors describe what they did to stimulate imagery, and audience members read copies of their poems and describe the images that they created.

Summary

There are three methods of building students' imagery capacities through CPI lessons: (1) deepening students' schema and domain knowledge, (2) invoking images through beautiful language, and (3) using poetry and art. The CPI Imagery Lessons 1–7 and the Comprehension Process Lesson 7 at the end of this chapter describe different media that can be used during instruction. These activities increase students' oral and written vocabulary, vivid word choices during composition periods, imagery experiences, and sensitivity to clues to meaning that stem from rhyme and rhythm patterns in our language. Using poetry and art also increases students' imagery during reading and writing because they teach students to visualize story grammar. CPI motions for feelings and visualizing, demonstrated to increase students' imagery abilities, were presented in this chapter, and along with other CPI lessons on imagery, are summarized in Figure 8.3. You can reference this figure for lesson planning purposes.

FIGURE 8.3. Summary of CPI imagery lessons.

Lesson 1:
Look Up and Away

Teach students to (1) pause as they are reading and (2) look away from the text to visualize all that they have read and reflect on it.

Lesson 2:
Write Similes and Idioms

Ask students to write similes or idioms to describe main ideas or themes from books read.

Lesson 3:
Create Mental Stories before Students Write Them

Ask students to tell you about events before they write them down.

Lesson 4:
Create Mental Transformations

Assign human traits to an animal or inanimate object.

Lesson 5:
Paint Mental Pictures and Learn CPI Feelings and Visualize Motions

Students are taught how to paint mental pictures.

Lesson 6:
Translate Audiotapes into Print

Ask students to listen to books on tape and write a summary of their most vivid mental image and what the author said to make that image so memorable.

Lesson 7:
Write Poems with Vivid Words and Phrases

Demonstrate how poets create images with words and ask students to write poems.

Comprehension Process Lesson 7:
CPI Visualizing Motion and Structured Mental Imaging

Enables students to recognize and report when they have created a mental image that assisted them to comprehend what they just read or heard.

Designed by Rachel R. Escamilla, Texas Christian University, Fort Worth, TX, and used by permission.

Reflecting on What You Have Learned

1. **Interpreting (Summarizing) the Main Points.** List the seven imagery lessons in an order that you would use them for kindergarten, first-, second-, or third-grade students. Explain why you ordered them as you did.

2. **Making Professional Decisions.** Select the imagery lesson that would be of greatest value for English-language learners. Defend your answer.

3. **Making Field Applications and Observations.** What advice will give to fellow educators concerning the first steps that should be taken to teach students how to image? How can you help students to comprehend and understand more accurately by increasing their imagery abilities?

4. **Keeping a Professional Poetry Journal.** In your journal, write poetry to be used as examples in Imagery Lesson 7. How would you implement the nine lessons in your classroom (e.g., once a month, as a thematic unit, once a week, and so on)? After you implement your plan, evaluate how effective it is and record your observations in your journal. How hard were the lessons to use? How practical were they?

5. **Making Multicultural Applications.** In one paragraph write a concise description of your understanding of teaching imagery to students. Describe your instruction and assessment plans for teaching imagery. This description will help you communicate to students, parents, and colleagues about how you are helping students that have difficulty using imagery.

6. **Meeting Students' Special Needs.** Many less able readers have difficulty imaging. Locate similes and books that are relevant to their lives. Teach all the lessons in this chapter using these personally relevant curricula. What specific benefits did the less able readers in your class gain from this approach? If you are not presently teaching, predict what benefits such curricula would be likely to offer.

7. **Checking Key Terms.** Following is a list of concepts introduced in this chapter. If you have learned the meaning of a term, place a checkmark in the blank that precedes that term. If you are not sure of the term's definition, increase your retention by reviewing it. If you have learned three of these terms on your first reading of this chapter, then you have constructed many meanings that are important for your work.

    _____Imaging (p. 132)

    _____Simile (p. 135)

    _____Idiom (p. 135)

    _____Format poetry (p. 141)

8. **Design a Comprehension Process Lesson.** The following Comprehension Process Lesson describes how to build mental pictures through mental imaging and using the CPI motion for visualizing. The lesson also demonstrates the basic CPI cycle of Strands 1, 2 and 3 lessons that are designed to teach imagery. It contains questions that you can ask during discovery discussions to assist students in overcoming blocks to imagery. The answers to these questions help young readers

understand how they can become more active comprehenders. Adapt this lesson to be developmentally appropriate for your students.

Comprehension Process Lesson 7: Structured Mental Imagery and CPM Visualizing Motion

Objective: To promote children's ability to recognize and report when they have created mental images increased their comprehension.

Listening and Drawing Mental and Visual Images

Prereading Stage

Step 1. Teach students to perform the CPM visualizing motion by following the basic Strand 1 lesson format and inserting Step 2 described in Figure 8.2. Demonstrate how to perform the visualization motion and model its use to signal when you create mental images while reading. Perform this motion three times while you read aloud from a text that students are reading silently with you. After you signal with the visualizing motion, describe (1) what you envisioned from the text and (2) the thought processes you followed to do so. Last, ask students to close their eyes and imagine a topic, event, or character about which they will read. Have them to perform the visualizing motion when that image is vivid in their minds. When most have signaled in this manner, ask all members of the class to open their eyes and draw what they saw in their minds from the vivid descriptions you gave to them orally.

Once students have completed their pictures, ask them to transform the object or event in accordance with the vivid description you will give them. For instance, if you had asked students to picture the big red ball about which they were scheduled to read, you would next ask them to transform their mental images several times, in accordance with the following alterations. Tell them to signal the visualizing motion when they have done so:

1. Picture a small red ball.
2. Place it on top of a white house.
3. Put it inside a large black dog's mouth.
4. Take the small red ball out of the dog's mouth and toss it in the air.
5. Picture another small white dog catching it and bringing it back to you.

Step 2. Have the students form groups of three in which to share their descriptions of what they did to create their mental images with two other students. Here they can talk about and analyze why they depicted the events as they did, using the words they heard or read. Ask them to explain the personal experiences and sources of information that helped them in their imaging.

Reading Stage

Step 3. Move to a Strand 2 lesson in the CPI cycle. Have students read the passage that you described orally in Step 2. Instruct them to keep the mental images created earlier in mind as they read.

Step 4. Engage in a small-group or whole-class discussion of the reading and then ask the students to develop a new visualization or change the existing one to correspond to the new information read.

After-Reading Stage

Step 5. Move into a Strand 3 lesson in the CPI cycle. Have students tell you (and list on a chart) the actions they took to image more as they read, and the actions they could take to add more imagery to their comprehension processes in the future. Allow those who wish to learn more about how to create more vivid and accurate mental images to meet as a student-led group, in which they read together in pairs (using one of the books they are presently reading) and pause at the end of each two-page sequence to discuss which words they could have used on these two pages to image as they read.

CHAPTER 9

Teaching Metacognition

Ms. Johnson was preparing her last science lesson of the year. She thought about the fast-paced world in which her students live. Thinking ahead to the summer, Ms. Johnson wanted to ensure that the higher-level thinking processes her students had acquired this year did not deteriorate. During the last 2 weeks, she prepared powerful CPI metacognitive process lessons. She wanted her first graders to use their own, self-regulated thinking when they read this summer. Ms. Johnson understood the importance of her students being able to take their comprehension to the metacognitive level.

Chapter Overview

Metacognition can be defined as a reader's awareness of (1) what he or she is thinking about while reading, (2) what thinking processes he or she initiates to overcome literacy challenges, and (3) how a he or she selects specific thinking processes to make meaning before, during, and after reading (Brown, 2002). Young students can learn how to correct misunderstandings in the process of comprehending (Delisle, 1997). The purpose of this chapter is to describe how this correction is accomplished. A second goal is to describe new methods of teaching students to generate personalized, automatic metacognitive thoughts during reading.

National committees on literacy have concluded that metacognition can be developed through instruction (Baker, 2002; Baker & Zimlin, 1989; Baumann, Jones, & Seifert-Kessell, 1993; Bereiter & Bird, 1985; Block, 1993; Collins, 1991; Miller, 1985; National Reading Panel, 1999; National Research Council, 1998; Payne & Manning, 1992). This chapter describes CPI lessons that enable students in grades K–3 to increase their metacognitive comprehension processes. By this chapter's end, you will be able to answer the following questions:

1. What can you do to improve less able comprehender's metacognitive processes?
2. How can you teach students to initiate metacognitive processes when they become confused?
3. What methods improve students' abilities to correct their own confusion as they read?

Theoretical Background

Readers think metacognitively when they (1) consider the implicit meanings in texts, (2) reflect on their own understanding, and (3) use multiple strategies to remove blocks that interrupt comprehension (Block, 2000c; Block & Johnson, 2002; Block & Pressley, 2002; Keene & Zimmerman, 1997). Metacognitive lessons are valuable because many of today's youngest students have had few adult mentoring experiences in which elders explained the thinking processes that they use when they encounter reading difficulties (Baker, 2002; Block & Mangieri, 1996a–c; Flavell, 1976). A second reason that metacognitive instruction is increasing in grades K–3 is that recent research proved that even young children have the ability to evaluate their own comprehension; however, most students will not engage such metacognitions without instruction (Baker, 2002; Block, 1998; Paris et al., 1991). Six metacognitive processes that can be taught effectively to students in grades K–3 (Baker, 2002; Block & Pressley, 2002) are described as follows:

1. *Semantic processes*—checking the meaning of individual words.
2. *Syntactic processes*—attending to the grammatical structure of sentences and phrases.
3. *Evaluating informational completeness*—verifying that all parts of a text that have been read are understood.
4. *Evaluating structural cohesiveness*—evaluating the hieratic capability of ideas throughout a text.
5. *Noting the direction of a character's thoughts*—identifying clues in a character's personality and interactions with other characters revealing the reason the author depicted the character in that way.
6. *Comparing what is read to similar events in readers' lives*—applying text to their individual lives by reflecting and thinking as they read.

When researchers taught young students to use metacognitive processes through the CPI lessons in this chapter, they found that both strong and weak comprehenders benefited equally from the instruction. Moreover, these researchers found that metacognition could be developed, even if literal (Block & Johnson, 2002) comprehension and decoding proficiencies were below grade level (Baker, 2002; Block, 2000c; Dyson, 2001).

When students become effective "metacognitivists," they are able to construct personalized "benchmarks" in a text that connect the textual events to their lives (Trimble, 1994). This pausing to reflect and apply is the ultimate goal of the lessons in this chapter, because it is positive evidence that students have guided their own minds to comprehend. For example, a student may mumble to him- or herself, "Hmm, that's the way Grandma spells her name," or "He's a pitcher, just like my brother." The more personal benchmarks students create as they read, the more new textual structures and knowledge will be related to their lives. Moreover, without the ability to make such links, many students will not approach new texts with a strong sense of self-efficacy.

Metacognition is crucial to (1) the development of real-world applications of the material students read; (2) learning how to learn—a highly advanced metacognitive ability, with an enduring affect on student achievement; (3) identifying and allocating appropriate attention to high-demanding text demands; and (4) the enhancement of young readers' motivation and positive attitudes toward reading (Chipman & Segal, 1985; Cullinan, 1999; Presseisen, 1987; Smey-Richman, 1988). Researchers have discovered that even young children can describe and monitor their own comprehension effectively when they talk about and hear their peers' descriptions of what they think while they read (Baker, 1984; Block, Gambrell, & Pressley, 2002; Glaubman, Glaubman, & Ofir, 1997).

As early as age 5, students can initiate metacognitive processes. Such energy positively increases their motivational drive, interest, and reading pleasure (Borkowski, Carr, Rellinger, & Pressley, 1990; Hacker, 1998; Paris & Winograd, 1990). This research is supported by the theoretical work of Vygotsky (1978), whose work demonstrated that children begin to mimic other people's thinking when an expert initially assists them in taking responsibility for regulating the metacognitive processes that they use. Such readers begin to see that planning before they read is necessary, and that they should ponder certain things during reading (see Block, Gambrell, & Pressley, 2002; Block & Pressley, 2002).

Overview of CPI Metacognitive Lessons

The CPI lessons in this chapter are based on this research foundation. Teachers are encouraged to perform oral renditions of their thinking—think-alouds—to support children's ability to fill in gaps and identify the explicit steps in their own metacognitive processes (Baker, 2002; Brown & Campione, 1998). CPI lessons develop three categories of metacognition: (1) controlling one's thoughts during reading; (2) developing text sensitivity; and (3) increasing knowledge of one's goals.

Before we discuss these categories, however, it might be helpful to distinguish between cognitive and metacognitive comprehension processes. *Cognitive comprehension processes* are comprised of thinking actions that can be conducted without students placing themselves in the text. That is, students can sum up, infer, and find evidence without questioning themselves as to how the summary, inference, or evidence would differ if they were reading a book from a different genre. On the other hand, *metacognitive comprehension processes* engage all cognitive processes in young readers, plus their ongoing monitoring of (1) their own understanding of text, (2) text features, and (3) their verification and application of new knowledge to their unique life experiences. To assist you in differentiating between cognitive and metacognitive comprehension processes, we have listed those presented in this book, to this point, as follows:

Cognitive	*Metacognitive*
Building Background	Establishing a Purpose for Reading
Tilling the Text	Clarifying
Summing Up	Making Connections
Main Idea	Skim and Scan until I Choose to Stop and Savor
Drawing Conclusion	Context Clues
Cause and Effect	Identifying Gaps in Knowledge

Predicting	Continuous Checks
Inferencing	Looking Up and Away
Paraphrasing	Imagery
Perspective	Visualizing
Reasons and Evidence	Feelings

CPI Lessons That Teach Semantic and Syntactic Processes

Because so many benefits result from increased metacognition, the subsequent CPI lessons assist students in focusing their thinking on key ideas while reading. To introduce metacognitive reading processes, first model what you do to overcome comprehension difficulties. Create and display an overhead transparency of a story and distribute a handout that describes two metacognitive processes (identified earlier in this chapter). After teaching how each process works, read a sentence orally and perform a think-aloud about how you use two (at first) or more (during subsequent lessons) of these metacognitive processes consecutively to enrich your comprehension of each sentence. For example, if you projected a sentence on an overhead, you could describe your metacognitive thinking to your class using a think-aloud similar to the example that follows. The projected sentence is: "The night sky was dark and a wolf howled." Think aloud:

> "Boys and girls, when I read this sentence, I think that the author is trying to make readers feel scared, because the words *dark night sky* and *a wolf howled* were chosen to remind us of times in our lives when we saw people in movies or on television who were scared by these two events occurring together."

Next, ask students to describe what they think their minds are doing while they read. List descriptions of what they are thinking on a chart. When we asked 678 children in grades K–3, "When you are reading alone and you understand what you're reading, what do you think your mind is doing?" they answered by citing many metacognitive processes (Block & Mangieri, 2003). Representative answers follow:

- Josh (kindergartner): "My mind is reading to me" (p. 17).
- Kasandra (first grader): "My mind is drawing pictures for me" (p. 28).
- Mesong (second grader): "It is doing what Amelia Buddleia is doing" (p. 39).
- Trisha (third grader): "My mind is wandering around in the story to see what it is about" (p. 60).

As students express their ideas, write them on a chart. After all students in this lesson have contributed, ask them to read the chart orally and compare the images that this reading created in their minds. You can end this Strand 1 lesson by asking students what new metacognitive process they would like you to model in a future lesson. For instance, if a student asked you to model "what to think when I come to a word I don't know," you could perform a metacognitive think-aloud similar to the following:

"When I come to a word I do not know, I think to myself about what I should do. That thinking to myself is a metacognition. I first look at how long the word is, and I check to see if there are any 'chunks' that I recognize. This helps me to decide if I should use phonics or if the word is a sight word that I must learn. While I am making this decision, I go back to the beginning of the sentence and reread the other words, so that I can put their meanings together with the sound of the first letter in the word I do not know. If I still do not know the word, I read to the end of the paragraph. At that time I have made a decision on whether or not I know the word. If I do not know the word, I will decide to either ask someone for the meaning, look it up in the dictionary, or read more to get more context clues. Now, try to use this metacognitive process to figure out this word [pointing to a word in a book a student has selected to read]."

Getting readers to talk about their metacognition helps them learn to do so on their own—but it may require repeated prompts, as illustrated in this exchange:

TEACHER: Jimmy, can you tell us one of the things we talked about that can help us figure out a new word?

JIMMY: First letter.

TEACHER: I'm not sure I understand what you mean. Could you give me some more words that will help us understand how the first letter can help figure out a new word in reading?

JIMMY: Look at the first letter.

TEACHER: How would looking at the first letter help us figure out a new word in reading?

JIMMY: Look at the first letter and think about what sound it makes. Then try to think of a word that starts with that letter and makes sense in the sentence.

TEACHER: Good, Jimmy. Now you've given enough words for us to understand how the first letter helps us figure out a new word. (Euler & Hellekson, 1993, p. 7)

In your curriculum, when it is time to schedule your next Strand 1 metacognitive lesson, you can teach readers to filter distracting thoughts from their minds. This CPI lesson also teaches them how to generate their own ideas as they read. Factors as general as age, gender, social class, the desire to communicate collectively, and the ability to interpret all influence a child's use of each of these positive metacognitive filters (Dyson, 2001). Because of this influence, it is important to teach children how to (1) control their own points of view and (2) reflect momentarily to make sense as they read. Students' personal worldview can help them decide what is relevant and overcome any comprehension difficulties. In addition, the schematic structure they devise to comprehend can be used as another resource to overcome other misunderstandings with similar text or contexts in the future.

In this CPI lesson, follow the traditional steps in Strand 1 lessons and perform think-alouds and CPM motions to describe what you think to filter distractions from your mind as you read. Then ask students to stop at the end of each page, for five consecutive pages, and describe what they were thinking as they read that page.

As students talk, write their comments in the first column of a two-column chart. Use the first column to describe any positive, meaning-building, metacognitive processes they used.

List statements students make about what they misunderstood on that page in the second column. Write the metacognitive filtering process that can be used to eliminate these confusions in parentheses (and in a different color marker from all others on the chart). Following is an example from a third-grade lesson in which students stopped at the end of reading *Volcano* (Lauber, 1986).

Positive metacognitive processes	*Metacognitive processes to be improved*
1. "When I read: 'For many years the volcano slept,' I thought that volcanoes were part of the earth like people, and I related this volcano to myself and how good it feels to sleep late on Saturdays. "Thinking about this book in my mind, like this, made it very interesting and I wanted to keep on reading."	1. "I stopped thinking when I came to a word I didn't know" (think to the end).

Another CPI lesson builds new metacognitive networks by presenting students with varying perspectives. As students reason through the differences between opposing or diverging positions and viewpoints, their minds draw on the metacognitive processes taught in prior lessons. To begin, have students read two texts that present slightly different versions of the same fairy tale, theme, or topic. Reading these texts consecutively strengthens students' abilities to notice similarities and differences. As each difference is noted, ask students to describe and list the values and issues that each involves.

Exposing young students to contrastive thinking is an effective megacognitive stimulant because it increases their sensitivity to authors' points of view. As a result, students learn how to draw contrasts between purposes as they read. They no longer cling to the author as the authority or to their own purpose, conceived before reading, to determine an author's intent in writing a text. Uniting an author's intended purpose with their own "purpose-setting process" increases students' active monitoring of their current levels of understanding, and is an excellent example of well-developed metacognition (Schwartz & Bransford, 2001; Vye et al., 1998). Develop these metacognitions by teaching the CPI Strands 1, 2, and 3 lesson cycle.

By age 10, most children can intertwine three different strands of metacognitive comprehension processes as they read. The CPI lessons described in this section can be used to increase the depth and frequency with which students self-initiate these metacognitions.

Developing Text Sensitivity: Teaching Structural Cohesiveness

Students in grades K–3 can be taught the patterns that authors use to communicate ideas. Authors organize their thoughts into recognizable writing patterns that allows readers to predict where main ideas and details will appear. When young readers learn to recognize the patterns that writers use, their ability to understand and recall ideas improves. You can teach the following patterns in a Strand 1 lesson to develop students' sense of textual structure so that they can more ably follow authors' ideas.

This CPI Strand 1 lesson begins by explaining each of the basic text patterns shown in Figure 9.1 (and Appendix A). After teaching each separately, allow students to practice recognizing the authorial writing patterns in Strand 2 lessons, using many different books, until students' metacognitive text sensitivities begin to emerge, unprompted.

Main Idea Pattern

The writing pattern of presenting main ideas followed by details explains a topic, concept, or theme by stating the main ideas (in a diagram/concept map, represented by circled ideas or overarching, curved lines) and elaborating on them with details (represented by lines that emanate from each main idea or occur horizontally beneath the overarching, curved-lined main idea). This pattern is used by many authors; the main ideas within this pattern can be recognized because they are repeated often and emphasized. Sometimes a tabletop

FIGURE 9.1. Recognizing the patterns that authors use in writing.

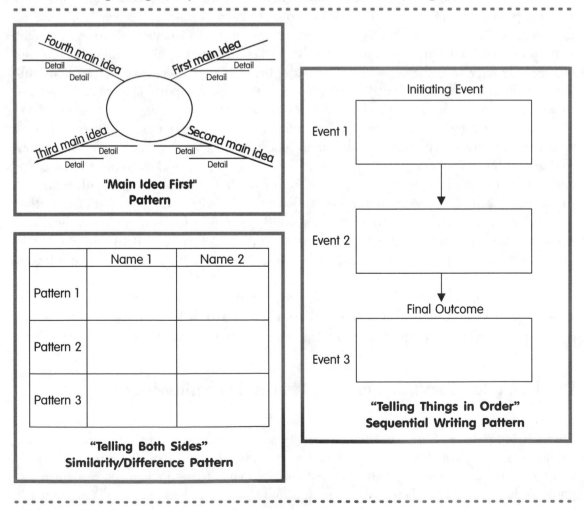

is used as the graphic or thinking guide to teach main ideas, as shown in the photograph on page 103.

Problem–Solution Pattern

The problem-to-solution pattern (see Figure 9.2 and Appendix A) occurs frequently in life. In literature, this writing pattern is signaled when a problem is presented, and three (or more) attempts to solve this problem occur before the climax (defined as the action that leads to the

FIGURE 9.2. **Example from <u>Princess Smarty Pants</u> of author's writing style that follows the problem-to-solution story pattern.**

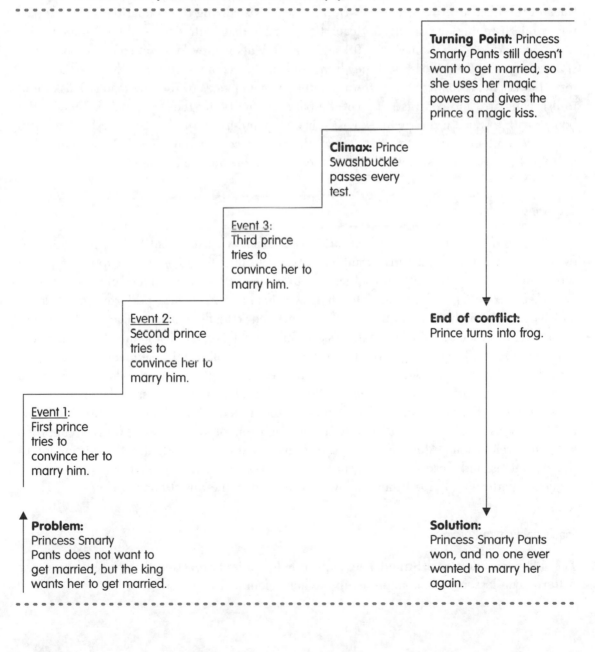

Turning Point: Princess Smarty Pants still doesn't want to get married, so she uses her magic powers and gives the prince a magic kiss.

Climax: Prince Swashbuckle passes every test.

<u>Event 3</u>: Third prince tries to convince her to marry him.

<u>Event 2</u>: Second prince tries to convince her to marry him.

<u>Event 1</u>: First prince tries to convince her to marry him.

End of conflict: Prince turns into frog.

Problem: Princess Smarty Pants does not want to get married, but the king wants her to get married.

Solution: Princess Smarty Pants won, and no one ever wanted to marry her again.

final significant turn of events) and solution occur. To teach this pattern, conduct a Strand 1 lesson in which you read, for example, *Princess Smarty Pants* (Cole, 1997) and display Figure 9.2 on an overhead projector. You can explain how you used your metacognitive comprehension process of attending to the author's problem-solving story map to sequence the important actions. As a class, students can diagram the events in that book to get the clearer sense of the problem–solution writing pattern, using Figure 9.2 as a thinking guide example.

Similarity/Difference Pattern

The "telling both sides" similarity/difference writing pattern defines how things are and are not, alike. People who think in this pattern often say things like "on one hand . . . but on the other hand"; "sort of . . . but," and "yes, but consider this . . ." It is easier for students to keep track of the ideas expressed in this writing style by visualizing the similarity/difference pattern while listening or reading. To teach this pattern, distribute copies of the "Telling Both Sides" pattern depicted on Figure 9.1 and ask students if they know anyone who uses this style to organize their ideas, or if they have read any books in which the author uses this pattern. If students recognize the pattern in either acquaintances or reading material, ask them to list, compare, and contrast a few of the patterns that typify these people's speech or the books writing style on their copies. Lastly, in a stop-and-ask Strand 2 lesson, ask students to read independently from a text that follows this pattern so that you can check the material in each of their columns as they fill them in, correcting errors immediately.

Sequential Pattern

The "telling things in order" or sequential writing pattern uses time to link thoughts and events. For example, historians or authors who write how-to guides or cookbooks follow a sequential pattern. This pattern is often easy to recognize by the sequence of words such as *first, then, next, after,* and *finally.* To teach this writing pattern, explain, perform a think-aloud, and use a section from a sequentially patterned book to demonstrate each of the metacognitions you used to follow the author's train of thought. Next, tell students that most directions that they will read throughout the rest of their lives will use this sequential writing pattern. Becoming familiar with this pattern can increase their ability to follow instructions. Demonstrate the pattern orally by giving directions to a location in the school without telling students the final destination. Before you begin the directions, explain: "Because you know that directions follow a sequential pattern, you can listen for key sequence words to improve your comprehension." After giving the directions, ask students to identify the destination of the directions and describe how using their metacognitive comprehension processes of sequence patterning helped them follow and remember the directions better.

Sequential Pattern Practice

The following additional Strand 1 lesson can help students practice the sequential writing pattern. The lesson uses a simple recipe to help them learn sequential order.

Strand 1 Objective: Students will be able to correctly prepare the recipe after putting the steps in sequential order.

Teaching Materials

- Recipe for chocolate sundae
- Recipe steps cut into strips
- Foods and materials needed:

  1. Ice cream
  2. Chocolate syrup
  3. Whipped topping
  4. Maraschino cherries
  5. Bowl
  6. Ice cream scoop

Teaching Directions

1. Cut the chocolate sundae recipe steps into individual strips.
2. Put strips into a plastic resealable bag.
3. Have students work in pairs.
4. Students must first put recipe strips in order (teacher should check for accuracy).
5. Then provide premeasured ingredients and allow them to make their own chocolate sundaes.

Chocolate Sundae Recipe
(makes 1 sundae)

Cooking Ingredients

2 scoops vanilla ice cream
¼ cup chocolate syrup
3 tbsp. whipped topping
1 maraschino cherry
10 ounce clear plastic cup

Cooking Directions

1. First place one scoop of vanilla ice cream in plastic cup.
2. Add chocolate syrup (use half).
3. Add another scoop of vanilla ice cream.
4. Add another layer of chocolate syrup.
5. Add whipped topping.
6. Finally, top with a maraschino cherry.

Once students have completed the activity, they may eat the sundae. (It is important to check for any allergies or medical conditions which would prohibit them from eating this food.)

CPI Lessons That Teach Students to Look for the Frequency with Which an Idea Is Repeated

Explain that looking for the frequency with which an idea is expressed helps students locate the most important information in a book or conversation. Demonstrate that frequently repeated ideas in a textbook are likely to be the most important pieces of information. During a shared reading, perform three think-alouds to describe how you apply metacognition to note main idea frequency and identify which type of detail is reported in subsequent sentences ("who" details, "what" details, "where" details, "how" details, or "why" details) as illustrated in Figure 9.3.

CPI Lessons That Teach Students to Note the Direction of a Character's Thoughts

Explain that noting the purpose of characters' and people's thoughts is a metacomprehension process that can be used to identify the direction an author's or speaker's thoughts take. Demonstrate this comprehension process by explaining how they can ask themselves: "Is this author trying to (1) inform me, as a reader, about something (by presenting new information), or (2) entertain me, or (3) persuade me." Explain that simply identifying an author's, literary character's, or speaker's purpose can improve comprehension. Furthermore, knowing characters' purposes makes it easier to predict what the main ideas of future paragraphs will be. As an example of identifying purpose, read a portion of a textbook from the middle of a chapter without revealing the title or the topic. Ask students if the characters are trying to inform, entertain, or persuade them. When you are sure that students can note the direction of characters' thinking, place them in Strand 2 lessons to practice these metacognitive thoughts, and then in Strand 3 lesson groups to analyze which aspects of these processes need to be retaught.

FIGURE 9.3. **Recognizing where an author places the main idea and what kind of details appear in the text.**

- -

Tree Frogs Example

Page 1–21:

Sentence 1: Main idea

Sentence 2: **How** detail, with new vocabulary word introduced and defined.

Sentence 3: **How** detail

Sentence 4: **How** detail

- -

CPI Strand 1 Lessons That Teach Students to Compare Similar Events in Their Lives to What Is Read

Explain that comparing literary events to those that occur in students' own lives is a fifth metacognitive strategy they should use when they do not understand something. At this point, read an excerpt from *The Magic School Bus: Inside the Human Body* by Joanna Cole (1990), a book that uses the familiarity of the classroom to explain how the human body functions. You can also list books they have read recently and identify any situations in which students could have compared what was happening in the book to something in their own life experiences to improve their comprehension.

Last, select any book that you are presently reading to the class, or read a selection from their anthologies. As you read each paragraph, stop at a difficult sentence and model what you want students to do if a misunderstanding occurs. You can demonstrate how, when they are tempted to say, while reading, "I don't know," instead they can choose to engage their metacognitive processes by saying, "I'm not sure, but I think it is like. . . ." Repeatedly model this type of think-aloud until you have finished two pages of the book. Close this section of the lesson by asking students to review their metacognitive processes and identify which ones they use most frequently. List these on the board. Tell students that these processes seem to be the ones that they can use most frequently to overcome misunderstandings—for the rest of their lives.

Increasing Knowledge of One's Goals

The ability to keep one's purpose and goals in mind throughout the reading of a text disciplines the mind and serves as a channel for metacognitive energy. Among the first studies demonstrating the close connection between students' control of their own purposes and metacognition occurred as early as 1901 (Thorndike & Woodworth, 1901). Current research has shown that when students improved their metacognition while they read, the quality of their postreading reflections increased (Lin et al., 1995; Pressley & Afflerbach, 1995). Another major finding concerning the power of teaching this third domain of metacognition is that this ability differs strikingly by age. For instance, when students are asked to generate questions on a particular issue about which they want to read, younger readers focus on single events rather than themes. Conversely, more expert readers or older readers draw diagrams in their mind of the total theme before they seek answers concerning single events (Vye, Schwartz, Bransford, Barron, & Zech, 1998).

Another component in goal setting and maintenance, to use Vye et al.'s (1998) phrase, is building students' desires to set those goals in the first place. As the work of Marzana (2001) demonstrated, learning to stay focused on goals while reading increases significantly during the first three lessons in which students attempt to use this new metacognitive process. To develop this ability, provide students with a checklist of comprehension processes to review before they read. Then, after reading a selection, ask them to place a checkmark in the blanks that precede each comprehension process that they used. Figure 9.4 (also in Appendix A) is useful for this purpose because it lists the metacognitive processes

FIGURE 9.4. **Student self-assessment of metacognitive processes.**

- -

_____ 1. Tilled the text.

_____ 2. Identified author's writing pattern as

       _____ a. Main idea pattern;

       _____ b. Problem–solution pattern;

       _____ c. Similarity/difference pattern (telling both sides);

       _____ d. Sequence pattern (telling things in order)

_____ 3. Looked for the author's sequencing patterns with words such as **first**, **then**, or **next**.

_____ 4. Determined whether the main idea was clear or reread if it was unclear.

_____ 5. Looked for frequency of ideas and if the same idea was repeated in different ways.

_____ 6. Noted the direction of the author's or characters' thinking.

_____ 7. Compared what I read to similar events in my life.

_____ 8. Organized the text in my mind as I read.

- -

described in this book. Other forms that can be used for students' self-assessment of metacognitive processes appear in Chapter 10.

Reteaching Comprehension Processes

It is important to take students through *all* levels of comprehension processes: basic, literal, inferential, and metacognitive. Unfortunately, many instructional programs for less able readers center on review and practice of separate skills—a method that reduces motivation and comprehension processing (Santa & Hoin, 1999). Indeed, most poor comprehenders do not catch up with their peers, and this achievement gap only increases as students age (Stanovich, 1986). Compounding the challenge faced by poor comprehenders is the reality that today's classes contain unprecedented academic diversity (Allington, 1996).

Typically, in a class of 26 children, (1) eight students display vast weaknesses in comprehension processes (Mangieri & Block, 1994); (2) three have a limited knowledge of English (Carnegie Foundation, 1995; Moll, 1997); (3) three have been raised in poverty (Children's Defense Fund, 1992); (4) seven have been diagnosed as being at risk for, or having, learning disabilities, mild mental challenges, emotional challenges, attention-deficit/hyperactivity disorder, attention-deficit disorder, or dyslexia (Council of Exceptional Children, 1997); (5) two take medication for hyperactivity or stress-related disorders (American Medical Association, 1996); (6) four have no or limited reading materials in their homes (American Library Association, 1996); and (7) five have *not* been taught by caregivers to value and appreciate the mental energy that is necessary to gain meaning and pleasure from reading.

Moreover, many students who are not good comprehenders today exert little or no effort to improve, because their schools do not address their cognitive needs. A strong meta-comprehension program is vital for these students. New methods must be created for students who are unable to (1) select appropriate books for independent silent reading (Shoemaker & Deshler, 1992), (2) visualize what they read (Shoemaker & Deshler, 1992), (3) ask themselves questions to monitor their understanding (Clark, Deshler, Shoemaker, Alley, & Warner, 1984), or (4) summarize what they read (Shoemaker & Deshler, 1992).

Research indicates that the CPI lessons described in this chapter improve less able readers' comprehension capabilities (Block & Rodgers, in press). These lessons present abstract concepts in concrete ways, teach the organizational structure of an author's writing style, make relationships among bits of information explicit, and distinguish between important and less important information. The needs for such lessons are increasing as today's textbooks grow thicker with more information that is written at a level that is above more students' instructional and independent reading levels than ever before (Fisher et al., 2002). The lessons described next build upon the early work in the "key word program" by Ashton-Warner (1966), literacy charts (McKay, Thompson, & Schabuh, 1970), dictation (Clay, 1979), and process reading and writing (Block & Johnson, 2002). Through these approaches, less able readers can begin to satisfy their need to set and reach their own comprehension goals independently.

In addition, many whole-class activities can be modified to meet these students' special comprehension needs. First, when material is read aloud, readers who are less skilled will profit by simultaneously reading the text silently. Second, when these students are placed in pairs for their reading activities, they benefit from the principles described in Chapter 4. Third, when concluding a discovery discussion, you can ask students who are less skilled readers to read orally and perform a think-aloud about a difficult comprehension process.

The activities and lessons in this section, which are designed for students who may be weak comprehenders or need more practice in developing their skills, have the following qualities in common: (1) they demonstrate the complexity of effective comprehension processing; (2) they teach comprehension in a challenging context, using methods that students may not have experienced previously; and (3) they embrace age-appropriate developmental realities.

Multisensory Additions

By grade 2, CPI lessons designed for weaker comprehenders will increase their effectiveness if they contain a multisensory component. Students who struggle to comprehend must quickly rise above their present levels or they may fall so far behind their peers that they give up and cease to exert themselves. Each lesson described up to this point can be retaught with additional multisensory elements. These new additions elicit kinesthetic and tactile dimensions that enable students to become more immersed in pleasurable comprehension than is possible through only reading print. For example, instead of teaching weak comprehenders to merely memorize the sequence signal words in Figure 9.5, you can bring in train car or train sets, or other such objects, so that weaker comprehenders can touch and see the effects of words like *next, third,* and *finally* as they use these directions to make a train of their choice. Teaching each of the six methods of ordering text, by grouping objects on a desk provides a concrete referent for cause–effect words, comprehension words, and time order words. For example, students can be given 20 beads of various colors. You would teach the time order words by saying and writing the word "before." Then you would use it (and all time order words) in a sentence such as "Put all the red beads before the blue beads in a long line."

CPI Fluency Lessons

Fluency lessons should be conducted weekly for weak comprehenders (Opliz & Rasinski, 1999). For 15 minutes, 1 day a week, students should practice reading 200 words fluently. To begin this lesson, read a page orally with fluent and appropriate phrasing. As you read, weak comprehenders read along silently, listening to your rendition. Next, you and one of the students read the text orally together, using the same pace and appropriate phrasing. Now, the student reads it to you, then moves into a Strand 2 lesson and pairs with a classmate to practice reading the text fluently and repeatedly. The student "performs" a text for an interested audience, usually a group of peers in the class that have not yet read that text. Last, the student and "audience" engage in a Strand 3 lesson in which they discuss what went well and what needs to be retaught in the area of fluency.

Creating Age-Appropriate Adaptations

By grades 2 and 3, instruction for less able comprehension must focus more on identifying the best bridge that individual students can use to cross over the major gaps between their comprehension abilities and those of the majority of their peers. Because the need to overcome each comprehension deficit at this age is so urgent, instruction for weaker comprehenders in second and third grades must become more personalized. You can accomplish this personalizing process by finding the right individual mixture, tempo, and context for each child's CPI catch-up lesson.

For children who have not yet learned to comprehend, by age 10, using the methods in their basic programs, CPI reteaching lessons are critical (Block, Oaker, et al., 2002). Moreover, by third grade, many less able readers could have spent *at least half* of their lives trying to catch up and comprehend independently. Many will need teachers to convince them that the efforts they will exert in CPI reteach lessons will be worthwhile.

For many years, a common practice among elementary school teachers was to divide students into small, same-ability groups for comprehension instruction. During the 1970s and 1980s, however, this prevailing practice "began to draw criticism on the grounds that ability grouping lowers self-esteem and motivation among students with reading problems, restricts friendship choices, and often widens the gap between high and low achievers" (Elbaum, Vaughn, Hughes, & Moody, 1999, p. 372). This criticism led more teachers to turn to cross-age tutoring groups. Such formats help classroom teachers accommodate the multiplicity of reading levels among students who have trouble comprehending. Research from impoverished but successful schools indicates that such tutoring also enables every child to receive

FIGURE 9.5. Signal words.

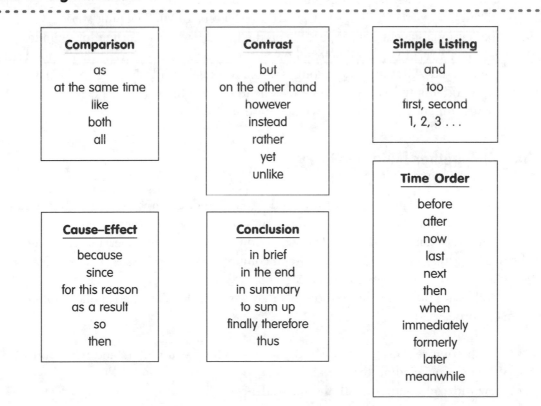

Comparison	Contrast	Simple Listing
as	but	and
at the same time	on the other hand	too
like	however	first, second
both	instead	1, 2, 3 . . .
all	rather	
	yet	
	unlike	

Cause–Effect	Conclusion	Time Order
because	in brief	before
since	in the end	after
for this reason	in summary	now
as a result	to sum up	last
so	finally therefore	next
then	thus	then
		when
		immediately
		formerly
		later
		meanwhile

instruction every day. After these tutoring sessions, students should spend time in small-group Strand 3 instructional settings, where they describe what they learned as well as misunderstood during their tutoring sessions. When these three-strand lessons conclude with home applications for parents to implement each evening, the comprehension reteaching process can be reinforced on an ongoing basis (Hiebert, 1999).

These CPI reteaching lessons can raise students' levels of comprehension because they help them become internally guided readers. To identify difficulties that are interfering with their own comprehension, they must learn to successfully (1) till the text before they read, (2) make meaning while they read, (3) reflect after they have read, and (4) select comprehension processes as the interact with what they read. However, providing choices about which book to read and which questions to ask while reading is not enough. The choices must be *challenging* (Ames, 1992). When choices are challenging, students develop their own desire to comprehend. In turn, this emotional response increases volition, persistence, and motivation.

Thus, through the quality of choices you provide, students can come to understand that comprehension is not merely a matter of terminating confusion but also of selecting appropriate thinking processes to remedy that confusion. Successful remediation of a misunderstanding does not guarantee that comprehension will take its place, however. Students must add active voices and choices, and they must develop their own abilities to determine whether incoming stimuli are coherent or incoherent. This process of making something one's own enlarges one's reference set of experiences so that relevance to new incidents within that domain can more quickly be established. When choices and challenges intertwine, children become strongly engaged in literacy (Cameron & Pierce, 1994). Teaching students to paraphrase a paragraph as accurately as possible on the literal level is important for them to retain new knowledge. Learning from that text, however, demands more—it requires "a good situational model linked with the reader's long term knowledge" (Kintsch, 1994, p. 321). In other words, *after* students tell you what they have learned, ask them when they think they will refer to or use this newly gained knowledge base in the future.

Pulling It Together Metacognitively

It is important to ask questions that are student centered. Do not ask a question unless it helps students (and not just yourself), and refrain from asking questions to which you already know the answer—and the students know that you know. On many occasions, the questions teachers ask address only the basic and literal comprehension processes. These questions do not promote more than recitation of facts.

The following questions help students in grades K–3 develop their metacognitive comprehension processes.

- Which comprehension process did you use to help you understand what you read?
- Why are you reading this book?
- How did you come up with the main idea?

- What information did you use to make that inference?
- How does that connection help you to understand what you have read?
- What do you think the author was thinking when [he or she] wrote this?

These questions cause the student to think about the material at a higher level. The student cannot simply return to the text to come up with an answer.

In addition, the K–3 reader may need more direct guidance in developing his or her metacognitive process. The following Strand 2 lessons model how students can "pull all their thoughts together" as they read.

CPI Pulling It Together Metacognitively, Lesson 1: "Ask My Teacher When I'm Confused"

When students are confused, teach them to stop and say to themselves:

"I don't understand. I need to stop and explain what I just read to myself or ask my teacher to explain why I misunderstood at this point."

You can also teach them to ask themselves the following questions:

"Was the sentence too complex?"
"Did an unknown word appear?"
"Did an event occur that I have never experienced?"

Once students have been taught to stop and ask such questions of themselves in a Strand 1 lesson, and have practiced doing so in three Strand 2 lessons, they can exercise the choice during future Strand 2 lessons of stopping to ask themselves questions as they read and verifying with their teacher if their answers were correct. Alternatively, they can signal the *clarify* CPM and ask their teachers to deliver a mini-intervention when they misunderstand a page of text. By the third round of posing these types of questions before, during, and after reading, most students have gained the ability to detect any confusion they may experience as they read.

CPI Pulling It Together Metacognitively, Lesson 2: "Mark Where I Am Confused"

Teach students how to use the strategy of jotting checkmarks and question marks in the margins of photocopied pages as they read silently in Strand 2 lessons. Alternatively, they can use a sheet of paper to record their comprehension by writing the page number, paragraph number, and the following shorthand to denote points of understanding and confusion while they read:

✓   I know that I understand this paragraph.
?   I know that I don't understand this paragraph.

For variety, provide students with sheets of acetate to cover the pages in a book. They can read and write the appropriate mark (i.e., ✓ or ?) beside each paragraph on the acetate to indicate how well they understand it. After students have read and recorded their comprehension successes and difficulties in 10 paragraphs, they bring their books to you for a discovery discussion. Work with students individually to analyze what the misunderstood paragraphs had in common. If students have difficulty detecting the similarities in their comprehension problems, you can describe the textual patterns that may be causing comprehension difficulties.

Summary

Every basic reading series published in the past 5 years includes lessons and activities that foster metacognition (Pressley et al., 1994; Schmitt & Hopkins, 1993). Although teachers' manuals provide information about how to teach some metacognitive processes, educators request additional assistance in developing these abilities in their students. The CPI lessons in this chapter build young readers metacognitive processes by helping them learn how to (1) control their thoughts during reading, (2) establish and maintain their own reading goals, and (3) initiate metacomprehension processes to overcome confusion. Instructional adaptations must be made for weaker comprehenders in the form of concrete CPI reteaching lessons, and five basic reteaching lessons were described.

Many teachers monitor students' silent reading and perform think-alouds that advance their thinking during reading (Block & Pressley, 2002). Few teachers are able to describe accurately their own metacognitive thinking. For this reason, it is important to increase teachers' awareness of their own metacognitive reading processes. The second goal of this chapter was to assist teachers in building that knowledge base (Edwards, 1999).

Reflecting on What You Have Learned

1. **Interpreting (Summarizing) the Main Points.** In your opinion, what is the most important metacognitive lesson in this chapter that we must address in a more focused manner at a grade level that you teach (or will teach)? Describe the instructional methods and books that you would use to teach this lesson.

2. **Summarizing the Key Points That You Have Learned Thus Far in the Book.** Make a graphic to depict your thought processes regarding these key points. How could this review method be adapted and used as an activity to increase your students' retention?

3. **Making Professional Decisions.** In one paragraph describe a new a research design that you believe should be undertaken to increase students' abilities to think metacognitively. In this design, describe the comprehension process to be researched and the method to be used in the research.

4. **Making Field Applications and Observations.** Describe the most effective method of teaching and assessing metacognition that you have observed or led in a preschool or primary-level classroom. Analyze which domain of metacognition the lesson was designed to develop. Be prepared to defend your answer.

5. **Keeping a Professional Metacognitive Journal.** In your journal, describe a professional difficulty you face. Journal for 12 days on what you do to overcome this challenge. The resultant diary could be used as a model for weak comprehenders. If you share your diary and discuss the benefits you received from this process, they may be motivated to begin their own diary to document what they are doing to overcome reading problems.

6. **Making Multicultural Applications.** Devise a think-aloud for a student who is having difficulties in one of the three metacognitive domains, because English is not his or her first language. Deliver your think-aloud, hold a discovery discussion, and evaluate the effects. How can you use the results of these actions to plan the next lesson that you will administer for that student? Be prepared to discuss your results with colleagues.

7. **Meeting Students' Special Needs.** Design a lesson using one of the metacognitive lessons discussed in this chapter to strengthen the comprehension process of a student with special needs.

8. **Checking Key Terms.** Following is a list of concepts introduced in this chapter. If you have learned the meaning of a term, place a checkmark in the blank that precedes it. If you are not sure of a term's definition, increase your retention by reviewing it. If you have learned eight of these terms on your first reading of this chapter, then you have constructed many meanings that are important for your work.

    ____Metacognition (p. 146)

    ____Semantic processes (p. 147)

    ____Syntactic processes (p. 147)

    ____Evaluating structural cohesiveness (p. 147)

    ____Noting the direction of a character's thoughts (p. 147)

    Comparing what is read to similar events in readers' lives (p. 147)

    ____Evaluating informational completeness (p. 147)

    ____Cognitive comprehension processes (p. 148)

    ____Metacognitive comprehension processes (p. 148)

    ____Main ideas followed by details authorial writing pattern (p. 152)

    ____Problem to solution pattern (p. 153)

    ____Similarity/difference authorial writing pattern (p. 154)

    ____Sequential authorial writing pattern (p. 154)

9. **Design a Comprehension Process Lesson.** CPI Lesson 8 demonstrates how students can integrate all the metacognitive processes that they have learned in this chapter. This lesson is a Strand 2 lesson. Before students read silently, remind

them to use the metacognitive processes depicted in Figure 9.4 or in the following chart that is placed beside their book as they read in this Strand 2 lesson. Instruct students to answer the questions on it as or after they read.

Comprehension Process Lesson 8: Thinking Metacognitively as You Read

- What do you need to do next?
- Can you think of another way a famous person we've studied would have solved this problem if he or she were here?
- What do you do when you come to a difficult word? What do you do when you do not understand the content/context?
- What thinking process did you follow, step by step, to reach this conclusion?
- How could we go about finding out if a statement is true?
- What helped you most to overcome a difficulty in reading?
    Construct a mental puzzle.
    Use illustrations.

Questions and Activities That Stimulate Higher-Level Thinking

- Does this story or nonfiction book remind you of another story you've read? Why? What specific characteristics does it have in common?
- What parts did you like more or less than the last one we read and why? Were there characters that you liked or disliked? Why?
- Why do you suppose that the author created this title? What kind of title would you have written and why?
- Could you give us an example of what you mean?
    Write in a journal.
    Draw a summary.

How Can You Express How This Story Made You Feel?

- After reading this story, has your perception or view of _____ changed? Explain.
- You seem to be approaching this issue from _____ perspective. Why did you choose this perspective?
- What might other groups say, and what would influence their perspective?
- How could you address the position that _____?
- What is an alternative?
    Create a diagram.
    Make graphs and charts.

How Can You Justify Your Reasons and Positions?

- Why is this reason better than that reason?
- What are your reasons for saying that?
- What does the author mean by _____?
- What do you mean by _____?
- You seem to be assuming _____. Why do you take this for granted?
- Why did you base your reasons on _____ rather than _____?

  Design a panel.
  Divide into groups.

CHAPTER 10

Assessment of Comprehension

"I want to tell you another success story," John Stoffel began in his letter to Dr. Block. "I used the assessment sheet that shows the different processes around the border, with blank lines in the middle [see Appendix A, p. 208]. Since I wanted to really concentrate on comprehension, not fluency, we listened to *Dream Wolf* by Paul Goble (1997) in our basal while students read along silently. I was using this experience as the culminating assessment of a mini-unit on Native Americans and the comprehension processes of wondering, predicting, and making connections.

"Upon my first prereading of the story, I wasn't all that excited about it, but it fit into our unit pretty well and was short enough to be our assessment content. However, by the time I finished the following evaluation lesson, I felt like I had been in my English class at Ball State University! Here's what we did. Like most good stories, there were several times in *Dream Wolf* that mini-climaxes occurred, and page breaks were appropriate for maintaining that suspense. I warned my students *not* to turn the page to see what was next in the upcoming pictures and text. Instead, we stopped at these suspenseful parts and about all I said to assess their comprehension was this: 'Now, tell me what comprehension process you're using right now. If you aren't using one, think of one you could use right now. Write down what you are thinking in the center of your sheet and put a corresponding number by the picture of the comprehension process motion that goes with it.'

"We did this four times in the middle of the story, but not at the end. The next day, we relistened to the story and stopped to share the thoughts that we were having at each point. Oh, what wonderful predictions and wonder we shared! We even made a few connections to other stories, along with feelings. At the end, we shared our final thoughts. Two students came up with one feeling and one wonder, and I told them that I thought that the author's main moral in this story was the combination of their two thoughts.

"If I had time to type in all the richness of this assessment in every savory detail, I could make your mouth water. As I said before, a story I anticipated with mediocrity, when used for a multiple comprehension process evaluation, actually left me with the feeling of having been in a college short-story discussion group. My students have learned to comprehend deeply, thoroughly, and richly through CPI lessons. Thank you, "

—JOHN STOFFEL, *Indiana*

Chapter Overview

How can we measure comprehension? This question has been asked for several decades, and many educators have answered that we need newer forms of comprehension evaluation. Most comprehension tests are based on brief paragraphs and often assess pupils' background experiences and short-term memory of literal facts rather than determining their ability to comprehend a novel piece of text. How often do students image? How often do students infer? How often do students engage effective metacognitive processes? How motivated are students to overcome confusion? Do they use what they read to make their lives better? These are questions that the CPI assessments in this chapter are designed to evaluate.

This chapter reports new research and more effective methods of assessing comprehension that unite the learning principles used in Strands 1, 2 and 3 of CPI instruction. First, the principles that new assessments should embody are explored and then new assessment measures are described. By the end of this chapter, you will be able to answer the following questions

1. How can the assessment of reading comprehension be improved?
2. What improvements are needed?
3. What methods can be used to assess comprehension at the primary, intermediate, and middle school levels?
4. What can administrators, teachers, and students use as evidence of individual comprehension successes?

Theoretical Background

The National Reading Panel (1999) and the Rand Reading Study Group (Sweet & Snow, 2002) agreed that additional professional development beyond a bachelor's degree is especially important for those who wish to teach reading comprehension. These scientists' synthesis of prior research found that the elementary school years are the most critical for diagnosing students' comprehension competencies. By third grade, most students have developed defense strategies to camouflage weaknesses in their abilities to make meaning from text. Only precise, effective assessment instruments can disarm these defenses. When students' comprehension weaknesses are detected and eliminated, their chances for developing richer interactions with their own cognitive processes increase exponentially. If their weaknesses are not detected, however, they are likely to develop even more effective methods of masking their reading failures (Block, 2002a).

Many studies are underway to examine new staff development programs designed to enhance teachers' abilities to instruct and assess comprehension. Many school districts are joining in these efforts, which are occurring through the Best Comprehension Practices Consortium, sponsored by the Institute for Literacy Enhancement in Charlotte, North Carolina. These training programs are researching new initiatives that would enable teachers to "see inside students' brains," while they independently apply the comprehension processes presented in this book. If your school district would like more information about these professional development programs, contact the director, Dr. John Mangieri, at *jmangieri@ carolina.rr.com.*

The work at this institute has also documented that teachers want new comprehension tools that not only assess what they have taught about comprehension but how much students are *actively* engaged in making meaning. When such measures are available, children's zones of proximal development (Vygotsky, 1978) and their rates of learning can be assessed, which are crucial to planning the pace of comprehension instruction. Building on this perspective and Vygotsky's (1978) theory, assessments should measure how rapidly a child can acquire new comprehension processes when these are modeled by more advanced comprehenders.

Dark and Gilmore (1999) challenge educators to address another need in comprehension assessment: that of *assisted performance evaluations.* These tests measure a student's degree of engagement in the process of comprehending, when a second person challenges the student beyond his or her independent reading level. These types of assisted performance, which are commonplace in everyday life (e.g., working side-by-side with a mentor for long periods of time to master a skill, sport, or leisure-time hobby), are less often used by teachers in classrooms. Instead, since the last century, comprehension instruction in North America has consisted mainly of assigning tasks and assessing individual development. This practice must change. Students cannot be left to learn on their own. Teachers cannot be content to merely provide opportunities to learn and then assess outcomes. Recitation must be deemphasized; responsive, assertive interactions must become commonplace in the classroom. When we do, more minds can be roused to life.

In support of this position, Tierney (1998) delineated several principles concerning comprehension assessment:

1. Assessments must contain a variety of comprehension experiences, including nonfiction.
2. Effective testing requires that teachers establish goals for what they are assessing and link those goals to learning.
3. Assessments should help students evaluate themselves. They should inform instruction. Scores and grades only give the illusion of accuracy and authority.
4. Assessments should be conducted judiciously, with teachers serving as advocates for students, ensuring their due process.
5. Research in assessment should extend beyond efforts to improve present tests and develop new tests that are more conceptually valid.
6. Diversity should be embraced, not slighted, in comprehension assessment. Informal tests can use culturally based texts to discern students' multicultural sensitivity. Unfortunately, in the past, test developers have tried to make tests culture free, which is impossible: "Cultural free assessments afford, at best, only a partial, perhaps distorted, understanding of a student's comprehension ability" (Tierney, 1998, p. 381).
7. Future comprehension tests must allow for a range of need in students. Some students have the potential to reveal their inner thoughts accurately; others do not, and still others do not process meaning as they read. Students need to receive differing amounts of encouragement and support, if we are to obtain accurate measurements of

the degree to which they are interrelating the various comprehension processes. When future tests are developed, individual performance assessments that tap into this knowledge-processing component more directly must be considered.

8. Some areas that are worth assessing can be evaluated only through the use of self-report instruments (e.g., degree of self-questioning employed whole reading, and level of engagement experienced). Interaction between multiple factors—speed, factual/literal recall, vocabulary development, inference accuracy, and metacognitive depth—must be developed. Presently, few tests measure such interactions. Educators need data that will help advance instruction at each level of comprehension competence.

9. Assessment should be developmentally sensitive and involve sustained reading rather than quick "dipstick approaches." For example, instead of measuring children's ability in 1 day, using only a few paragraphs or page-length passages, tests should continue for several days and be calculated from longer-term engagements.

10. Assessments must be viewed as ongoing and suggestive rather than "fixed or definitive" (Tierney, 1998, p. 385).

Based on the current status of reading assessment, three specific actions can be taken. First, culturally sensitive assessments must be developed that are directly related to the teaching process. Second, these assessments should be ongoing, involve students in goal setting, and be related to students' developmental stages. Third, these data can then be used to make better instructional decisions. Teachers should not have to repeat the same lessons several times; they should evaluate growth effectively, so that comprehension becomes active and exciting for students. To utilize the assessment process correctly, collaborative planning with students is essential. New tests, discussed in the next section, can use new resources to address the complexity of comprehension.

New Comprehension Tests

Eleven new comprehension assessment tools that serve as models are discussed in the following sections.

Assessment 1: "What Do We Need to Fill In?" Test

Based on the research of Oakhill and Yuill (1999), one of the most effective comprehension assessments is a test that allows students to report what is missing to make a text comprehensible. For children in grades K–3, this test involves a blank sheet of paper, landscape style, divided into eight numbered boxes. In each box, students are asked to write a sentence or draw a picture that could be used to complete the idea in a test text. This test allows children to tell us what needs to be "fixed" in a particular passage so that the information in adjacent sentences is connected. These boxes can also be used to assess students' abilities to initiate simultaneous literal and inferential comprehension processes. When used in this way, the boxes in the upper row would be labeled *Prediction*, and the lower row of boxes would be labeled *Facts Omitted*. (Children who need more work in integrating their inferences with their literal comprehension will not perform well on this test.) You would read, or ask students to read, a section of text in which you placed numbered Post-it Notes over sentences that communicated vital literal information. Students are told to stop at each covered portion of text and write (1) the literal sentence that should appear in this stop to make the text coherent, and (2) the inference/prediction that they made to assist them in drawing that conclusion.

This test can also be given orally and individually. You ask a child to come to your desk to read a passage similar to the following, which was used in Oakhill and Yuill's research (1999):

> A scarecrow was dressed by someone else. A scarecrow is tied down to a pole forever. He is not allowed to turn his head at all. He must stand in the rain without an umbrella all day long. When the winter comes, no one lends him a coat. But a scarecrow's life is all his own. (modified from *Scarecrow* by Cynthia Ryland, 1998; quoted in Oakhill & Yuill, 1999, p. 114)

After a student has read the passage, he or she performs a retelling. Then ask: "What do we need to fill in to make this story more complete for others to read?" When children tell *what* needs to be added *where* to make the text easier for others to comprehend, they reveal what *they* need to comprehend better. As each student answers this question, write down as many of the comments as possible in the first box of the "What Do We Need to Fill In?" test. Date your entry. Keep a separate test for each child, and readminister the assessment three more times during the year. Progress individuals are making should become vivid as well as their rates of growth in literal and inferential comprehension processing. When the next pupil comes to read the same passage, diagnose the type of instruction that this particular child needs. Write his or her name in the next column of the "What Do We Need to Fill In" instructional planner, shown in Figure 10.1 (also in Appendix A). During the next week, place children into groups based on the types of processes they need to be retaught which is reflected in the last column of Figure 10.1.

This test format can be modified in many ways, as shown in the first- and second-grade samples in Figures 10.2 and 10.3. In Figure 10.2, Ms. Painter, a first-grade teacher, used one full sheet as a single box and asked students to write the comprehension processes they used to deduce (and to draw a picture of) what the last picture in the test book would be. In Figure 10.3, Ms. Zinke, a second-grade teacher, asked students to use four boxes to fill in pictures and/or text of what was needed at marked sections of the story to make it fit together; then she used the bottom portion of the test as a single unit, on which students were to write the moral that the author was communicating in the story. Notice that Dannielle can interpret literal and inferential meanings while simultaneously drawing a conclusion as to the moral of a story.

Assessment 2: "What's the Problem?" Test

This test is designed to measure students' imagery and metacognition processes. To administer it, create two passages that children are to read aloud. In each of the passages, substitute "×'s" for a word that could be a visually imaged (using the same number of ×'s as are letters in the correct word). Continue to make substitutions in alternating sentences: One correct sentence is followed by one sentence that has an ×××××'d word inserted; then another

FIGURE 10.1. **Example of the "What Do We Need to Fill In?" test.**

●●

Directions: (1) Put names of group members above each column. (2) Put a tally mark in the appropriate box each time a group member contributes that comprehension process in writing or orally. (3) Make notes on the back when interesting things happen that are not captured by the categories.

Ms. Whalen's Class	Suzanna	Jonathan	Kaitlin	Marcus	Roberto	Total
1. Contributes ideas from other sources	///	/			/	5
2. Describes feelings and makes connections	/	/	/	/	/	5
3. Paraphrases main ideas		///		/		4
4. Recalls sequence	//	//	///	/	//	10
5. Makes inferences	//	///	/	///	///	12
6. Summarizes	/	//		/		4
7. Images	⊦⊦⊦	////	/	⊦⊦⊦	//	17
8. Uses authorial writing pattern	///	///	//	//	//	12
9. Draws conclusions and summarizes	//	//	//		//	8

correct sentence followed by a sentence with ✕✕✕✕'s inserted, etc. Remove easily visualized verbs and nouns. For example, if you were to use sentences from *My Chinatown: One Year in Poems* (2002) by Kam Mak, you would rewrite the italicized word into an ✕✕✕✕'ed word in the two sentences that follow: "I pass the cobbler every day sitting and working on shoes. I stop and watch him cutting the leather in small curves, pulling the needle, tugging the *thread* tight" (Mak, 2002, p. 7).

Thread was chosen to be rewritten as ✕✕✕✕✕ because the context clues supply the answer: *Thread* is the only word that would fit in that testing passage. Therefore, if a young reader did not recognize that ✕✕✕✕✕ stood for *thread*, you could deduce that this student needed additional catch-up lessons on how to image.

This assessment would not be based on only two sentences, however. As noted previously, new comprehension tests should use more than one page of text to assess comprehension. This test should have at least 20 sentences and 10 words removed. Such a length would ensure that students have several opportunities to demonstrate their imagery abilities. How-

FIGURE 10.2. **Example of a first grader's comprehension processes in the "What Do We Need to Fill In" test.**

I predict Santas New Suit will look like this because I read all the facts together and made a main idea.

FIGURE 10.3. **Example of a second grader's comprehension processes in the "What Do We Need to Fill In" test.**

ever, if a student misses the first three words, you can stop this test—she would not be able to score 80% proficiency, even if she were allowed to continue. Three errors would demonstrate a need to reteach imagery to her.

Assessment 3: "Did You Till the Text?" Test

Oakhill and Yuill (1999) also explored the effectiveness of creating a test to identify whether students noticed inconsistencies separated by several sentences. According to their research, a significant interaction occurs between students' abilities to till a text and to retain literal information. Less skilled comprehenders were more affected by the distance that existed between incongruent information than were more skilled students.

To create a "Did You Till the Text?" test, identify a passage where a sentence is inserted on every other page that does not make sense and needs to be changed. Then, ask children to read silently to determine if the passage does or does not make sense. This test indicates if students can till a text and follow authorial writing patterns so carefully that they notice clues that new information is about to be presented. The error pattern on this test helps you understand the quality of students' memory loads and how much information can be retained. Short-term memory is needed to store and integrate information, whereas long-term memory is necessary to store this information as permanent background knowledge that can be accessed in making inferences. Poor readers are less able to monitor texts, detect anomalies, and make inferences involving different parts of a text. Integration is especially difficult if unusually large portions of memory must be allocated to decoding (Oakhill & Yuill, 1999; Perfetti & Lesco, 1979; Stanovich, 1986; Tergeson & Wagner, 1987). The comprehension processes listed in Figure 10.4 (and Appendix A) can be assessed at the kindergarten level if you use it to guide a discovery discussion. At first grade, add a "Know How Text Works" section; at second grade add a "Think Metacognitively" section, asking about these processes.

FIGURE 10.4. **"Did You Till the Text?" Test.**

Name: _____Jeannette_____   Grade: ___3___   Date: ___9-30-03_____

Circle the appropriate numbers to describe your most recent silent reading.

	Always do by myself				Can't do
1. Set my purpose for reading	5	(4)	3	2	1
2. Make predictions	(5)	4	3	2	1
3. Tilled the text	(5)	4	3	2	1
4. Summarized every so often	5	4	(3)	2	1
5. Infer	5	(4)	3	2	1
6. Raise questions about unknown information	5	4	3	(2)	1
7. Connected ideas in 2 sentences	5	(4)	3	2	1
8. Recognize details and main ideas in paragraphs	5	4	(3)	2	1

Assessment 4: "The Importance of Rereading to Remember More Information" Test

First teach students the CPM for rereading, shown in Figure 10.5. To make this motion, hold up the left hand, open and palm toward you (representing a book); bring up the right hand, formed into a V-shape (representing two eyes), and make a zigzag motion (representing the eye movements of reading).

This evaluation assesses how much students remember after a first and second reading of the same text. To administer, distribute a blank copy of the test, which has been provided in Appendix A (p. 203). Ask students to read a text or chapter. In the left column have them write all they remember in a 5- to 10-minute writing period. Then have them reread the same text. In the right column have them write all that they remember after the rereading. The types of information absent in the left column indicate weaknesses in comprehension processing. The absences in the right column document what students are unable to accomplish even with the support of extra reading time. An example of a first grader's completed assessment appears in Figure 10.6.

Assessment 5: "Telling What Comprehension Processes I'm Using" Test

This assessment was the one used by Ms. Stoffel in the description he reported at the beginning of this chapter. An example of a first grader's test appears in Figure 10.7, and a blank form for your use or modification (by inserting different processes that have been taught) appears in Appendix A. To administer, stop students' reading at strategic points in a text in which a particular comprehension process could be used to increase their understanding. Ask students to write the number you say, write what they are thinking after that number on the

FIGURE 10.5. The CPM for rereading.

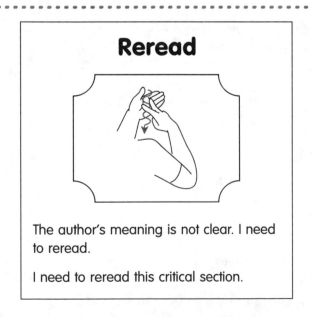

Reread

The author's meaning is not clear. I need to reread.

I need to reread this critical section.

FIGURE 10.6. **Example of a first grader's test of the importance of rereading to remember more information.**

- -

Use a different colored pen and write every detail you remember from the story after reading it one time.

1. That a flying incet was out of the window.
2. I remember that the tittle is Pete's story.
3. I third rember that Pete was telling a story to his brother.
4. I rember that Pete wanted to be a fireman.
5. I rember reading that a cat tried to catch a insect.

Use a different colored pen and write every detail you remember from the story after reading it a second time.

1. I remembered it by reading a second time was that Pete rescues hes brother.
2. Pete little brothe took a nap.
3. Pete told his brother a story.
4. Pete rescues and helps people get out a buring building.
5. I rember that Pete did a story about a cat that tried to get a insect, and a bird.
6. I rembered that Pete said, it's not bad having a little brother.
7. I seveth rembered that the cat in the story that Pete read to his brother was mean.
8. I also rembered that Pete had a aunt named Ant that was her nickname.
9. I rembered that Pete's mother said great job to him because he helped to savral the people.
10. I rember that Pete got in a fire station suit to help the people.
11. In Pete's story their was a clever acrobat.
12. The cat grew angery and meaner.
13. The story was mostily about a boy named Pete that is a fire slation helper that helps people get out of fire.
14. The setting is the outside of bolding.
15. The hairy cat wanted to get an eat the dranger fly.
16. The hairy cat tride to catch a bird to.
17. The hairy cat's eye's was very bright.
18. Outside the window (Pete's window) he saw the yellow hairy cat.
19. In the story that Pete read to his little brother his said that the cat was nerby a huge moutain.
20. When Pete was still telling the story he said one day the cat look down the moutain and then saw the acrobat.
21. The cat got more bigger a lot of years.
22. Pete brother like the story.

- -

Designed by Rachel Escamilla, School of Education, Texas Christian University, Fort Worth, TX, and used by permission.

FIGURE 10.7. Example of a first grader's "Telling What Comprehension Processes I'm Using" test.

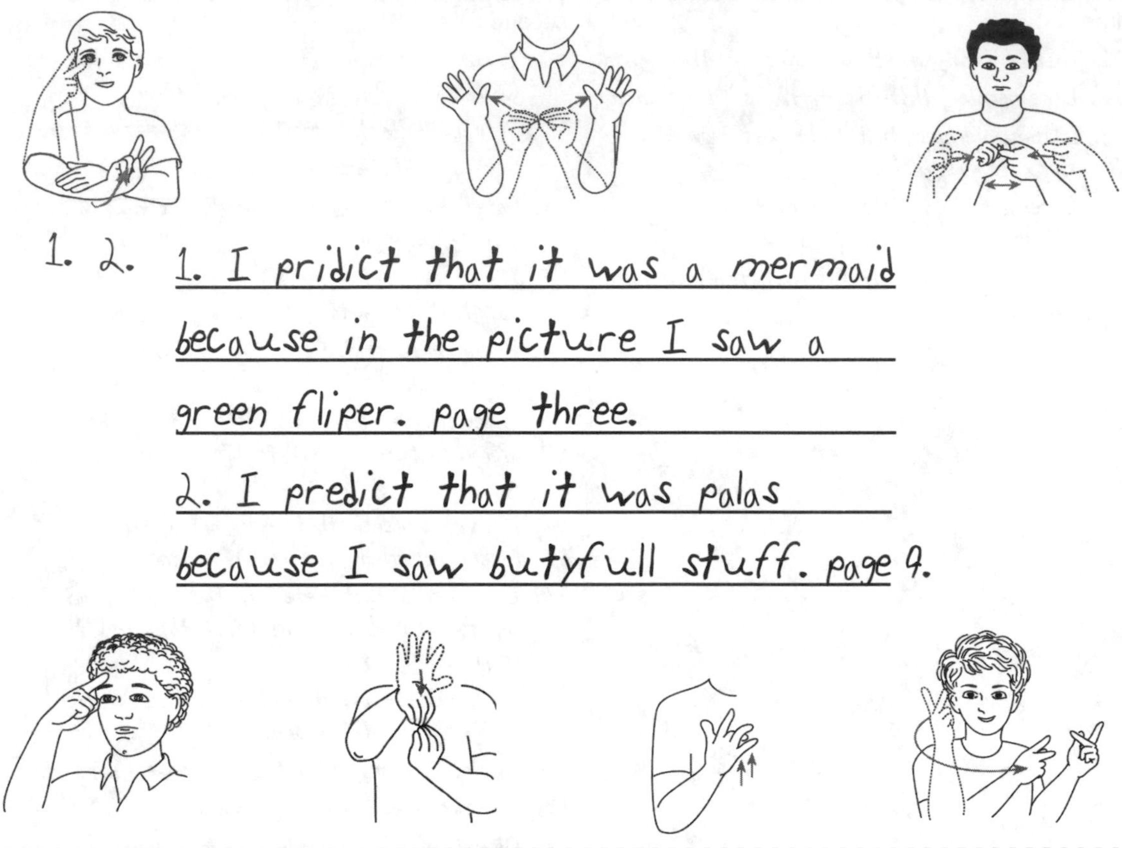

1. 2.
> 1. I pridict that it was a mermaid because in the picture I saw a green fliper. page three.
>
> 2. I predict that it was palas because I saw butyfull stuff. page 4.

lines in the center of the test, and write the number of their answer beneath the CPM that depicts that thinking process. For this assessment stop students' reading twice for kindergarten children, three times for first graders, and four times for second and third graders. After the written portion of the test is complete, collect the papers to grade them and place the students in groups for reteaching (using a form similar to the one in Figure 10.1), or conduct a Strand 3 whole-class lesson in which you ask students to share their answers orally. Discuss what they have learned and need to learn about each of the comprehension processes that were assessed.

Assessment 6: Self-Assessment Tests

These assessments enable students to measure their own comprehension. Several examples of student self-assessment tests appear for your use and modification in Appendix A (pp. 205–209). Also, students can select the format they like best, which can be (1) a checklist in which they list the comprehension processes taught that week and give themselves a rating of 5, 4, 3, 2, or 1 as to how well they learned each; (2) an essay form in which they describe what they want to learn next; or (3) work samples that they grade, stating the criteria they used to determine their own comprehension. Guthrie et al. (2000) recommend that students conduct self-assessments each 6 weeks at the beginning of the year, and no more frequently than once every 3 weeks in the second half of the year. Children store these forms in their portfolios or reading folders and share them during discovery discussion meetings.

For younger students, instead of asking what they are thinking in their minds (which Pressley [1976] determined to be a very difficult task), ask them to play school and teach someone else to read. You can also have younger students draw pictures to depict the end of what they read. As the children draw, you can deduce what they are thinking and assess the quality of their imagery abilities.

Assessment 7: Color-Coded Comprehension Portfolios and Comprehension "Happy-to-Sad Face" Assessments

In this assessment, students insert examples of a correctly used process in a color-coded folder, or shade happy, average, or sad faces to indicate how well they think they are performing individual comprehension processes. These work samples are stored for a year. For example, after teaching students how main ideas build in a story, use a yellow highlighter, with the students, to mark the pages (e.g., across the top edge of the page) that they want to place in their portfolios (or turn in at the end of the week). In addition, students can store magazines or computer text pages, marking the pages with the yellow highlighter, to indicate that they located the main ideas in that material.

Alternatively, you keep a yellow folder (change colors for each process) and students mark their papers and insert them into your folder when they feel they know how to locate a main idea. Then, when you are ready to assess a student's ability to discern main ideas, you can reference the material in that folder and ask the student to describe how the main ideas in the passage he or she selected became vivid. When teaching another process, highlight the papers to be used for pupils' independent practice with a different color.

With color-coded comprehension folders, students learn processes faster; the use of color is an excellent learning tool with which they easily identify and associate concepts. Furthermore, students can be assessed using passages for which they know they have achieved mastery of a comprehension process. In so doing, you can strengthen their motivation, self-efficacy, and ability to choose wisely. "Happy-and-sad" face assessments are important for students in kindergarten through grade 2. Students can make a   beside reading activities they enjoyed, on their individual papers, or on class charts. Happy and sad faces can also be used as an indicator of how well they feel they did on a retelling or writing.

Assessment 8: "Tell Me What I Should Do and I'll Do It" Test

This assessment measures metacognition, fluency, and ability to process the varying writing styles found in expository and narrative texts. As noted previously, in the past, teachers did not model comprehension processes frequently or explicitly enough for students to understand what their minds should be thinking when they are comprehending well. Some teachers still do not demonstrate how to understand phrases, how to connect meanings between paragraphs, and how to put single pieces of information together in the writing formats of different genres. Some do not talk about how we read faster when we have a large data bank of past experiences on the topic. To model all these comprehension processes, you can read orally to children and then allow them to do an assisted reading or a repeated reading.

To make repeated reading into a test for comprehension, you need to add an initial step first. Take a passage that has been written by a child and type it (or have the child type it) as a final draft. Read the passage silently to understand where to pause when modeling what your mind is doing. Then read the passage orally, demonstrating to the child how to stop after phrases to make the passage memorable and how to convey the beauty and rhythm of the English language. Immediately after reading the passage, ask the child to read it orally, mimicking the manner in which you read it. You can then ask the child to describe what was different in his or her mind—the speed or the thoughts—from prior reading experiences.

For students who are unable to describe this process another step is necessary. This step must precede all others, and all steps are tape-recorded. Ask the child to read his or her writing before you read it. Then you read it silently, followed by your oral reading of it. As before, now ask the child to mimic your reading of it. Have the child listen to how he or she read it first, how you read it, then how the child mimicked your reading of it, and then to describe any differences that he or she heard. Last, teach the child how to think while reading so that the differences he or she heard in this lesson can be reproduced in the future.

Assessment 9: Long-Term Memory Test

To assess pupils' long-term memory, you can ask them to list all the books that they have read (or all of the stories that have been taught from the literature anthology) within the past 2 weeks. This list allows you to identify gaps in long-term memory (e.g., the title of a story you know the child has read during the past 2 weeks is not listed). Then you can ask the child to tell you about that story, jotting down the specific things that the child says. You then pass out Figure 10.8 and ask the child to fill it out by describing the most memorable book that she or he has read that year. When the child has finished, you can hold a discovery discussion and ask the child to tell you any differences in how much was remembered and comprehended from both of the books in this assessment and why those differences exist.

Assessment 10: Improving the Specificity of Report Cards and Observation Reports Sent Home to Parents

It is important to communicate an expanded vision of comprehension instruction to parents as well as to children. This can be accomplished by listing the types of processes that have been taught in school on report cards and observation forms. This method was described by Block (in press). You can note whether children demonstrate these processes *always*, *usually*, or *occasionally*. Doing so will ensure that your plans for the next 6 weeks of comprehension instruction will contain each of the steps necessary to enhance all children's full range of abilities.

FIGURE 10.8. Long-term memory test.

- -

<u>Jeannette</u>
<u>November 1, 2003</u>
<u>Ms. Whalen</u>

Dear Reader,

The book I am going to describe is the best book I have read. I would now like to write you this letter to let you know why I think it is the best.

Before I read the book <u>Silkworms</u> I didn't know anything about how silk was made. I now remember all the steps even I read it so long ago. It was the first book that I read this year in September. I remember every step from a silk worm's birth till blooses are made. Worms make silk threads that are 1,000 feet long. They use these threads to make cocoons. The cocoons are heated so that the threads can undo and be woven together. An Emperor's wife in China discovered how to make silk.

Sincerely,

Jeannette

- -

Assessment 11: Coordinating Assessments at School and Home

Often observations are used to assess comprehension. It is important to increase the value of these observations. The following evaluations can help improve comprehension assessments.

Book sharing assessments are one example of how to coordinate comprehension assessment so it mirrors work that the child does at home and at school. Harwayne (2000) provided a list of 10 books that could be recommended to parents as benchmarks for each grade level to assess book sharing experiences at home. These books could be used by parents at the beginning and at the end of the school year, so that they can begin to hear the progress in comprehension, fluency, and decoding skills that their children are making. Parents can also be shown how to use these books by sending home instructions in which you describe the strengths and weaknesses parents can observe as their children read silently and orally.

The specific books recommended by Harwayne (2000) for first graders entering second grade are *Town Mouse and Country Mouse* by Val Biro (2002) and *Morris Goes to School* by B. Wiseman (1983). For second graders entering third grade, she recommends *Nate the Great* by Margerie Weiman Sharmat (2000) and *The Growing Up Feet* by Beverly Cleary (1987). For third graders entering fourth grade, she recommends *Busybody Nora* by Johanna Horwtz (1976) and *Teddy's Scrapbook* by Debra and James Howe (2002).

Another method of assisting parents to build on the instruction that children receive at school is to ask them to complete the Home Comprehension Checklist shown in Comprehension Process Lesson 9. When this information is acquired from parents, you can use it to communicate at school to students about how proud you are of the steps they are taking at home. You can also use the information to plan new instruction to fill any gaps. Last, there is a website that can help parents reinforce the comprehension instruction given at school. This site offers home tutorials that are correlated to state comprehension standards. It also helps parents find books geared to their child's interest level: *www.nclb.gov/parents*.

Summary

All of the assessments discussed in this chapter are graphically depicted on Figure 10.9. This chapter described new comprehension tests. Each test is intended to demonstrate comprehension processes in action. Many are performance based, such as (1) assisted-performance assessments, (2) "What Do We Need to Fill In" tests, (3) "What's the Problem" tests, or (4)

FIGURE 10.9. Summary of Comprehension Process Instruction tests.

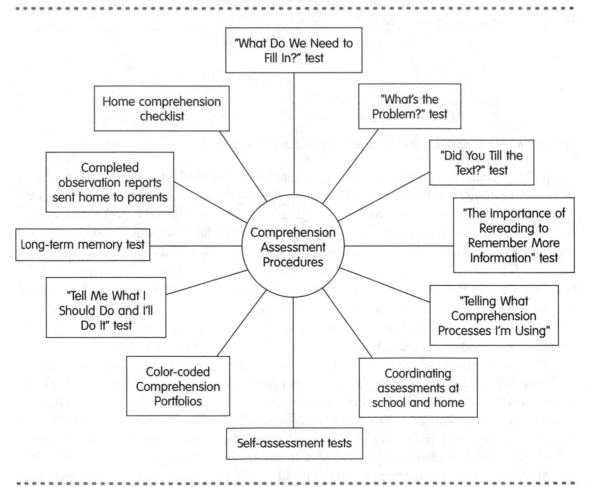

Designed by Rachel R. Escamilla, School of Education, Texas Christian University, Fort Worth, TX, and used by permission.

"Did You Till the Text" tests. Other tests assess students' abilities to reflect on their own comprehension processes, such as (1) "The Importance of Rereading to Remember More Information" test, (2) the "Telling What Comprehension Processes I'm Using" test, (3) the "Tell Me What I Should Do and I'll Do It" test, and (4) the "Long-Term Memory Test." Many involve parents' participation or written forms, folders, and multiple work samples (e.g., self-assessment systems, color-coded comprehension portfolios, report cards or observations, integrating assessments at home and school, and the Home Comprehension Checklist). By using these evaluations, teachers can provide valuable comprehension experiences for students by identifying specific limitations in individual students' past comprehension experiences.

Reflecting on What You Have Learned

1. **Interpreting (Summarizing) the Main Points.** List as many of the assessment tools as you can remember without referring back to the textbook. When you have finished compare your list to the list in question 7. What does your list tell you about your comprehension ability? Why did you not remember some of the assessments covered? This type of assessment is similar to one that you would give to children (Assessment 10, as described in this chapter) about the books that they have read.

2. **Summarizing the Key Points You Have Learned Thus Far in the Book.** Select the type of self-assessment systems that you want to administer once every 3 weeks (or once every 6 weeks based on the age of your students). Make a list of these and describe why you want to use them.

3. **Making Field Applications and Observations.** Select one assessment method that you would like to use to coordinate school and home assessments of comprehension. What will your first step be in using this instrument? How can this information be used to include parents in the development of their children's comprehension on a more frequent basis?

4. **Making Professional Decisions.** In approximately one paragraph, write a concise description of your philosophy for instructing and assessing comprehension. Describe how you would explain the process underlying your assessment decisions to students, parents, and administrators.

5. **Keeping a Professional Assessment Journal.** Summarize the key principles of assessment in this chapter. What do these principles have in common with the principles that were cited relative to instruction in Chapters 1–9?

6. **Making Multicultural Applications.** Select the assessment in this chapter that you most appreciated. Modify it to better meet the needs of students from a minority culture. Specify the adaptation that you recommend, prepare an example, and share it with colleagues. In addition, what advice can you give to teachers at your school (or a future school) concerning the information that you have read in this chapter that could help them improve their comprehension assessment? In your opinion, what is the first step that your school must take to improve its students' comprehension assessment?

7. **Checking Key Terms.** Following is a list of concepts introduced in this chapter. If

you have learned the meaning of a term, place a checkmark in the blank that precedes that term. If you are not sure of a term's definition, increase your retention by reviewing it. If you have learned 10 of these terms on your first reading of this chapter, then you have constructed many meanings that are important for your work.

_____Assisted-performance assessments (p. 170)

_____"What Do We Need to Fill In?" test (p. 171)

_____"What's the Problem?" test (p. 172)

_____"Did You Till the Text?" test (p. 175)

_____"The Importance of Rereading to Remember More Information" test (p. 176)

_____"Telling What Comprehension Processes I'm Using" test (p. 176)

_____Self-assessment tests (p. 178)

_____Color-coded comprehension portfolios (p. 179)

_____"Tell Me What I Should Do and I'll Do It" test (p. 179)

_____Long-Term Memory Assessment (p. 180)

_____Improving Report Cards and Observation Reports Sent Home to Parents (p. 180)

_____Coordinating assessments at school and home (p. 181)

_____Home Comprehension Checklist (p. 184)

8. **Design a Comprehension Process Lesson.** Comprehension Process Lesson 9 demonstrates how students can assume the responsibility of assessing their own comprehension at home and when they select a book. You can use this lesson in your classroom to improve conversations about self-assessment of comprehension. Students' answers to these questions will assist them to become more active in increasing their own abilities to make meaning. Adapt for your class.

Comprehension Process Lesson 9: Self-Assessing Reading at Home and Choosing the Best Book to Read

Name: _____ Grade: _____

Teacher: _____ Date: _____

Home Comprehension Checklist

Readers can evaluate their home study by reading each sentence in the checklist and putting an ✕ on the line under the appropriate column: *Always, Sometimes, Never.*

	Always	Sometimes	Never
1. I have a quiet, private place to read at home.	_____	_____	_____
2. My home reading comprehension place has good light.	_____	_____	_____
3. My study place has a comfortable temperature.	_____	_____	_____
4. There is a desk or table large enough to hold all of the materials in my home study place.	_____	_____	_____
5. There is a comfortable chair to sit in at my home reading comprehension place.	_____	_____	_____
6. I keep all the required work and reference materials that I will need to complete my content assignments in my home study place.	_____	_____	_____
7. There are no distractions of any kind at my home reading comprehension study place.	_____	_____	_____
8. My home reading comprehension place is kept private from my brothers or sisters, who might disturb me.	_____	_____	_____
9. I can use my home reading comprehension place whenever I need or want to.	_____	_____	_____
10. I enjoy studying at my home reading comprehension place.	_____	_____	_____

Teaching the Comprehension Process of Choosing the Best Book to Read

Step 1

Expert readers know that they can read more advanced books on topics about which they have read extensively in the past. Teach students to identify the topic about which they want to read based on what they want this particular reading experience to achieve: learning, relaxing, reviewing, or escaping into another person's world. As students approach a set of books, their reading goals will determine the thickness of the book they choose to examine. For example, if they want to relax, they may choose a shorter book than if they wanted to learn very specific information about a topic.

Step 2

Expert readers read books by authors that they enjoy. Teach students to survey the authors and titles of book that are about the length that they desire. If a favorite author or captivating title attracts their attention, they should examine that book first.

Step 3

Teach students to thumb through the book to determine the density of the text and the amount of effort they will have to exert to enjoy this author's writing. Then have them select a single page near the middle of the book to read to determine whether they know the majority of words. As they read that page, students can count the words that they do not know by pressing down one finger on the opposite page each. If students press down all five fingers before they finish reading a single page, they will know that this book may cause frustration in decoding and interfere with their comprehension and enjoyment. Students should return to Step 1 in this case.

APPENDIX A

Reproducible Forms

Flashcards to Enhance Students' Use of Think-Aloud Strategies

1 — How to select and begin to think about a book	1 — Looking for important information	1 — Connect to author's big ideas
1 — Activate relevant knowledge	1 — Put yourself in the book	2 — Revise prior knowledge and predict
2 — Infer author's intention and depth of writing style	2 — Determine word meanings: Decode, use context, and learn new vocabulary	2 — Think strategically: Question, confirm, and disconfirm
3 — Notice novelties in the structure of the text and converse with author	3 — Summarize, evaluate, reflect, and paraphrase	3 — Use knowledge in the future

Note. 1 = Think-alouds that begin before and as one reads the first few pages; 2 = think-alouds that occur after one has read the first few pages; 3 = think-alouds that occur after a large amount of text has been read.

Light Bulb Think-Aloud Assessment Strategy

Names of reading processes are written in blanks after student demonstrates an effective think-aloud.

Teacher–Reader Group Thinking Chart

Name of the group: _____

Members of the group are: _____

Comprehension process taught: _____

Where and how do you use this process?

1.

2.

3.

4.

5.

6.

What new things have you learned that help you use this comprehension process more easily and better?

1.

2.

3.

4.

5.

6.

Thinking Guide: Questions to Clarify

1. Why?

2. Is the most important point _____ or _____?

3. What do you mean by "_____"?

4. If I understand, you mean _____. Is that right?

5. Where will the point you are making not apply? How does _____ relate to _____?

6. If your idea is accepted, what is the greatest change that will occur?

7. Would you say more about _____?

8. What is the difference between _____ and _____?

9. Would this be an example?

10. Is it possible that _____? What else could we do?

11. If _____ happened, what would be the result?

Story Frame Form

Student's name: _____ Date: _____

Name of book: _____ Author: _____

Setting: (When and where does the story take place?) _____

_____

I know this because the author uses these words: _____

_____

Main characters: (Who are the most important people in the story?) _____

_____

I know they are important because: _____

_____

The problem starts when: _____

_____ or

The main character's goal is: _____

_____

The plot: (What happened?)

Event 1: _____

_____

After that . . .

Event 2: _____

_____

Next . . .

Event 3: _____

_____

Then . . .

Event 4: _____

_____

Turning point: (How I know the plot is reaching a solution) _____

_____

The resolution: (How did it end?) _____

_____

I know this because the author uses these words: _____

Author's moral or purpose (or, purpose for me): _____

_____

I think this is the moral because: _____

_____

Practice Sheet for Main Idea Strand 2 Lesson

Who? _____

Did what? _____

Where? _____

When? _____

Why? _____

Main idea was _____

_____

Strand 2 Main Idea Practice Sheet for Main Idea, Sum Up, and Draw Conclusions Comprehension Processes

1. What is your favorite main idea? Give 2 reasons why.

2. Sum up your favorite part of this book and say why.

3. Sequence three events in the story (tell the beginning, middle, and end).

4. What is the conclusion the author is building toward?

Designed by Rachel R. Escamilla, School of Education, Texas Christian University, Fort Worth, TX, and used here by permission.

Thinking Guide: Drawing Inferences

Name: _____ Date: _____

What is said or read	+ What you know	= What is meant
1.		
2.		
3.		
4.		
5.		

First-Person Narrative

Lunch made me sleepy, so I curled up to take a nap. With sleep came a wonderful dream. I was stretched out on a lovely green lawn with the sun warming my body. Birds were singing gaily overhead, and little yellow daffodils peeked out through the grass. I reached out to touch one—and suddenly there was no sun.

A heavy shadow had shut out the light. Something grabbed me and I cried out, fighting to get free. It was no use; I was traveling through space. This was no dream. It was real. I had been captured, and there was nothing I could do about it.

CLUE #2

Soon I felt something solid at my feet. I could move, but it was hard to stand. My legs felt limber. Where was I?

Cautiously, I stepped forward. OUCH! I bumped into a wall and went in the other direction, but every time there was a wall. Four walls and no door. I'm in a cell!

All of a sudden there was a blast of cold air from above. I looked up but could see nothing. Where was the air coming from? Suddenly I knew. there was no roof on my cell! I had discovered a way out.

CLUE #3

Creeping carefully toward a wall, I attempted to reach the opening. I wasn't big enough, so I curled up and began to think. The cell was still rocking. Maybe I could throw myself against one of the walls and tip the cell over. Again and again I rushed at the wall, but I finally gave up, defeated.

I tried to gather the energy for one more try. If that didn't work —wait, the movement stopped!

A minute later I heard an earthshaking bang as I felt a different motion. My cell was moving up and down, not back and forth. I couldn't keep my balance. I said to myself I'd swat whatever it was. I'd be ready. In an instant there was a horrible crunch, and the wall nearest me was ripped away. Beyond the opening I could see a dazzling light.

CLUE #4

"Now's your chance," I told myself, cautiously crawling to the opening. At first, I saw nothing but a shiny wood floor. Then I saw **them**!

Feet! Giant feet! They seemed about to surround me, so I quickly retreated. I could be ground to smithereens out there! Of course, that's what they were planning—that's why they made it easy for me to escape! Well, I'd fool them; I wouldn't move.

No, I couldn't stay. I had to try to get out.

CLUE #5

Once again I crept to the opening, but the feet were still there. Then I noticed something else. Near two of the feet, four round posts rose from the floor. The posts were topped by a thick, low roof. I could easily crawl under it, but those giant feet couldn't.

I took a deep breath and moved quickly. Racing out of my cell, I pranced rapidly until I was under the thick roof. I made it! My legs felt like rubber again, but I was safe for the moment.

CLUE #6

What would happen next? I wondered. I didn't have long to wait, however, for I heard voices high above the roof.

"Oh, Donald, she's afraid of us!"

"Well, naturally," came the reply. "That must have been a very frightening trip for such a little _____."

[Answer: kitten]

From *Comprehension Process Instruction: Creating Reading Success in Grades K–3* by Cathy Collins Block, Lori L. Rodgers, and Rebecca B. Johnson. Copyright 2004 by The Guilford Press. Permission to photocopy this form is granted to purchasers of this book for personal use only (see copyright page for details).

Recognizing the Patterns That Authors Use in Writing

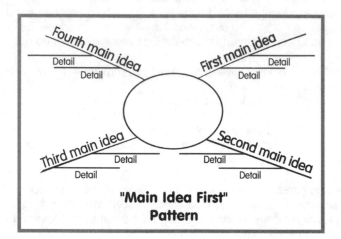

"Main Idea First"
Pattern

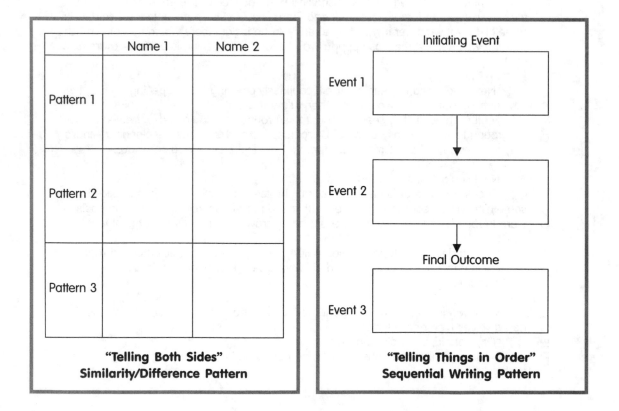

"Telling Both Sides"
Similarity/Difference Pattern

"Telling Things in Order"
Sequential Writing Pattern

Problem-to-Solution Story Pattern

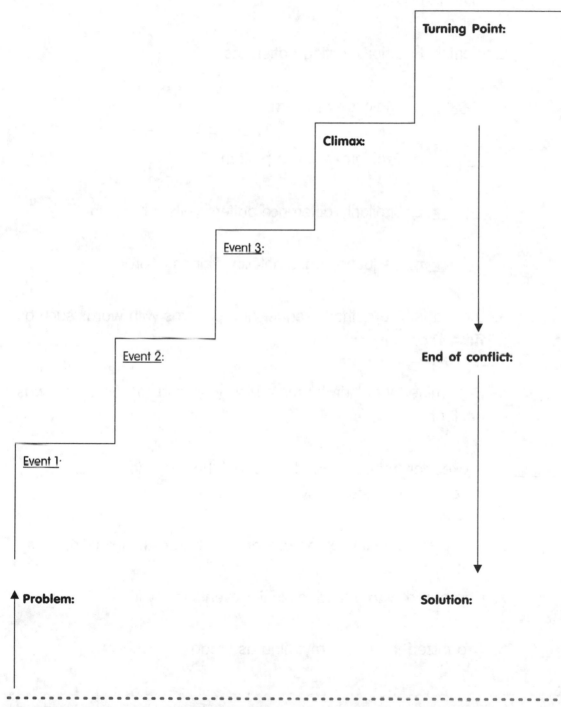

Student Self-Assessment of Metacognitive Processes

_____ 1. Tilled the text.

_____ 2. Identified author's writing pattern as

      _____ a. Main idea pattern;

      _____ b. Problem–solution pattern;

      _____ c. Similarity/difference pattern (telling both sides);

      _____ d. Sequence pattern (telling things in order)

_____ 3. Looked for the author's sequencing patterns with words such as **first**, **then**, or **next**.

_____ 4. Determined whether the main idea was clear or reread if it was unclear.

_____ 5. Looked for frequency of ideas and if the same idea was repeated in different ways.

_____ 6. Noted the direction of the author's or characters' thinking.

_____ 7. Compared what I read to similar events in my life.

_____ 8. Organized the text in my mind as I read.

"What Do We Need to Fill In?" Test

Directions: (1) Put names of group members above each column. (2) Put a tally mark in the appropriate box each time a group member contributes that comprehension process in writing or orally. (3) Make notes on the back when interesting things happen that are not captured by the categories.

Student's name:						Total
1. Contributes ideas from other sources						
2. Describes feelings and makes connections						
3. Paraphrases main ideas						
4. Recalls sequence						
5. Makes inferences						
6. Summarizes						
7. Images						
8. Uses authorial writing pattern						
9. Draws conclusions and summarizes						

"Did You Till the Text?" Test

Name: _____ Grade: _____ Date: _____

Circle the appropriate numbers to describe your most recent silent reading.

	Always do by myself				Can't do
1. Set my purpose for reading	5	4	3	2	1
2. Make predictions	5	4	3	2	1
3. Tilled the text	5	4	3	2	1
4. Summarized every so often	5	4	3	2	1
5. Infer	5	4	3	2	1
6. Raise questions about unknown information	5	4	3	2	1
7. Connected ideas in 2 sentences	5	4	3	2	1
8. Recognize details and main ideas in paragraphs	5	4	3	2	1

The Importance of Rereading to Remember More Information

Use a different colored pen and write every detail you remember from the story after reading it one time.	Use a different colored pen and write every detail you remember from the story after reading it a second time.

- -

Reteaching Skill Development Chart: One-on-One Intervention Strategy to Build on Students' Home Literacy Richness

Name: _____

	Book or magazine and author	Pages read	Parent signature	Parent or student comment
Monday				
Tuesday				
Wednesday				
Thursday				
Friday				
Saturday				
Sunday				

What did I do this week that good readers do? _____

_____

Parents' comment: What my child did better as a reader or writer this week was _____

_____

- -

Self-Assessment:
Directions for Student Self-Responsibility Guides

Self-responsibility guides are used as outlines you can follow to develop new literacy and effective thinking behaviors. You can make self-responsibility guides yourself to improve in many areas. A sample guide appears here. It is a self-responsibility guide to help you learn a new reading process. Complete each blank below.

1. Start simply to achieve initial success.

   I am doing so by _____.

2. Old literacy habits take time to modify or replace with effective comprehension processes.

   I am learning how to replace my old habit of _____
   by doing _____.

   I am replacing this ineffective habit because _____
   _____.

3. Learning to do new comprehension processes takes time; therefore, I will revisit this self-responsibility guide at least once a week.

   I did so on these dates: _____.

Student Self-Responsibility Guide

Name: _____ Date: _____

Homeroom teacher: _____

Reading specialist: _____

Read the following list. Check the statements that apply to you:

_____ Not decoding well

_____ Forgetting what I read

_____ Coming late to school or class

_____ Reading too slowly or too fast to comprehend

_____ Losing my books or forgetting to bring them

_____ Losing my place when I read

_____ Not writing complete sentences

_____ Not using vivid verbs and precise nouns

_____ Rambling when I write or speak

_____ Having limited interest in reading and writing

_____ Not reading or writing very often to solve problems in life or for personal pleasure

_____ Other _____

_____ Other _____

Books (or topics) I'd like to read: _____

_____

Activities I've enjoyed this week: _____

_____

Using My Processes

Name: _____

Directions: Circle the processes you used as you read, then write the page number where you
used it and how it helped you.

_____

_____

_____

_____

_____

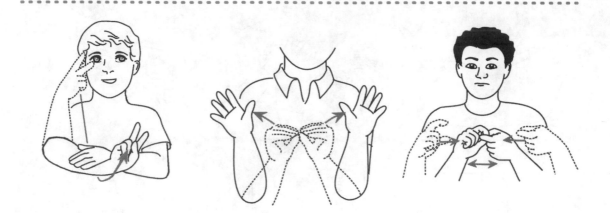

Using My Favorite Processes

Name: _____

Directions: Circle the process you used as you were reading. Describe below which one was the one you did the best or liked the best and why.

_____

_____

_____

_____

_____

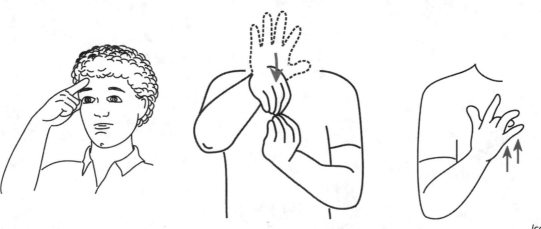

(cont.)

APPENDIX B

*Reproducible Comprehension Process
Motion Posters*

Ask Questions

Do I understand the author?

Why did the author _____?

Cause and Effect

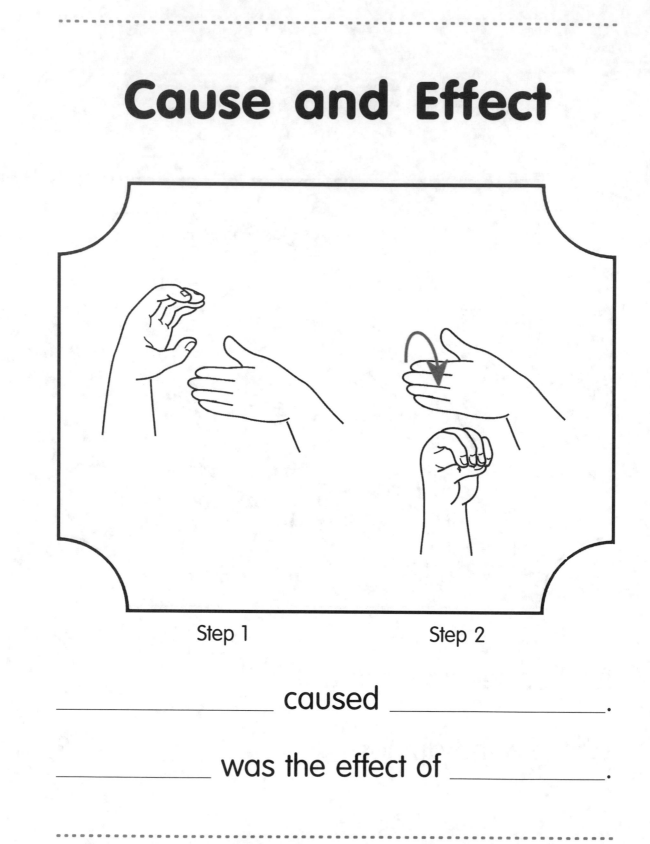

Step 1   Step 2

_____ caused _____.

_____ was the effect of _____.

Clarify

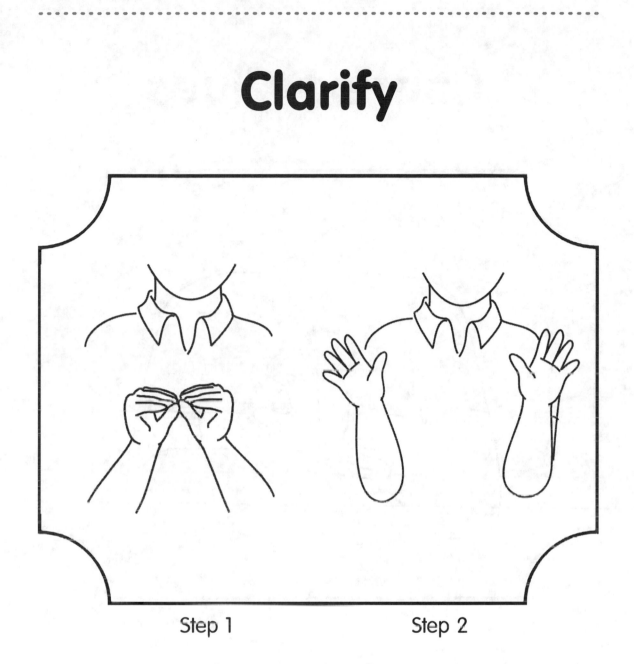

Step 1   Step 2

Why do you say that?

Could you explain that further?

Context Clues

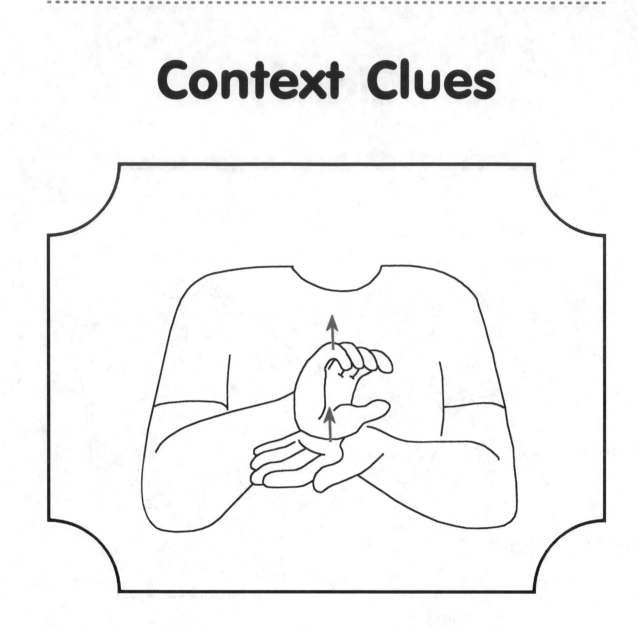

What context clues give the words a
bigger leap forward in meaning?

Draw Conclusions

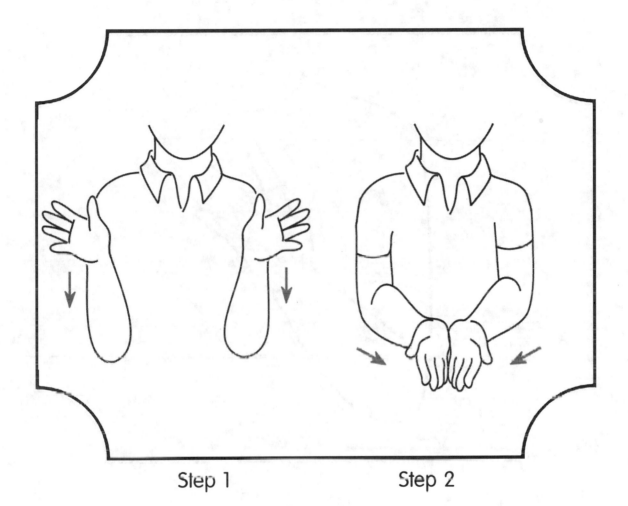

Step 1   Step 2

The author's words tell me _____,
but the idea is _____.

What idea is the author trying to give me?

Feelings

How are the characters feeling?

How does what I'm reading make me feel?

Inference

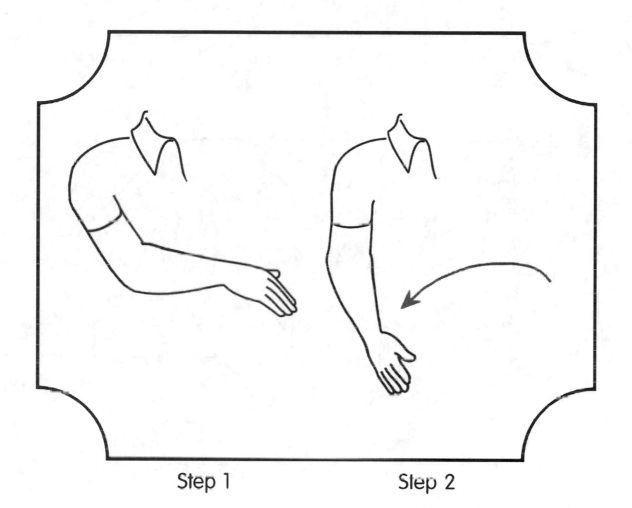

Step 1   Step 2

Take what the author says, add what you know, and you end up with what was meant.

Main Idea

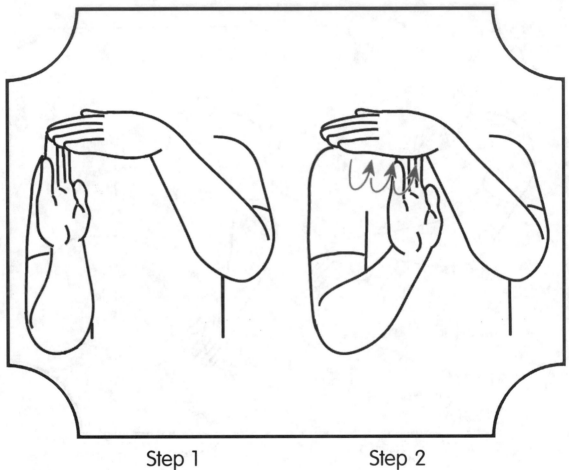

Step 1   Step 2

How did you decide on the main idea?

What details supported the main idea?

Make Connections

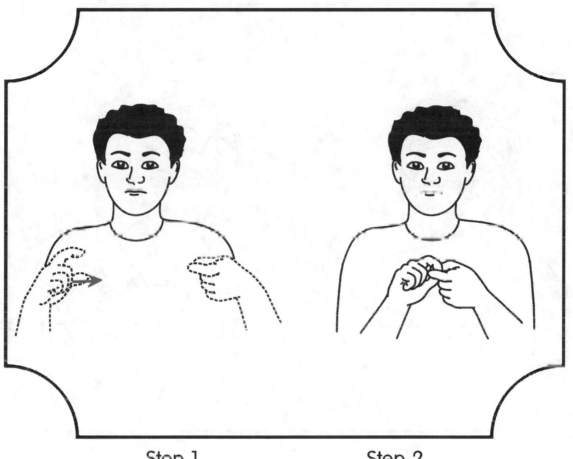

Step 1   Step 2

What does this remind me of?

Perspective

Step 1   Step 2

My eyes are seeing through someone else's eyes because I pretend I am that person.

Did this change your understanding of the character? of the story?

Prediction

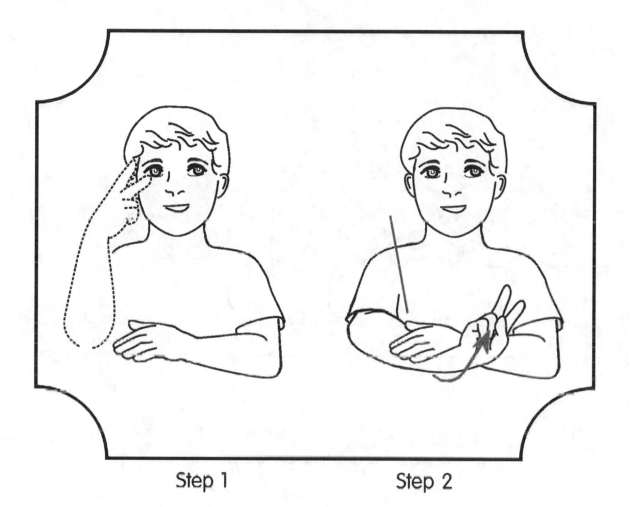

Step 1   Step 2

Which picture helped me predict?

What did I already know that helped me predict?

Reasons and Evidence

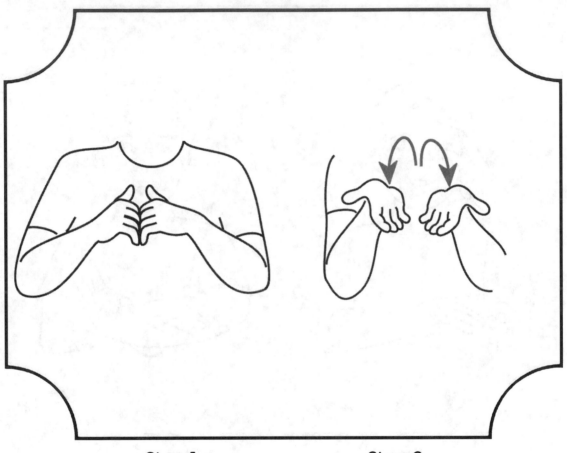

Step 1   Step 2

How do you know?

Could you explain your reasons to us?

Reread

The author's meaning is not clear. I need to reread.

I need to reread this critical section.

Sum Up

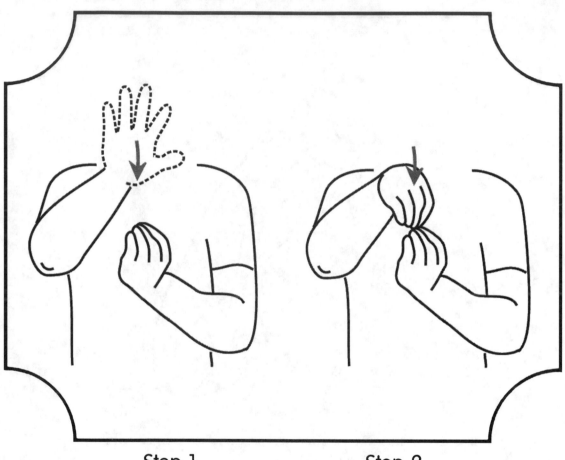

Step 1   Step 2

What is this selection about?

Can I find out more if I look back?

Visualize

What image does this text create in my mind?

List of Children's Books

Aaseng, N. (1980). *Winners never quit*. New York: Lerner.

Adler, D. (2000). *Cam Jansen*. New York: Viking.

Aesop. (1999). *The hare and the tortoise*. Minneapolis: Millbrook.

Aiki. (1999). *Fossils*. New York: BT Bound.

Arnold, P. (2002). *Goodbye*. New York: Scholastic.

Birdwell, N. (1985). *Clifford*. New York: Scholastic

Biro, V. (2002). *Town mouse and country mouse*. In M. Winter (Ed.), *The Aesop for children*. New York: Barnes and Noble Books.

Brett, J. (2003). *Town mouse and country mouse*. New York: HarperTrophy

Brown, M. (2000). *Arthur*. New York: Random House.

Bunting, E. (1989). *Wednesday surprise*. Boston: Scott Foresman.

Cleary, B. (1987). *The growing up feet*. New York: William Morrow.

Cole, B. (1997). *Princess Smarty Pants*. New York: Puffin.

Cole, J. (1990). *The magic school bus: Inside the human body*. New York: Scholastic.

Demi. (1990). *Empty pot*. New York: Holt.

Farrell, L. (2002). *The true story of the tree little pigs*. New York: Anvil Books.

Florian, D. (1998). *Insectlopedia*. New York: Harcourt.

Florian, D. (1999). *Laugh-eteria*. San Diego, CA: Harcourt Brace.

Fox, P. (1984). *One-eyed cat*. Scarsdale, NY: Bradbury Press.

Frasier, D. (2000). *Miss Alaineus: A vocabulary disaster*. San Diego, CA: Harcourt.

Gaines, E. (1982). *The autobiography of Miss Jane Pittman*. New York: Bantam.

Greenfield, E. (1978). *Honey I love*. New York: HarperCollins.

Greene, C. *Martin Luther King, Jr.: A man who changed things*. Chicago: Children's Press.

Grimm, J. (1997). *Rapunzel*. New York: Dutton Books.

Ginsburg, M. (1988). *The chick and the duckling*. New York: Aladdin Library.

Goble, P. (1997). *Dream wolf*. New York: Aladdin Library.

Granowski, A. (1995). *Dinosaur fossils*. Austin, TX: Raintree/Steck-Vaughn.

Grant, J. (1994). *I hate school*. Boston: Modern Learning Press.

Hilton, S. E. (1997). *The outsiders*. Boston: Prentice Hall.

Hoffman, M. (1991). *Amazing Grace*. Boston: Scott Foresman.

Horwtz, J. (1976). *Busybody Nora*. New York: HarperTrophy.

Howe, D. & Howe, J. *Teddy's scrapbook*. New York: Scholastic.

Kasahara, K. (2003). *Creative origami*. New York: Oxford University Press.

Kimmel, E. A. (1993). *Anansi goes fishing*. New York: Holiday House.

Lauber, P. (1995). *Volcano*. New York: Houghton Mifflin.

Mak, K. (2002). *My Chinatown: One year in poems*. New York: HarperCollins Juvenile Books.

Mayer, M. (2000). *Just a mess*. New York: Golden Books.

Miles, M. (1985). *Annie and the old one*. Boston: Little Brown.

Milne, A. A. (1998). *Pooh goes visiting*. San Diego, CA: Trafalgar Square.

Monjo, F. N. (1993). *The drinking gourd*. New York: HarperTrophy.

Munson, D. (2000). *Enemy pie*. San Francisco: Chronicle Books.

Muth, J. (2002). *The three questions: Based on a true story by Leo Tolstoy*. New York: Scholastic.

Numeroff, L. (1991). *If you give a moose a muffin*. New York: HarperCollins.

Parish, P. (1995). *Amelia Bedelia*. New York: HarperCollins Juvenile Books

Pattou, E. (2001). *Mrs. Spitzer's garden*. San Diego, CA: Harcourt.

Pinkney, J. (2000). *Aesops fables*. New York: SeaStar Books.

Robinson, V. (2002). *Our eyes*. Chicago: McGraw-Hill/Wright Group.

Ross, T. (1992). *The boy who cried wolf*. New York: Puffin.

Rucki, A. (1992). *Turkey's gift to the people*. Toronto: Northland Publishers.

Scieszka, J. (1993). *The three little pigs*. New York: Viking Press.

Scieszka, J., & Smith, L. (2001). *Baloney*. New York: Viking Children's Books.

Scieszka, J. (2002). *The stinky cheese man*. New York: Viking Childrens Books.

Sharmat, M. W. (2000). *Nate the great*. New York: Sagebrush Education Resource.

Shreve, A. (2002). *Sea glass*. Boston: Little Brown.

Silverman, E. (1999). *Don't fidget a feather*. New York: Simon & Schuster.

van Allsburg, C. (1988). *Two bad ants*. New York: Houghton Mifflin.

Viorst, J. (1998). *Alexander—The terrible, horrible, no good, very bad day*. New York: Simon & Schuster.

Wiesner, D. (1997). *Tuesday*. Chicago: Scott Foresman.

Wiseman, B. (1983). *Morris goes to school*. New York: HarperTrophy.

References

Adams, M. (1990). *Beginning to read.* Cambridge, MA: Harvard University Press.

Afflerbach, P. (2002). Teaching reading self-assessment strategies. In C. C. Block & M. Pressley (Eds.), *Comprehension instruction: Research-based best practices* (pp. 96–111). New York: Guilford Press.

Alexander, P. A., & Jetton, T. L. (2000). Learning from text: A multidimensional and developmental perspective. In M. L. Kamil, P. B. Mosenthal, P. D. Pearson, & R. Barr (Eds.), *Handbook of reading research* (Vol. 3, pp. 285–310). Mahwah, NJ: Erlbaum.

Allington, R. L. (1996, December). *What we need instructionally.* Presidential address at the annual meeting of the National Reading Conference, Charleston, SC.

Allington, R. L. (2001) *What really matters for struggling readers: Designing research-based interventions.* New York: Longman.

Alverman, D., & Mosie, R. (1991, December). *Sociological perspectives on literacy in content areas.* Paper presented at the annual meeting of the National Reading Conference. Austin, TX.

Ambruster, B. B. (1991). Silent reading, oral reading, and learning from text. *The Reading Teacher, 45,* 154–155.

American Library Association. (1996). *Annual national survey of U.S. public and school librarians, 1996.* Washington, DC: Author.

American Medical Association. (1996). *Principles of professional practice in psychological analyses.* Washington, DC: Author.

Ames. W. (1992). Children's motivation. *Review of Research in Education, 23,* 156–174.

Applebee, A. N., & Langer, J. A. (1983). Instructional scaffolding: Reading and writing as natural language activities, *Language Arts, 60,* 168–175.

Ashton-Warner, S. (1966). *The teacher.* New York: Macmillan.

Au, K. (1993). *Literacy instruction in multicultural settings.* Fort Worth, TX: Harcourt.

Baker, L. (1984). Children's effective use of multiple standards for evaluating their comprehension. *Journal of Educational Psychology, 76,* 588–597.

Baker, L. (2002). Metacognition in comprehension instruction. In C. C. Block & M. Pressley (Eds.), *Comprehension instruction: Research-based best practices* (pp. 77–95). New York: Guilford Press.

Baker, L., & Anderson, R. I. (1982). Effects of inconsistent information on text processing: Evidence for comprehension monitoring. *Reading Research Quarterly, 27,* 281–294.

Baker, L., & Zimlin, L. (1989). Instructional effects on children's use of two levels of standards for evaluating their comprehension. *Journal of Educational Psychology, 81,* 340–346.

Bakhtin, M. M. (1993). *Toward a philosophy of the act* (V. Liapunov & M. Holquist, Eds.; V. Liapunov, Trans.). Austin, TX: University of Texas Press.

Bales, R., & Gambrell, L. (1985). *Visual imagery and the comprehension monitoring performance of fourth and fifth grade poor readers*. Unpublished paper, University of Maryland, Baltimore, MD.

Bandura, A. (1986, April). *Achievement goal orientations: Research for choice must have challenge*. Paper presented at the annual meeting of the American Educational Research Association. San Francisco, CA.

Barrows, H. S. (1985). *How to design a problem-based curriculum for the preclinical years*. New York: Springer.

Baumann, J. F., Jones, L. A., & Seifert-Kessell, N. (1993). Using think alouds to enhance children's comprehension monitoring abilities. *The Reading Teacher, 54*(5), 235–241.

Beal, C. R. (1996). The role of comprehension monitoring in children's revision. *Educational Psychology Review, 8*, 219–238.

Beck, I. L., & Dole, J. (1992). Comprehension schema in science and social studies content areas. In C. C. Block & J. Mangieri (Eds.), *Teaching thinking: An agenda for the 21st century* (p. 466). Hillsdale, NJ: Erlbaum.

Beck, I. L., McKeown, M. G., Hamilton, R. L., & Kucan, L. (1997). *Questioning the author: An approach for enhancing student engagement with text*. Newark, DE: International Reading Association.

Bereiter, C., & Bird, M. (1985). Use of thinking aloud in identification and teaching of reading comprehension strategies. *Cognition and Instruction, 2*, 131–156.

Beyer, B. (1986). *Overcoming blocks to creativity*. New York: Wiley/Jossey-Bass.

Blachowicz, C., & Fisher, C. (2002). *Teaching vocabulary*. Boston: Allyn & Bacon.

Blair-Larson, L. S., & Williams, K. (1999). *The balanced reading program*. Newark, DE: International Reading Association.

Block, C. C. (1992). Improving reading and thinking: From teaching or not teaching skills to interactive interventions. In M. Pressley, K. Harris, & I. Guthrie (Eds.), *Promoting academic competence and literacy in schools* (pp. 149–167). San Diego: Academic Press.

Block, C. C. (1993). Strategy instruction in a literature-based reading program. *Elementary School Journal, 33*, 123–147.

Block, C. C. (1996, April). *Increasing students self-initiated comprehension*. Paper presented at the annual conference of the American Educational Research Association, San Francisco.

Block, C. C. (1997a). *Literacy difficulties: Diagnosis and instruction*. Fort Worth, TX: Harcourt Brace.

Block, C. C. (1997b). *Teaching the language arts* (2nd ed.). Boston: Allyn & Bacon.

Block, C. C. (1998, November 19). *New millennium reading*. Presentation to the Nobel Learning Communities' Biannual Board Meeting. Philadelphia, PA.

Block, C. C. (1999). The case for exemplary teaching especially for students who begin first grade without the precursors for literacy success. *National Reading Conference Yearbook, 49*, 71–85.

Block, C. C. (2000a). The case for exemplary instruction especially for students who came to school without the precursors for literacy success. *National Reading Conference Yearbook, 50*, 155–167.

Block, C. C. (2000b). Reading instruction in the new millennium. In A. Costa (Ed.), *Developing minds* (3rd ed., pp 472–490). Alexandria, VA: Association for Curriculum and Instruction.

Block, C. C. (2000c). *How can we teach all students to comprehend well?: Research paper No. 4*. New York: Scholastic, Inc.

Block, C. C. (2001a). *Teaching the language arts: Expanding thinking through student-centered instruction* (3rd ed.). Boston: Allyn & Bacon.

Block, C. C. (2001b). A spotlight on exemplary practices that significantly increase students' literacy even when they enter first grade without the precursors for literacy success. In T. Shananan (Ed.), *National Reading Conference yearbook* (pp. 43–55). Chicago: National Reading Conference.

Block, C. C. (2001c, May). *Reading to learn: Comprehending non-fiction.* Paper presented at the annual meeting of the International Reading Association, New Orleans, LA.

Block, C. C. (2001d, May). *Effects of teacher change on student achievement.* Paper presented at the annual meeting of the International Reading Association. New Orleans, LA.

Block, C. C. (2002a). *Literacy difficulties: Diagnosis and instruction for reading specialists and classroom teachers* (2nd ed.). Boston: Allyn & Bacon.

Block, C. C. (2002b, October). *Effects of books on tape on students' comprehension abilities.* Paper presented at the 30th Plains Regional Conference of the International Reading Association, Topeka, KS.

Block, C. C. (2003). *Teaching comprehension: The comprehension process approach.* Boston: Allyn & Bacon.

Block, C. C. (2004). What are metacognitive assessments? In S. Israel, C. C. Block, K. Bauerman, & T. Kaucer (Eds.), *Metacognitive literacy research theory and teacher education* (pp. 79–92). Mahwah, NJ: Erlbaum.

Block, C. C., & Beardon, P. (1997, April). *Student initiative in literacy instruction.* Paper presented at the annual meeting of the American Educational Research Association, San Francisco, CA.

Block, C. C., & Cavanagh, C. (1998). Teaching thinking: How can we and why should we?" In R. Bernhardt, C. N. Hedley, G. Cattaro, & V. Svolopooulous (Eds.), *Curriculum leadership: Rethinking schools for the 21st century* (pp. 301–320). Boston: Allyn & Bacon.

Block, C. C., & Dellamura, R. (2000/2001). Better book buddies. *The Reading Teacher, 61,* 79–91.

Block, C. C., Gambrell, L., & Pressley, M. (Eds.). (2002). *Rethinking comprehension.* San Francisco: Jossey-Bass.

Block, C. C., & Israel, S. (2004). *The ABC's of teaching think-alouds.* Manuscript submitted for publication.

Block, C. C., & Johnson, R. (2002). The thinking process approach to comprehension development: Preparing students for their future comprehension challenges. In C. C. Block, L. B. Gambrell, & M. Pressley (Eds.), *Improving comprehension instruction: Rethinking research, theory, and classroom practice* (pp. 54–80). San Francisco: Jossey-Bass.

Block, C. C., & Mangieri, J. N. (1996a–c). *Reason to read: Thinking strategies for life through literature* (Vols. 1, 2, & 3). Palo Alto, CA: Addison-Wesley.

Block, C. C., & Mangieri, J. N. (2003). *Exemplary literacy teachers.* New York: Guilford Press.

Block, C. C., & Mangieri, J. N. (2004). *Power thinking for leaders.* San Francisco, CA: Jossey-Bass.

Block, C. C., Oaker, M., & Hurt, N. (2002). Exemplary literacy teachers: A continuum from preschool through grade 5. *Reading Research Quarterly, 33,* 115–134.

Block, C. C., & Pressley, M. (Eds.). (2002). *Comprehension instruction: Research-based best practices.* New York: Guilford Press.

Block, C. C., & Reed, K. (2003). *Effects of trade books, basal workbooks, and sustained silent reading on students' literacy achievement.* Charlotte, NC: Institute for Literacy Enhancement.

Block, C. C., & Rodgers, L. (2004). *Effects of comprehension process motions on the reading achievement of kindergarten through grade 5 students.* Charlotte, NC: Institute for Literacy Enhancement.

Block, C. C., & Rodgers, L. (in press). Developing K–3 students' comprehension abilities: Using comprehension motions. *The Reading Teacher.*

Block, C. C., Schaller, J., Joy, J., & Gaines, P. (2002). Teaching students to think about comprehension as a process and more than strategies. In C. C. Block & M. Pressley (Eds.), *Comprehension instruction: Research-based best practices* (pp. 33–56). New York: Guilford Press.

Block, C. C., & Stanley, C. (2004). *To inference, image, or summarize.* Manuscript in preparation.

Bloome, D. (1986). Building literacy and the classroom community. *Theory into Practice, 15* 71–76.

Borkowski, J. G., Carr, M., Rellinger, E., & Pressley, M. (1990). Self-regulated cognition: Interdependence of metacognition, attributions, and self-esteem. In B. F. Jones & L. Idol (Eds.), *Dimensions of thinking and cognitive instruction* (pp. 53–92). Hillsdale, NJ: Erlbaum.

Bransford, J. D., & Schwartz, D. L. (1998). *Rethinking transfer: A simple proposal with multiple implications* (Research Paper 13). Nashville, TN: Vanderbilt University Press.

Britton, B. K., & Graesser, A. C. (1996). *Models of understanding text*. Mahwah, NJ: Erlbaum.

Broudy, H. S. (1989). Types of knowledge and purposes of education. In R. C. Anderson, R. J. Spiro, & W. E. Montague (Eds.), *Schooling and the acquisition of knowledge* (pp. 1–17). Hillsdale, NJ: Erlbaum.

Brown, A. L. (1978). Knowing when, where, and how to remember: A problem of metacognition. In R. Glaser (Ed.), *Advances in instructional psychology* (pp. 279–284). Hillsdale, NJ: Erlbaum.

Brown, A. L., & Campione, J. C. (1998). Designing a community of young learners: Theoretical and practical lessons. In N. M. Lambert & B. L. McCombs (Eds.), *How students learn: Reforming schools through learner-centered education* (pp. 153–186). Washington, DC: American Psychological Association.

Brown, R. (2002). Straddling two worlds: Self-directed comprehension instruction for middle schoolers. In C. C. Block & M. Pressley (Eds.), *Comprehension instruction: Research-based best practices* (pp. 419–432). New York: Guilford Press.

Bruner, J. (1978). *Scaffold instruction*. Cambridge, MA: MIT Press.

Bruner, J. (1985). The model of a learner. *Educational Researcher, 14*(6), 5–8.

Cain-Thoreson, C., Lippman, M. Z., & McClendon-Magnuson, D. (1997). Windows on comprehension: Reading comprehension processes as revealed by two think-aloud procedures. *Journal of Educational Psychology, 89*(4), 579–590.

Caine, R. N., & Caine, G. (1997). *Education on the edge of possibility*. Alexandria, VA: Association for Supervision and Curriculum and Development.

Calkins, L. (1997). *Whole language classrooms* (2nd ed.). Portsmouth, NH: Heinemann.

Cameron, J., & Pierce, W. D. (1994). Reinforcement, reward, and intrinsic motivation: A meta-analysis. *Review of Educational Research, 64*, 363–423.

Carnegie Foundation. (1995). *Understanding: New developments*. New York: Author.

Carnegie Foundation. (2000). *What Is the New Generation "Y"?* (Research Report 31). New York: Author.

Carr, K. (1998, May). *Instructional implications for inferencing and interpreting*. Paper presented at the annual meeting of the International Reading Association, New Orleans, LA.

Carver, R. (1994, December). *Can all of the variance in word identification be explained by cipher knowledge?* Paper presented at the annual meeting of the National Reading Conference, Austin, TX.

Carver, R. (1995, December). *Can all of the variance in word identification be explained by cipher knowledge and lexical knowledge?* Handout presented at the National Reading Conference, Austin, TX.

Cazden, C. (1991). *Balancing whole language*. Portsmouth, NH: Heinemann.

Chall, J. (1998). *Teaching children to read*. Cambridge, MA: Brookline.

Chambliss, M. (1993, December). *Science textual awareness*. Paper presented at the annual meeting of the National Reading Conference, Miami, FL.

Chi, M. T. H., Slotta, J. D., & deLeeuw, N. (1994). From things to processes: A theory of conceptual change for learning science concepts. *Learning and Instruction, 4*, 27–43.

Children's Defense Fund. (1992). *Impact of literacy achievement on future earning potential* (Report 122). New York: Author.

Chipman, S., & Segal, E. (1985, April). *Literacy achievement: Effects of decoding and comprehension instruction for at-risk students*. Paper presented at the annual meeting of the American Educational Research Association, New York, NY.

Clark, H. H., Desheler, D., Shoemaker, M., Alley, R., & Warner, T. (1984). Understanding what is meant from what is said: A study of conversationally conveyed requests. *Journal of Verbal Learning and Verbal Behavior, 14*, 56–72.

Clay, M. (1979). *Observation survey*. Portsmouth, NH: Heinemann.

Collins, C. (1991). Reading instruction that increases thinking abilities. *Journal of Reading, 34*, 510–516.

Cornoldi, C., & Oakhill, J. (1998). Constructive processes and pronoun resolution in skilled and less-skilled comprehenders: Effects of memory load and inferential complexity. *Language and Speech, 29*, 25–37.

Council of Exceptional Children. (1997). *Reading instruction through infusion in regular classrooms* (Research and Policy Report 56). Washington, DC: Author.

Cullinan, B. (1999). Imagery is of the essence. *Instruction/UMI*. Retrieved July 23, 2003, from *http://www.texshare.edu*.

Culp, M. (1985, April). *Comprehension research: Review of research*. Paper presented at the annual meeting of the American Educational Research Association, Washington, DC.

Daniels, H. A. (1990). Developing a sense of audience. In T. Shanahan (Ed.) *Reading and writing together: New perspectives for the classroom* (pp. 99–125). Norwood, MA: Christopher–Gordon.

Dark, L., & Gilmore, J. (1999, April). *Assessment of comprehension in this Internet society*. Paper presented at the annual meeting of the American Educational Research Association, New Orleans, LA.

Delisle, R. (1997, March). *How to use problem-based learning in the classroom*. Paper presented at the annual meeting of the Association for Supervision and Curriculum Development, Alexandria, VA.

Diamond, B. (1999). Students' role. *Educational Leadership, 79*, 381–394.

Duke, N. K. (2000). 3.6 minutes per day: The scarcity of informational texts in first grade. *Reading Research Quarterly, 35*(2), 202–224.

Duke, N. K., & Kays, J. (1998). "Can I say 'once upon a time'?" Kindergarten children developing knowledge of information book language. *Early Childhood Research Quarterly, 13*, 295–318.

Durkin, D. (1978). What classroom observations reveal about reading comprehension. *Reading Research Quarterly, 14*(4), 481–533.

Durkin, D. (1981). Reading comprehension instruction in five basal reading series. *Reading Research Quarterly, 16*, 515–544.

Dyson, A. H. (2001). Transforming transfer: Unruly children, contrary texts, and the persistence of the pedagogical order. In A. Iran-Nejad & P. D. Pearson (Eds.), *Review of Research in Education, 24*, 23–49.

Edwards, M. (1999). The aim is metacognition: For teachers as well as students. In J. Hancock (Ed.), *The explicit teaching of reading* (pp. 80–96). Newark, DE: International Reading Association.

Elbaum, S., Vaughn, S., & Hughes, M., & Moody, S. W. (1999). Grouping practices and reading outcomes for students with disabilities. *Exceptional Children, 65*(3), 391–420.

Elster, J. (2000, December). *Inferencing for at-risk adolescents*. Paper presented at annual meeting of the National Reading Conference, Miami, FL.

Euler, R., & Hellekson, B. (1993, April). *Imagery training and effect on retention*. Paper presented at the annual meeting of the American Educational Research Association, San Francisco, CA.

Fisher, J. B., Schumaker, J. B., & Deshler, D. D. (2002). Improving the reading comprehension of at-risk adolescents. In C. C. Block & M. Pressley (Eds.), *Comprehension instruction: Research-based best practices* (pp. 431–447). New York: Guilford Press.

Fisher, D., & Trabasso, T. (2001). Teaching readers how to comprehend text strategically. In C. C. Block & M. Pressley (Eds.), *Comprehension instruction: Research-based practices* (pp. 156–177). New York: Guilford Press.

Fitzgerald, J., & Spiegel, D. (1983). Teaching main ideas and the effect on student achievement. *National Reading Conference Yearbook, 14,* 116–129.

Flavell, J. C. (1976). Metacognitive aspects of problem solving. In L. B. Resnick (Ed.), *The nature of intelligence* (pp, 94–106). Hillsdale, NJ: Erlbaum.

Fleckenstein, F. (1991, April). *Inferencing and impact on comprehension.* Paper presented at the annual meeting of the American Educational Research Association, Toronto, Canada.

Frederiksen, C. H. (1981). Structure and process in discourse production and comprehension. In M. A. Just & P. Carpenter (Eds.), *Cognitive processes in comprehension* (pp. 719–740). Hillsdale, NJ: Erlbaum.

Freire, P. (1999). *Pedagogy of the heart.* New York: Continuum.

Galda, L. (1998). Mirrors and windows: Reading as transformation. In T. Raphael & K. Au (Eds.), *Literature-based instruction: Reshaping the curriculum* (pp. 156–169). Norwood, MA: Christopher–Gordon.

Gambrell, L., & Koskinen, P. (2001). Imagery: A strategy for enhancing comprehension. In M. Pressley & C. C. Block (Eds.), *Teaching comprehension* (pp. 397–419). New York: Guilford Press.

Garcia, K. (2002, December). *ELL needs for literacy lessons: Language variance increases as grade levels advance.* Paper presented at the annual meeting of the Greater Association of National Reading Conferences, Miami, FL.

Gaskins, R. W., Gaskins, J. C., & Gaskins, I. W. (1991). A decoding program for poor readers—and the rest of the class, too! *Language Arts, 68,* 213–225.

Glaubman, R., Glaubman, H., & Ofir, L. (1997). Effects of self-directed learning, story comprehension, and self-questioning in Kindergarten. *Journal of Educational Research, 90,* 361–372.

Graham, M., & Block, C. C. (1994). Elementary students as co-teachers and co-researchers. *Greater Washington Journal of Literacy, 12,* 34–48.

Guthrie, J. T., Cox, K. E., Knowles, K. T., Buehl, M., Mazzoni, S. A., & Fasulo, L. (2000). Building toward coherent instruction. In L. Baker, M. J. Dreher, & J. T. Guthrie (Eds.), *Engaging young readers: Promoting achievement and motivation* (pp. 209–236). New York: Guilford Press.

Hacker, D. J. (1998). Self-regulated comprehension during normal reading. In D. J. Hacker, J. Dunlosky, & A. C. Graesser (Eds.), *Metacognition in educational theory and practice* (pp. 165–191). Mahwah, NJ: Erlbaum.

Haenggi, D., Kintsch, W., & Gernsbacher, M. (1995). Spatial situation models and text comprehension. In J. R. Anderson (Ed.), *The architective of cognition* (pp. 293–321). Cambridge, MA: Harvard University Press.

Hansen, J. (1980, May). *When writers read for comprehension development.* Paper presented at the annual meeting of the International Reading Association, New Orleans, LA.

Hansen, J., & Pearson, P. D. (1983). An instructional study: Improving the inferential comprehension of good and poor fourth-grade readers. *Journal of Educational Psychology, 75,* 821–829.

Hapgood, J., Palincsar, A., & Magnusson, J. (2000). The role of dialogue in providing scaffolded instruction. *Educational Psychologist, 21,* 211–225, 229.

Hiebert, E. (1999). *Creating communities of teachers and learners across school districts.* San Diego, CA: International Reading Association.

Holmes, A. (1987, April). *Predictive thinking and its development.* Paper presented at the annual meeting of the American Educational Research Association, San Francisco, CA.

Horne, J. (2000, December). *Reading instruction: From the past to the future.* Paper presented at the annual meeting of the National Reading Conference, Scottsdale, AZ.

Hunt, M. A., & Vipond, R. (1985). *A multimedia approach to children's literature.* Chicago: American Library Association.

Invenez, M., Mendon, B., & Juel, C. (1999, December). *Building students' vocabulary through book buddies.* Paper presented at the annual meeting of the National Reading Conference, San Diego, CA.

James, W. (1890). *Elementary reading instruction.* New York: World.

Johnson, D., & Johnson, R. (1986). *The achieving student in the heterogeneous learning groups.* Paper developed for a workshop at the University of Minnesota, Minneapolis.

Johnston, J., Invernizzi, M., & Juel, C. (1998). *Book buddies.* New York: Guilford Press.

Keene, E. O., & Zimmerman, S. (1997). *Mosaic of thought: Teaching comprehension in a reader's workshop.* Portsmouth, NH: Heinemann.

King, A. (1994). Guiding knowledge construction in the classroom: Effects of teaching children how to question and how to explain. *American Educational Research Journal, 31*(2), 338–368.

Kintsch, W. (1991). A theory of discourse comprehension: Implications for a tutor for word algebra problems. In M. Pope, R. J. Simmons, J. I. Poso, & M. Caretero (Eds.), *Proceedings of the 1989 EARLI conference* (pp. 235–253). London: Pergamon Press.

Kintsch, W. (1993). Information accretion and reduction in text processing: Inferences. *Discourse Processes, 16*, 193–202.

Kintsch, W. (1994). Learning from text. *American Psychologist, 49*, 294–303.

Kintsch, W. (1998). *Comprehension: A paradigm for cognition.* New York: Cambridge University Press.

Kintsch, W. (1999, April). *Comprehension transfer model.* Paper presented at the annual meeting of the American Educational Research Association, New Orleans, LA.

Kintsch, W. (2000, April). *Coherence memory: Theoretical perspectives.* Paper presented at the annual meeting of the American Educational Research Association, San Francisco, CA.

Kintsch, W. (2001, April). *Nodes of memory.* Paper presented at the annual meeting of the American Educational Research Association, St. Louis, MO.

Kintsch, W., & Otero, O. (1992, April). *Inference: A model for understanding.* Paper presented at the annual meeting of the American Educational Research Association, Washington, DC.

Kintsch, W., & van Dijk, T. A. (1978). Towards a model of text comprehension and production. *Psychological Review, 85*, 363–394.

Kletzien, L. (1991). Strategy used by good and poor comprehenders. *Reading Research Quarterly, 26*(1), 70–94.

Koslyn, A., Brunn, B., Cave, T., & Wallach, S. (1984, May). *Metacognitive thinking and its effect on literal comprehension abilities.* Paper presented at the annual meeting of the International Reading Association, New Orleans, LA.

Krashen, S. (1993). *The power of reading.* Englewood, CO: Libraries Unlimited.

Kucan, L., & Beck, I. L. (1996). Four fourth graders thinking aloud: An investigation of genre effects. *Journal of Literacy Research, 28*, 259–287.

Langer, J. (1991). *Levels and types of scaffolding* (Research Report 43). Albany, NY: National Center for Language and Literature Achievement.

Langer, J. (1999). Reading comprehension. *Research in the Teaching of English, 14*, 55–88.

Lanham, G. P. (1993). *Hypertext: The convergence of contemporary critical theory and technology.* Baltimore, MD: Johns Hopkins University Press.

Lauber, P. (1986). *Volcano: The eruption and healing of Mount St. Helens.* New York: Macmillan.

Learning First Alliance. (1998). *Every child reading: An action plan of the Learning First Alliance.* Washington, DC: Author.

Lee, A. Y. (2001). Transfer as a measure of intellectual functioning. In S. Soraci & W. J. McIlvane (Eds.), *Perspective on fundamental processes in intellectual functioning: A survey of research approaches* (Vol. 1, pp. 351–366). Stamford, CT: Ablex.

Lehr, S., & Thompson, D. (2000). Comprehension: Semantic maps revisited. *The Reading Teacher, 53*(6), 480–487.

Leslie, L., & Allen, L. (1999). Factors that predict success in an early literacy intervention project. *Reading Research Quarterly, 34*(4), 404–424.

Leslie, L., & Caldwell, J. (2001). *Qualitative reading inventory.* Boston: Allyn & Bacon.

Levin, J. R. (1980, April). *Mnemonics and key word methodology.* Paper presented at the annual meeting of the American Educational Research Association, Chicago, IL.

Levin, J. R. (1991). A comparison of semantic and mnemonic-based vocabulary learning strategies. *Reading Psychology, 5,* 1–16.

Levin, J. R., Barry, I. K., Miller, G., & Bartel, R. (1982, April). *Metacognition and key word method.* Paper presented at the annual meeting of the American Educational Research Association, St. Louis, MO.

Levin, J. R., Johnson, D. D., Pittelman, S. D., Levin, K. M., Shriberg, L. K., Toms-Bronowski, S., & Hayes, B. L. (1985). Child's developing sense of vocabulary as a response to learning strategies. *Journal of Educational Psychology, 54,* 334–356.

Levin, J. R., & Pressley, M. (1981). Improving children's prose comprehension: Selected strategies that seem to succeed. In C. M. Santa & B. L. Hayes (Eds.), *Children's prose comprehension* (pp. 44–71). Newark, DE: International Reading Association.

Leu, D., & Kinzer, C. (1995). The convergence of literacy instruction with networked technologies for information and communication. *Reading Research Quarterly, 35,* 108–127.

Lewin, J. (1999). Site reading the World Wide Web. *Educational Leadership, 56,* 16.

Lin, X. D., Bransford, J. D., Kantor, R., Hmelo, C., Hickey, D., Secules, T., Goldman, S. R., Petrosino, A., & the CTGV (1995). Instructional design and the development of learning communities: An invitation to a dialogue. *Educational Technology, 35*(5), 53–63.

Linden, L., & Wittrock, R. (1981). Vocabulary Development. In P. D. Pearson et al. (Eds.), *Handbook of reading research* (pp. 566–690). New York: Macmillan.

Lion, R., & Betsy, B. (1996, December). *Teacher improvement: Research concerning student achievement.* Paper presented at the annual meeting of the National Reading Conference, Miami, FL.

Lipson, M. Y., Mosenthal, J. H., & Mekkelson, J. (1999). The nature of comprehension among Grade 2 children: Variability in retellings as a function of development, text, and task. In T. Shanahan & F. Rodriquez-Brown (Eds.), *National Reading Conference yearbook* (Vol. 48, pp. 104–119). Chicago: National Reading Conference.

Lipson, M. Y., & Wixson, K. K. (1997). *Assessment and instruction of reading and writing disability: An interactive approach* (2nd ed.) New York: Longman.

Locken, R. (1981, December). *Literal comprehension: Influenced by decoding abilities.* Paper presented at the annual meeting of the National Reading Conference, Austin, TX.

Long, G. (1994). *Spatial learning strategies: Techniques, applications, and related issues.* New York: Academic Press.

Loxterman, J. A., Beck, I. L., & McKeown, M. (1994). The effects of thinking aloud during reading on students' comprehension of more or less coherent text. *Reading Research Quarterly, 29*(4), 353–366.

Lysaker, J. T. (1997). Learning to read from self-selected texts: The book choices of six first graders. In C. K. Kinzer, K. A. Hinchman, & D. J. Leu (Eds.), *Inquiries in literacy theory and practice: National Reading Conference yearbook* (Vol. 46, pp. 399–407). Chicago: National Reading Conference.

MacKenzie, A. (1972). *The time trap*. New York: Macmillan.

Mackey, M. (1997). Good-enough reading: Momentum and accuracy in the reading of complex fiction. *Research in the Teaching of English, 31*(4), 428–458.

Mackey, M. (1998, April). *Erasing good-enough reading forever*. Paper presented at the annual meeting of the American Educational Research Association, New Orleans, LA.

Maduram, I. (2000). "Playing possum": A young child's response to information books. *Language Arts, 77*(5), 391–397.

Mandler, J. M. (1978). A code in the node: The use of a story schema in retrieval. *Discourse Processes, 1*, 14–35.

Mangieri, J. N., & Block, C. C. (1992). *Creating powerful thinking for teachers and students: Diverse perspectives*. Fort Worth, TX: Harcourt, Brace.

Mangieri, J. N., & Block, C. C. (1996). *Power thinking for success*. Cambridge, MA: Brookline.

Marschark, M., Richman, C. L., Yuille, J. C., & Hunt, R. R. (1987). The role of imagery in memory: On shared and distinctive information. *Psychological Bulletin, 120*, 28–41.

Marzana, R. (2001). Teaching for understanding. *Educational Leadership, 87*, 12–20.

Maslow, B. (1968). *Human nature and man's hierarchy*. Cambridge, MA: Harvard University Press

McDaniel, M. A., & Einstein, G. O. (1986). Bizarre imagery as an effective memory aid: The importance of distinctiveness. *Journal of Experimental Psychology: Learning, Memory, and Cognition, 12*(1), 54–65.

McDermott, J. (2000). The effects of production system implementation. In D. A. Waterman & F. Hays-Roth (Eds.), *Pattern directed inference systems* (pp. 519–543). New York: Academic Press.

McDermott, J. (2001, April). *Tracking of production system implementations*. Paper presented at the annual meeting of the American Educational Research Association, New Orleans, LA.

McKay, D., Thompson, E., & Schabuh, R. (1970). Effect of imagery upon retention. *Journal of Educational Psychology, 52*, 118–126.

McKenna, M. C., Robinson, R., & Miller, J. (1993). Whole language and research. In D. Leu & C. Kinzer (Eds.), *Examining central issues in literacy research: National Reading Conference yearbook* (Vol. 43, pp. 141–152). Chicago: National Reading Conference.

McNamara, D. S., & Kintsch, W. (2000). Learning from texts: Effects of prior knowledge and text coherence. *Discourse Processes, 22*(3), 247–288.

Means, B., & Knapp, M. (1991). Introduction: Rethinking reaching for disadvantaged students. In B. Means, C. Chaiemer, & M. Knapp (Eds.), *Teaching advanced skills to at-risk students* (pp. 333–347). San Francisco, CA: Jossey-Bass.

Meichenbaum, P., & Biemiller, A. (1990, May). *In search of student expertise in the classroom: A metacognitive analysis*. Paper presented at the Conference on Cognitive Research for Instructional Innovation, University of Maryland, College Park, MD.

Melo, T. (1994, December). *Metacognition and effects on student achievement*. Paper presented at the annual meeting of the National Reading Conference, San Diego, CA.

Meyer, B. J. F. (1975). *The organization of prose and its effect on memory*. Amsterdam: North-Holland.

Mezynski, W. (1983). *Literal comprehension instruction and the correlations with detail versus main idea retention*. Unpublished dissertation, University of Wisconsin, Madison.

Miholic, V. (1994). An inventory to pique students' metacognitive awareness. *Journal of Reading, 38*, 84–86.

Miller, G. E. (1985). The effects of general and specific self-instruction training on children's comprehension monitoring performance during reading. *Reading Research Quarterly, 20,* 616–628.

Miller, G. E. (1987). The influence of self-instruction on the comprehension monitoring performance of average and above average readers. *Journal of Reading Behavior, 19,* 303–317.

Miller, G. E. (1999, April). *Metacognitive comprehension monitoring performances of below average readers.* Paper presented at the annual meeting of the American Educational Research Association, Seattle, WA.

Miller, J. R., & Kintsch, W. (1980). Readability and recall of short prose passages: A theoretical analysis. *Journal of Experimental Psychology: Human Learning and Memory, 6,* 335–354.

Moll, L. (Ed.). (1990). *Vygotsky and education: Instructional implications and applications of sociohistorical society.* Cambridge, MA: Cambridge University Press.

Moll, L. (1997, March). *Cultural bearings upon early literacy development.* Paper presented at the School of Education, Texas Christian University, Fort Worth.

Moss, E. F. (1989). *Macroprocessing in expository text comprehension.* Unpublished dissertation, University of Colorado, Boulder.

Muth, J. J. (2002). *The three questions.* New York: Scholastic Press.

Myers, I. B. (2001). *Myers–Briggs personality trait assessment: Battery 7 research manual.* San Antonio, TX: Psychological Corporation.

Nagy, W., & Herman, P. (1987). Incidental vs. instructional approaches to increasing reading vocabulary. *Educational Perspective, 23,* 16–21.

Narvaez, D. (2002). Individual differences that influenced reading comprehension. In C. C. Block & M. Pressley (Eds.), *Comprehension instruction: Research-based best practices* (pp. 178–205). New York: Guilford Press.

National Reading Panel. (1999, February 22). *Progress report to the National Institute on Child Health and Human Development,* Washington, DC.

National Reading Panel. (2000). *Progress report to the National Institute on Child Health and Human Development,* Washington, DC.

National Research Council. (1998). *Preventing reading difficulties in young children.* Washington, DC: National Academy Press.

Nell, A. (1988). *Teaching themes: Effects on student comprehension.* Unpublished dissertation, University of New York, Albany.

Norman, D. A. (1981). The trouble with UNIX. *Datamation, 13,* 139–150.

Oakhill, J. (1993). Children's difficulties in reading comprehension. *Educational Psychology Review, 5,* 223–227.

Oakhill, J., & Yuill, N. (1999). Higher order factors in comprehension disability: Processes and remediation. In C. Cornoldi & J. Oakhill (Eds.), *Comprehension difficulties.* Mahwah, NJ: Erlbaum

O'Flahavan, J. O. (1989). *Second graders' social, intellectual, and affective development in varied group discussions about narrative texts: An explanation of participation structures.* Unpublished doctoral dissertation, University of Illinois, Urbana–Champaign.

Omanson, R., Warren, R., & Trabasso, T. (1978, April). *Comprehending text through strategies.* Paper presented at the annual meeting of the American Educational Research Association, New Orleans, LA.

Opliz, M., & Rasinski, T. (1999). *Goodbye round robin reading.* Portsmouth, NH: Heinemann.

Orellana, M. F. (1995). Literacy as gendered social practice: Tasks, texts, talk, and take-up. *Reading Research Quarterly, 30*(4), 674–709.

Otero, J., & Kintsch, W. (1992). Failures to detect contradictions in a text: What readers believe versus what they read. *Psychological Science, 3*(4), 229.

Owocki, G. (2003). *Comprehension: Strategic instruction for K–3 students*. Portsmouth, NH: Heinemann.

Palincsar, A. S. (1986). The role of dialogue in providing scaffolded instruction. *Educational Psychologist, 21*, 73–98.

Pappas, C. C. (1991). Young children's strategies in the "book language" of information books. *Discourse Processes, 14*, 203–225.

Pappas, C. C. (1993). Is narrative "primary"? Some insights from kindergartners' pretend readings of stories and information books. *Journal of Reading Behavior, 25*, 97–129.

Pardo, L. S. (1997). Criteria for selecting literature in upper elementary grades. In T. Raphael & K. Au (Eds.), *Literature-based instruction: Reshaping the curriculum* (pp. 71–89). Norwood, MA: Christopher–Gordon.

Paris, S. G. (1986). Teaching children to guide their reading and learning. In T. E. Raphael (Ed.), *The contexts of school-based literacy* (pp. 115–130). New York: Random House.

Paris, S. G., Cross, D. R., & Lipson, M. Y. (1984). Informed strategies for learning: A program to improve children's reading awareness and comprehension. *Journal of Educational Psychology, 76*, 392–409.

Paris, S. G., Wasik, B. A., & Turner, J. (1991). Portfolio assessment for young readers. *The Reading Teacher, 44*, 680–682.

Paris, S. G., & Winograd, P. (1990). How metacognition can promote academic learning and instruction. In B. F. Jones & L. Idol (Eds.), *Dimensions of thinking and cognitive instruction* (pp. 15–51). Hillsdale, NJ: Erlbaum.

Paris, S. G., & Winograd, P. (2001). *The role of self-regulated learning in contextual teaching: Principles and practices for teacher preparation*. Ann Arbor, MI: Center for the Improvement of Early Reading Achievement.

Payne, B. D., & Manning, B. H. (1992). Basal reader instruction: Effects of comprehension monitoring training on reading comprehension, strategy use and attitude. *Reading Research and Instruction, 32*, 29–38.

Pearson, P. D., & Fielding, L. (1991). Comprehension Instruction. In P. D. Pearson, E. Barr, P. Mosenthal, & M. Kamil (Eds.), *Handbook of reading research* (Vol. 2, pp. 815–860). Mahwah, NJ: Erlbaum.

Pearson, P. D., Hansen, J., & Gordon, C. (1979). The effect of background knowledge on young children's comprehension of explicit and implicit information. *Journal of Reading Behavior, 9*(3), 17–26.

Pearson, P. D., & Johnson, D. (1978). *Teaching comprehension*. Fort Worth, TX: Harcourt, Brace.

Perfetti, C. (1998). The limits of co-occurrence: Tools and theories in language research. *Discourse Processes, 25*(2 & 3), 363–377.

Perfetti, C., & Lesco, R. (1979). Sentences, individual differences, and multiple texts: Three issues in text comprehension. *Discourse Processes, 23*, 337–355.

Perfetti, C. A., Marron, M. A., & Foltz, P. W. (1999). Sources of comprehension failure: Theoretical perspectives and case studies. In C. Cornaldi & G. Oakhill (Eds.), *Research explorations into literacy challenges* (pp. 59–79). Mahwah, NJ: Erlbaum.

Piaget, J. (1963). *Play, dreams, and imitation in childhood*. New York: Norton.

Piaget, J., & Inhelder, B. (1971). *Mental Imagery*. New York: Basic Books.

Poltrock, A., & Brown, A. L. (1984). Reciprocal teaching of comprehension-fostering and comprehension-monitoring activities. *Cognition and Instruction, 1*, 117–125.

Prawatt, G. (2001, April). *Theoretical models for comprehension development*. Paper presented at the annual meeting of the American Educational Research Association, Seattle, WA.

Presseisen, B. (1987). *Teaching thinking: Piagetian influences*. Paper presented at the annual meeting of the American Educational Research Association, Chicago, IL.

Pressley, M. (1976). Mental imagery helps eight-year-olds remember what they read. *Journal of Educational Psychology, 68*, 355–359.

Pressley, M. (1998). *Balanced reading instruction*. New York: Guilford Press.

Pressley, M. (1999). *Reading instruction that works*. New York: Guilford Press.

Pressley, M., & Afflerbach, P. (1995). *Verbal protocols of reading: The nature of constructively responsive reading*. Hillsdale, NJ: Erlbaum.

Pressley, M., Almasi, J., Schuder, T., Bergman, J., Hite, S., El-Dinary, P. B., & Brown, R. (1994). Transactional instruction of comprehension strategies: The Montgomery County, Maryland, SAIL program. *Reading and Writing Quarterly: Overcoming Learning Difficulties, 10*, 5–19.

Pressley, M., Goodchild, F., Fleet, J., Zajchowski, R., & Evans, E. D. (1989). The challenges of classroom strategy instruction. *Elementary School Journal, 89*, 301–342.

Pressley, M., Harris, K., & Guthrie, J. (1995). Mapping the cutting edge in primary level literacy instruction for weak and at-risk readers. In D. Scrubles & M. Mastropileri (Eds.), *Advances in learning and behavioral disabilities*. Greenwich, CT: JAI Press.

Rand Reading Study Group. (2002, December). *Review of literature concerning comprehension research*. Symposium papers presented at the annual meeting of the National Reading Conference. Scottsdale, AZ.

Raphael, T., & Au, K. (Eds.). (1997). *Literature-based instruction: Reshaping the curriculum*. Norwood, MA: Christopher–Gordon.

Read, S., & Roller, C. (1987). Constructing causal scenarios: A knowledge structure approach to causal reasoning. *Journal of Personality and Social Psychology, 52*, 288–302.

Rosenblatt, L. M. (1978). *The reader, the text, the poem: The transactional theory of the literary work*. Carbondale, IL: Southern Illinois University.

Ruffman, M. (2000, December). *Literal comprehension of details and the effect on retention of causal relationships and inferences*. Paper presented at the annual meeting of the National Reading Conference, Scottsdale, AZ.

Sadoski, M. (1985). The natural use of imagery in story comprehension and recall: Replication and extension. *Reading Research Quarterly, 20*, 658–667.

Sadoski, M., & Paivio, A. (1994). A dual coding view of imagery and verbal processes in reading comprehension. In R. B. Ruddell, M. R. Ruddell, & H. Singer (Eds.), *Theoretical models and processes of reading* (4th ed., pp. 582–601). Newark, DE: International Reading Association.

Santa, C. M., & Hoin, R. (1999). An assessment of early steps: A program for early intervention of reading problems. *Reading Research Quarterly, 34*(1), 54–79.

Schmitt, M. C. (1988). The effects of an elaborated directed reading activity on the metacomprehension skills of third graders. In J. E. Readance & R. S. Baldwin (Eds.), *Dialogues in literacy research: National Reading Conference yearbook* (Vol. 37, pp. 167–181). Chicago: National Reading Conference.

Schmitt, M. C., & Hopkins, C. J. (1993). Metacognitive theory applied: Strategic reading instruction in the current generation of basal readers. *Reading Research and Instruction, 32*, 13–24.

Schraw, G. (1998). Promoting general metacognitive awareness. *Instructional Science, 26*, 113–125.

Schunk, D. H. (1990). Goal setting and self-efficacy during self-regulated learning. *Educational Psychologist, 25*, 71–86.

Schunk, D. H., & Zimmerman, B. J. (1997). Developing self-efficacious readers and writers: The role of social and self-regulatory processes. In J. T. Guthrie & A. Wigfield (Eds.), *Reading engagement: Motivating readers through integrated instruction* (pp. 34–50). Newark, DE: International Reading Association.

Schwartz, D. L., & Bransford, J. D. (2001). A time for telling. *Cognition and Instruction, 41(4)*, 291–321.

Scott, J. A., Jamieson, D., & Asselin, M. (1999). Instructional interactions in upper elementary classrooms: An observational study. In T. Shanahan et al. (Eds.), *Theory and practice in literacy: National Reading Conference yearbook* (Vol. 48, pp. 167–177).

Shoemaker, M., & Deshler, D. (1992). Effects of strategy instruction on at-risk students' comprehension. *Journal of Educational Psychology, 98*, 668–679.

Singer, M., & Ritchot, K. F. M. (1996). The role of working memory capacity and knowledge access in text inference processing. *Memory and Cognition, 24*, 733–743.

Smey-Richman, B. (1988). *Involvement in learning for low-achieving students.* Philadelphia: Research for Better Schools.

Smolkin, C. (2002). Teaching non-fiction. *The Reading Teacher, 57(2)*, 123–130.

Snow, C. C. (2002, December). *What research has to say about the teaching of less able readers.* Paper presented at the annual meeting of the National Reading Conference, San Diego, CA.

Stahl, S. (1998). Four questions about vocabulary knowledge and reading and some answers. In C. Hynd, S. Stahl, M. Carr, & S. Glynn (Eds.), *Learning from text across conceptual domains* (pp. 73–94). Hillsdale, NJ: Erlbaum.

Stanovich, K. E. (1986). The Matthew effects in reading: Some consequences for individual differences in the acquisition of literacy. *Reading Research Quarterly, 21*, 360–407.

Sweet, A., & Snow, C. (2002). The RAND Corporation: New perspectives on comprehension. In C. C. Block, L. Gambrell, & M. Pressley (Eds.), *Comprehension instruction: Building on the past to influence the future* (pp. 474–523). San Francisco, CA: Jossey-Bass and the International Reading Association.

Taylor, B. M., & Beach, R. W. (1984). The effects of text structure instruction on middle-grade students' comprehension and production of expository texts. *Reading Research Quarterly, 19*, 134–146.

Taylor, B., Graves, M., & van den Brock, P. (2000). *Reading for meaning: Fostering comprehension in the middle grades.* New York: Columbia University, Teachers College.

Tergeson, J. K., & Wagner, J. (1987). What it means to learn to read. *Child Development, 56(5)*, 1134–1144.

Thomas, K. F., & Barksdale-Ladd, M. A. (2000). Metacognitive processes: Teaching strategies in literacy education courses. *Reading Psychology, 21*, 67–84.

Thorndike, R., & Woodworth, R. (1901). *Reasoning and Comprehension.* New York: World.

Tierney, R. J. (1998). Literacy assessment reform. *The Reading Teacher, 51(5)*, 371–393.

Torrance, P. (1981). *The study of creativity.* Athens, GA: University of Georgia Press.

Torrance, P., & Sisk, D. (2001). *Spiritual intelligence.* Washington, DC: Association for Gifted Children.

Trimble, S. (1994). The scripture of maps, the names of trees: A child's landscape. In G. P. Nabhan & S. Trimple (Eds.), *The geography of childhood: Why children need wild places* (pp. 15–32). Boston: Beacon Press.

van Dijk, T. A. (1980). *Macrostructures.* Hillsdale, NJ: Erlbaum.

van Dijk, T. A., & Kintsch, W. (1983). *Strategies for discourse comprehension.* New York: Academic Press.

Vye, N. J., Schwartz, D. L., Bransford, J. D., Barron, B. J., & Zech, L. (1998). SMART environments that support monitoring, reflection, and revision. In D. J. Hacker, J. Dunlosky, & A. C. Graesser (Eds.), *Metacognition in educational theory and practice* (pp. 305–346). Mahwah, NJ: Erlbaum.

Vygotsky, L. S. (1978). *Mind in society.* Cambridge, MA: MIT Press.

Weaver, C. A., III, & Kintsch, W. (1996). *Handbook of reading research* (Vol. 1). Mahwah, NJ: Erlbaum.

Wigfield, A., Eccles, J. S., & Rodrigues, D. (1999). The development of children's motivation in school contexts. *Review of Research in Education, 23*, 73–118.

Wiley, J., & Voss, J. F. (1999). Constructing arguments from multiple sources: Tasks that promote understanding and not just memory for text. *Journal of Educational Psychology, 91*(2), 301–311.

Wittrock, M. C. (1998). Students' thought processes. *Educational Psychologist, 35,* 76–87.

Wittrock, M. C., & Alesandrini, K. (1990). Generation of summaries and analogies and analytic and holistic abilities. *American Research Journal, 27,* 489–502.

Wood, D. J., Bruner, J. S., & Ross, G. (1976). The role of tutoring in problem solving. *Journal of Child Psychology and Psychiatry, 17,* 89–100.

Yuill, N., & Oakhill, J. (1991). *Children's problems in reading comprehension.* Cambridge, UK: Cambridge University Press.

Zecker, L. B., Pappas, C. C., & Cohen, S. (1998). Finding the "right measure" of explanation for young Latina/o writers. *Language Arts, 76*(1), 49–60.

Zimmerman, B. J., & Bonner, S. (2000). Models of self-regulatory learning and academic achievement. In B. J. Zimmerman & D. H. Schunk (Eds.), *Self-regulated learning and academic achievement: Theory, research, and practice* (pp. 1–25). New York: Springer-Verlag.

Index

Metacognition category of question, 30
Momentum, developing, 95–96
Monitoring paired reading, 49–51
Motivation
   discovery discussions and, 60
   metacognitive processes and, 148
   self-efficacy and, 93
   skimming and scanning nonfiction text and,
      95–96
   See also Initiative, helping students develop
Multisensory additions to lessons, 160
My Chinatown: One Year in Poems (Mak), 173

N

Nonfiction text
   attitude toward, 92
   building bridges, 108–110
   choice of, 93
   comprehension instruction for, 93–94
   Comprehension Process Motions (CPMs)
      and, 99
   grouping, 99
   inferring, interpreting, predicting, and, 114
   skimming and scanning, 95–96, 97
   teaching by reading two texts consecutively,
      95
   tilling the text, 96–97

O

Object inferences, 112
Observation reports, improving specificity of,
   180
One-Eyed Cat (Fox), 120
Our Eyes (Robinson), 52

P

Painting mental pictures, 138
Paired reading, 49–51
Paragraphs
   literal comprehension and, 73–74
   predicting function of, 97–99
Paraphrasing, 122
Peer think-aloud game, 44–45
Perspective of another person, gaining, 124,
   126, 222
Photographs, using to teach inferencing, 120
Pivotal point scaffolding, 48–49
Poetry, teaching imagery using, 138, 141

Point of need
   teaching after, 10, 13–16, 55–56
   teaching at, 9–10, 41
   teaching before, 7–9
Portfolios, color-coded, 179
Posters, of CPMs. *See* Forms
Post-it Notes, think-aloud, 46, 47, 190
Power of three technique, 34–35
Praise-Ask-Raise (PAR) feedback, 46, 48
Predicting
   Comprehension Process Motion (CPM) for,
      115, 116, 223
   difficulty of, 113–114
   functions of paragraphs, 97–99
   as type of inference, 112
   writing hypotheses or predictions, 115
Previewing, 96
Princess Smarty Pants (Cole), 153–154
Problem-solution inferences, 112
Problem solving category of question, 30
Problem-to-solution story pattern, 153–154, 199
Purpose for reading, establishing, 76–77, 78

Q

Question-and-answer sessions, 6
Questions
   asking, 69, 77, 79–82, 163, 213
   respondent-centered, 30, 34

R

Reader of the day, 67
Reading
   empathetic, 82–83
   "good enough," 19
   monitoring paired, 49–51
   purpose for, establishing, 76–77, 78
   responses to, 4
   See also Book buddy format; Weekly reading
      program
Reasons and evidence, identifying, 120, 121, 224
Relevance, personal, 119–120
Report cards, improving specificity of, 180
Rereading, Comprehension Process Motion
   (CPM) for, 176, 225
Research
   on comprehension instruction, 3–4
   Comprehension Process Instruction (CPI)
      principles and, 11
   on imagery, 133–134